Gathering God's People

Signs of a Successful Parish

Gathering God's People

Signs of a Successful Parish

edited by
J. Stephen O'Brien

National Catholic Education Association
with
Our Sunday Visitor, Inc.

© *Our Sunday Visitor, Inc. 1982*
All rights reserved.

ISBN: 0-87973-656-9
Library of Congress Catalog Card Number: 81-85241

Published by the
National Catholic Education Association
and
Our Sunday Visitor, Inc.

Printed and bound in the U.S.A. by
Our Sunday Visitor, Inc.
200 Noll Plaza
Huntington, Indiana 46750

656

Acknowledgments

The editor wishes to thank all those individuals, besides the authors, who have made this book possible. Among them are:

• Dr. Mary-Angela Harper and the editorial committee at NCEA (Rev. Msgr. William Baumgartner, Rev. Francis D. Kelly, and Rev. Frank J. Murphy).

• Edward J. Murray of Our Sunday Visitor, whose knowledge and humor made it fun.

• Rev. Msgr. John F. Meyers and Rev. Msgr. Francis X. Barrett of NCEA for their support and confidence.

• Rev. Philip Murnion of The Parish Project, for generously supplying the names of possible authors.

• Joy Gadway Payne of Richmond, Virginia, for invaluable assistance in preparing the manuscript and for sustaining enthusiasm.

Scripture texts used in this book are taken from the Revised Standard Version of the Bible, © 1946, 1952, 1971, and 1973 by the Division of Christian Education of the National Council of Churches of Christ in the U.S.A. Used by permission.

The quotes used from *Vatican Council II: The Conciliar and Post Conciliar Documents,* © 1975 (Austin Flannery, O.P., general editor), have been used with permission of Costello Publishing Company, Northport, N.Y.

The parish is for most Catholics
the single most important part of the Church.
This is where for them
the mission of Christ continues.
This is where they publicly express their faith,
joining with others
to give proof of their communion
with God and with one another.

FROM
THE PARISH: A PEOPLE, A MISSION, A STRUCTURE
U.S. BISHOPS' COMMITTEE ON THE PARISH
MARCH, 1981

Table of Contents

Foreword

The questionings and perhaps the doubts that once surrounded the future of the parish are over. There will be room for other kinds of communities and groupings, but the basic unit for the Church's outreach will be through the parish.

As the study from the American bishops has shown, the parish is a versatile kind of tool, rather than a single pattern for coming together. It can offer a variety of liturgical and devotional experiences, a community that can exist amid great diversity, and the opportunity for many ministries as well as continuing formation in them.

This book deals with the two poles within parish life relating to spirituality and to activity. A generation ago Etienne Gilson wrote: "Piety is no substitute for technique." A decade ago others might have stated: "Technique is inadequate in the absence of piety."

A blessing of our time is the joining together in our mentality of spirituality and skills. We seek good tools in the hands of well-formed ministers.

This demand is ongoing. This book is a contribution to that continuing development.

Most Rev. John S. Cummins
Bishop of Oakland and
Chairman, NCEA Board of Directors

1

Preface

As its name implies, the National Catholic Education Association (or NCEA) is primarily an educational association. The people at NCEA are concerned with learning and teaching, with proclaiming the Word of God effectively, with all aspects of Catholic education.

For most Catholics, formal and informal learning takes place within the parish community. Thus it was fitting for NCEA to undertake a major new work directed toward total parish ministry. The outline of this book was taken from the United States bishops' statement "The Parish: A People, A Mission, A Structure," since that statement contains the best summary of parish life in the Church today.

Gathering God's People: Signs of a Successful Parish has been written by parish people for parish people. It is for all those who share in parish ministry. Pastors and associates, administrative staff, principals and directors of parish programs, members of parish councils, committees, and boards, volunteers, and even those who do not volunteer — all will find this book a useful tool for understanding parish ministry. Our hope is that *Gathering God's People* will help people who work in parishes to share the good news and to build up the kingdom of God.

NCEA is proud to publish this work in cooperation with Our Sunday Visitor.

Rev. Msgr. John F. Meyers
President, NCEA

Introduction

The American bishops recently reminded us that the Church touches most American Catholics through the parish. It is here that the overpowering love of the Father calls people together as Jesus' brothers and sisters. In the parish, people empowered by the Holy Spirit gather together in faith to celebrate birth, love, and death made hopeful by resurrection.

Those who minister in parishes have become increasingly aware in recent years that effective parish ministry demands work. More than work, it demands faith, patience, a willingness to risk, personal loyalty, and a variety of skills. Parish ministers, whether ordained or appointed, are always looking for new ways to improve their ministry. This book has been written for them.

What This Book Will Do

This book will do several things for those involved in parish ministry:

1. It will support people in their work by reinforcing the good things they do. Those people who are successful will find their efforts mirrored here and will be supported in their efforts.

2. Reading this book will guide those who are actively seeking to improve their parish ministry in a particular area. Each chapter contains practical, proven ways to minister in a parish. The insights gained will help people to improve their work, making it more efficacious.

3. For those whose parish is just beginning systematic ministry in a given aspect of parish life, sections of this book will give them a starting point and some concrete directions to follow.

Some chapters will be more concrete than others. Some are basic how-to-do-it essays. Others are more reflective, evoking thoughts (and even some feelings) on how to serve people as a disciple of Christ. Each chapter is practical, springing from the experiences of parish life.

How to Use This Book

The following are five ways to get started:

1. Read the book from cover to cover and think about it.

2. Use the book as an educational tool for the parish council. Have two members of the council read one chapter each for every meeting, for a year. Have those people present the major ideas to the other members of the council for ten minutes each. Allow ten minutes for discussion. (A twenty-minute education period for each meeting is not outrageous.)

3. Make this book the outline for a Sunday morning adult education program. Have parishioners make presentations on a chapter each week, with time for discussion. This kind of discussion session will surface enough items to help create additional programs.

3

4. Have parish committees read the chapters that apply to their areas of interest. They can then evaluate their work based upon their insights gleaned from reading and discussion.

5. Use the book for staff enrichment. Discussing a book together, especially one that focuses on mutual concerns, is an excellent way to find out where people are. Open discussion allows for greater cooperation and support.

The people who have worked hard on this book to share their knowledge hope that it is helpful in making the kingdom of God a little more present in our world, in your parish.

J. Stephen O'Brien
Richmond, Virginia
January 1, 1982

The Pastor as Enabler

The Rev. Edward F. Haggerty

Ordained for the Archdiocese of Detroit in 1966, Father Haggerty holds a degree in guidance and counseling and a Master of Divinity degree. Actively involved in many organizations within the diocese, including the Senate of Priests and the Engaged Encounter program, Father Haggerty is currently pastor of St. Mary's of Redford, Detroit.

Where We Were and Where We Are

In an age marked by change, the understanding of the role of the pastor has changed significantly. Sometimes it has been difficult for the pastor to keep up. "I'm no longer a priest," he says, "I'm a presider, or a facilitator, or a celebrant, or a delegator." There is another possibility: the pastor as enabler. Pastors have a new challenge: to enable people to recognize, develop, and use their own ministries for the good of the whole community and for the continuation of Christ's work.

The challenge confronts pastor and parishioner alike. What is my role? my place? my task? What is allowed? How far should I go? Multiple questions point to diverse problems. Not the least of these "problems" is the "sacred apartness" which has characterized the ordained priesthood for many centuries. The roots of this notion go as far back as the cultic priesthood of the Hebrew Testament.[1]

When the early Church began to dwell on the Eucharist as sacrifice, the cultic notion of the ordained minister gained more and more weight. Gradually, the ordained minister (the priest or bishop) assumed more and more ministries. The "sacred apartness" relegated the other members of the baptized community to less visible and less active roles.

In recent years, there has been a renewed sense of the ministry, of the priesthood, of all the baptized. This period of renewal has included the Catholic Action movement, "participation of the laity in the apostolate of the hierarchy," which grew in the forties and fifties, resulting in an increased understanding of the ownership of ministry on the part of all. More recently, it has included the notion of the Church as the People of God, with its realization that all have a task and that divisions and castes are not part of the nature of the Church.

This renewed understanding does not deny that specialized ministries are part of the Church's life. They are. The Second Vatican Council document "The Dogmatic Constitution on the Church" has an instructive passage that makes some distinctions and offers some foundation for reflection:

> Though they differ essentially and not only in degree, the common priesthood of the faithful and the ministerial or hierarchical priesthood are none the less ordered one to another; each in its own proper way shares in the one priesthood of Christ. The ministerial priest, by the sacred power that he has, forms and rules the priestly people; in the person of Christ he effects the eucharistic sacrifice and offers it to God in the name of all the people. The faithful indeed, by virtue of their royal priesthood, participate in the offering of the Eucharist. They exercise that priesthood, too, by the reception of the sacraments, prayer and thanksgiving, the witness of a holy life, abnegation and active charity (No. 10).

Other council documents, episcopal statements, and the writings of theologians speak of the priest-officeholders in the Church as having the task of preserving the original revelation, communicating it, and making it present in the experience of the Christian community. They speak of the importance of assuring sacramental service, the consolation of the gospel, the seeking of justice, and the reception of new candidates for the community.

When all of these elements are viewed together, many people see them as a heavy and tiring burden, especially since it appears that one person must take all of these ministries completely unto himself. Fortunately, it is within these and many other ministries that the pastor-enabler helps the whole community to live its priesthood. It is through the enabling task that the parish, which for most Catholics is the single most important part of the Church, can continue to grow and to flourish.

The United States Bishops' Committee on the Parish is not unaware of the problem. In their recent document "The Parish: A People, A Mission, A Structure," the bishops wrote:

> The foremost leader of the parish remains the pastor (or team where it is in effect). The pastor is the point of unity between the worship of the parish and its activities, between the spiritual aspects of the parish and the organizational, between the specific character of the parish and the mission of the larger Church. This leadership is greatly enhanced when it continually develops the skills and structures that invite open dialogue, shared decision making and effective action. As a result, the goal of leadership is not simply to provide service for the people of the parish, but to enable them to minister to one another, to become part of a people and to extend their Christian commitment into everything they do. People can better take advantage of such opportunities for ministry

when they are offered the encouragement and training necessary to be effective (No. 32).[2]

Paul's letter to the Ephesians reminds us that the gifts Christ gave us were bestowed "to equip the saints for the work of ministry, for building up the body of Christ" (4:12). The work of enabling is one of equipping. It is a work of helping parish members to recognize and put into action the power to follow their baptismal call as a "chosen race, a royal priesthood, a holy nation, God's own people" (1 Peter 2:9).

The pastor can only aid this development if he takes seriously the variety of gifts in the Church (1 Corinthians 12:4ff) and if he works to cultivate the seeds which God has planted. Such a pastor is willing to make himself dispensable. He does not need to have all power residing in himself. He recognizes the importance of powerlessness, as Henri Nouwen describes it in "The Monk and the Cripple."[3] He resists the temptation to hold on to power through Word and sacrament or through individualism. And he brings to the task what James C. Fenhagen describes in *Mutual Ministry:* "A high degree of security, genuine skill, and the ability to see things through. He recognizes and deals with the enormous pressures, within and without, against this kind of ministry."[4]

Setting the Tone — Sharing a Vision

In recent years, some pastors have been making statements of philosophy and purpose to the parish as they begin new assignments. In the statements they set forth something of their vision of the Church, of their own ministry, and of their local parish Church. One statement, for example, included such notions as: "The authority of the pastor is not to dominate or control people, but to serve them." "The pastor must help to apply the gospel to the daily life of people, challenge them, and help them make their life decisions."

This practice has set in motion the possibility of subsequent evaluations of the pastor's effectiveness. More importantly, it has helped to begin the process of developing a vision for the whole parish. As time goes on, pastor and parishioners together continue to develop the vision.

The key factor here is a dialogue with as many people as possible. The purpose of such dialogue is to help people take ownership of the problems which blur the vision and to develop a knowledge of the processes which will fulfill that vision. Often this dialogue calls for a rather prophetic stance on the pastor's part. He must state his intention of enabling as many people as possible. He must offer hope. He must invite people to move beyond the limits they might otherwise set for themselves.

The Vatican Council II "Decree on the Apostolate of the Laity" addresses the mutuality of this dialogue:

> The laity should develop the habit of working in the parish in close union with their priests, of bringing before the ecclesial community their

own problems, world problems and questions regarding man's salvation, to examine them together and solve them by general discussion (No. 10).

One key to success is the pastor's ability to discern the potential within the parish to deal with reality. Regular and consistent census work, needs surveys, and commitment requests are some general tools for drawing an overall picture. The picture of realities includes, of course, both limitations and possibilities.

A parish council renewal weekend helps council members to share in the establishment of a parish picture and a parish vision. An outside facilitator is usually necessary to foster communication. Out of such experiences can grow follow-up programs in skills training programs frequently offered by the diocese for parish council members, or by outside consultants.

Throughout the course of the year, time should be set aside at each council meeting for "vision." This is the portion of the meeting that does not involve business, but provides for reflection on the meaning of our parish life, and a time for expanding the council's notion of Church. Council members and the pastor may take turns preparing this part of the meeting.

Jesus as Enabler

Just as it is of utmost importance for the pastor to help the congregation to reflect consistently on the mission of Jesus, so is it helpful for the pastor (and anyone in a leadership position) to reflect on how Jesus went about enabling. Jesus in his earthly ministry took a group of rather ordinary people and enabled them to do far more than they ever dreamed. In fact, he told them they would do works far greater than his own (John 14:11).

How did Jesus go about enabling? First, he went searching, making contacts. "Come, follow me" is what he said to the Twelve. Jesus did not stop there. He continued the formation in many different ways: through storytelling, teaching, praying, encouraging, challenging, bringing conflict into the open and utilizing it (Mark 9:30-37).

After a time, Jesus sent out those whom he was enabling. He sent them two by two to do the works that were his (Mark 6:7-13). He was not threatened by their efforts nor by their successes or failures. He received them upon their return and helped them reflect on their experiences. He supervised them and helped them grow (Luke 9:10-11). In the end, Jesus enabled his disciples to continue the work his Father had sent him to do (John 17:1-11).

Formation and Supervision

In the tradition of the Gospels, spiritual formation continues to be essential to the development and enablement of ministers today. This becomes evident when, after many years, people come up and say, "Do you remember that scripture course you conducted in the parish? That really got me started on what I'm doing now." Or, "Do you remember those sessions on prayer we used to have? I'm still finding them to be a big help in my life."

Parishioners who answered either a general or individual call to work in catechetical ministries have been in the forefront of those who have taken ownership of the parish and its mission. The reason seems to be the confidence and skills they have developed as they constantly seek instruction, receive supervision, and do their own reflecting. Their deeper search into the history, background, and meaning of their faith has contributed immensely to their ability as catechetical ministers and as sharers in the parish life.

Expanded liturgical ministry has been an equally important factor in enabling people. For example, the practice of having special ministers of the Eucharist, whether during Eucharist or in visitation of the sick and shut-ins, has helped break down old barriers between clergy and parishioners. Other forms of liturgical involvement, such as the ministry of the Word (lector) and liturgical planning, have brought about a fresh look at the meaning of the Church's life and of the possibilities this life holds. An unwarranted and unwanted mystique that placed all Church things in the hands of the clergy has given way to a newer age in the Church with a greater sense of responsibility on the part of all members for the Church's life and mission.

Simply to say that it is no longer the case, is not enough. Enabling must take on concrete action. Thus it is important that prospective liturgical ministers go through formation programs which dwell on history, theology, and practice. The development should not stop there. Periodic refresher programs and evenings of reflection are essential. Such programs foster feelings of mutual encouragement when forty or sixty baptismally commissioned ministers come together in the parish and spend time in prayer.

Liturgy planning groups, each with a staff member or experienced planner, meet to prepare Sunday, feast day, or special liturgies. The continuing development of scripture, prayer, and art skills give participants a sense of being enabled. They see their efforts flower before the whole parish and before God each week.

Through such guided involvement young members of the parish, from an early age, develop the same sense of ownership of the Church and of their place in it. Other programs, such as Peer Counselors, in which students are an adjunct of the high school counseling office, enhance the relational skills of young people. Hours of training and continued supervision make the students a valuable asset to the school. The students take justifiable pride in their contribution to the parish/school community.

Job Descriptions

People generally like to know what they are getting into. While the topic of job descriptions, expectations, and requirements may be designated more strictly as being part of recruitment, it seems that it can be an important element in the overall enabling process. Suffice it to say that the job description should include some designated length of time. Rather explicit opportunities should be given for people to move in and out of specific functions and services. This provides a freedom that in itself may be enabling.

Legitimation

Even enabled people need some sort of public approval or affirmation of their ministry or function. Some people call this "legitimation." Legitimation happens frequently with liturgical ministries through short installation ceremonies which involve an interrogation, or acceptance, by the congregation, and an affirmation in word or gesture. Usually the pastor is the one who speaks the word or makes the gesture of affirmation. Legitimation ceremonies may be done for parish councils, for officers, pastoral care visitors, and for a wide variety of ministries. In addition, there are other kinds of affirmation and legitimation such as issuing certificates of completion at the end of education and formation programs.

The Budget

One other area of formation and training toward enablement that is very important is money. The budget may be a strong statement of an intention to enable ministers. It may also be a very effective way of doing so. Each section of the parish budget, whether for staff or various commissions, indicates a certain amount of money set aside for the continuing education of those involved. Classes, conventions, and conferences are encouraged whenever possible.

Enabling the Enablers

In many parishes it would be impossible for the pastor to be the only enabler. His task is often one of overseeing. His job is to state a vision of enabling, and to see to it that others become enablers (for example, the religious education coordinator, various staff members, and committee workers). One parish which recently experienced a change in pastoral leadership found itself within one year to have a great number of enabled people. The two new pastors had involved many parishioners in leadership and enabling programs, such as Cursillo, Marriage Encounter, and various courses.

In enabling parishes, staff members do not simply recruit bodies; staff members become resources with a wide variety of skills and experience which they liberally share. They come to know local programs such as Meals on Wheels or Retired Senior Volunteer Programs in order to make the necessary linkages. They work toward helping the community itself become an enabling community, where the laity are not defined negatively, as those without certain skills or powers. Rather, everyone makes up the *laos,* the single body.

In the midst of the enabling parish, the pastor is like Barnabas, whose name means "son of encouragement." He is open, innovative, and eager to share the life of the community. He tries to be consistent, coherent, patient, and efficient. He continues to give priority to study and prayer. (It is good for parishioners to know he does these things.) He continues consciously to develop enabling skills in group work, spiritual direction, supervision, and in communication.

Perhaps Bishop Raymond G. Hunthausen's remarks in the National Federation of Priests' Councils Proceedings — 1980 can serve as a vision within which all people find their ministry:

> So let's take our stand imaginatively with our friend the helmsman (on a Greek or Roman sailing vessel) as he goes about his labor of governing. It's interesting: he doesn't create the wind, the power, you know. That comes from somewhere else. Nor is he the one who placed the stars by which he navigates; they've been around for a little while before he undertakes the voyage, and will be there long after he's gone. And he's not really the one who chooses the destination, that's been established by the purposes of the owner of the ship, of the passengers who are paying for the trip. And the helmsman is not the one who actually cranks the winches or reefs in the sails, although he may give the orders concerning which sails to put on or lower and when.
>
> No, the helmsman just moves the tiller. The helmsman just steers — on a boat staffed by others, toward purposes set by others, according to markers set by God, using power he doesn't create. But without him and his craft the whole enterprise can founder. And what is his steering designed to do? To harness the power, to make as much of it as possible serve the purpose of getting the ship to the right port with the minimum loss or waste of energies.

Although he speaks as a bishop, so much of what he says describes the enabling pastor.

SUMMARY

1. In recent years the role of the pastor has undergone great scrutiny. Official Church documents, theological reflection and writing, and pastoral practice have promoted the concept of the pastor as enabler. He sees to it that God's people are equipped for work in his service to the building up of the body of Christ (Ephesians 4:12).

2. The pastor's role is a specialized one, carried out within the body of the Church which has grown to appreciate the gifts of all the baptized. As enabler, the pastor may feel that he is giving up a good deal of his power; but he also finds that he can enrich the ministry of the whole parish with a ripple effect that can have great consequences.

3. The pastor is the chief intercommunicator in helping the parish establish a vision of and for itself. Open dialogue and regular reflection are essential to this task.

4. Jesus is the model of the enabling pastor. Just as Jesus instructed,

formed, equipped, sent out, and supervised his disciples, so the pastor-enabler sets about using these skills in order to empower the members of the parish. Through these efforts, people of all ages can become more and more aware that the parish is *their* parish.

5. Public affirmation or legitimation of enabled ministers enhances the ministries and the parish. Job descriptions and budget considerations are essential for ensuring that all the skilled tools of enabling are in place.

6. Pastors are not the only enablers in a parish, but pastors do oversee the whole work of empowering. They, too, must consistently work on their own skills, spend time in study and prayer, and encourage all who minister in the body of Christ.

CHAPTER NOTES

1. For a good history of the priesthood, see Bernard Cooke, *Ministry to Word and Sacraments* (Philadelphia: Fortress Press, 1976).
2. United States Bishops' Committee on the Parish, "The Parish: A People, A Mission, A Structure." NC Documentary Service (March 26, 1981), Vol. 10, No. 41, pp. 641-46.
3. Henri J. M. Nouwen, "The Monk and the Cripple," *America* (March 15, 1980).
4. James C. Fenhagen, *Mutual Ministry* (New York: Seabury Press, 1977), p. 104.

SUGGESTED READINGS

Cooke, Bernard. *Ministry to Word and Sacraments.* Philadelphia: Fortress Press, 1976. Cooke's historical approach and development provides an excellent perspective. This is especially true for contemporary Catholics in the section on ministry to the Church's sacramentality.

Elsesser, Suzanne E., ed. *Parish Ministry.* National Conference of Catholic Bishops and Paulist Press. Published six times a year. New York: Paulist Press. These publications frequently deal with the theory of enablement and with implementation.

Fenhagen, James C. *Mutual Ministry.* New York: Seabury Press, 1977. The truly alive congregation is one that ministers to one another rather than depending on the pastor to do all the ministering. The chapter on enabling the pastor is quite valuable.

National Conference of Catholic Bishops. *As One Who Serves.* Prepared for the Bishops' Committee on Priestly Life and Ministry. Washington, D.C.: United States Catholic Conference, 1977. Reflections prepared by a committee of priests. Topics include ministerial relationships and parish ministry.

Wentz, Frederick K., *Getting Into the Act.* Nashville: Abingdon, 1978. Some practical approaches to developing a congregation of mutual ministry.

Staff
Relationships

Barbara Valuckas, SSND

A member of the School Sisters
of Notre Dame, Sister Barbara is
the director of the Foundation
for Community Creativity in
Washington, D.C. The purpose
of the foundation is to foster local
leadership in the Church. Part of
that process includes
interviewing parish staff
members in an effort to provide
data from lived experience for
theological reflection. Prior to
the work with the foundation,
Sister Barbara was active in
diocesan administration, in
educational television, and in
school teaching.

The Issue

The local Church in the United States is still very much in the process of translating the Vatican II People of God ecclesiology into pastoral practice. An integral part of this development has been the expansion and diversification of parish staffs.

Twenty years ago, a parish priest could gaze around a staff meeting table (if indeed such meetings were held) and see his own white, male, Roman-collared self mirrored in all the other persons present. There was a general similarity of background and training.

Today, the same parish priest is planning and making decisions with trained lay colleagues, with women in ecclesial communities, with black, Hispanic, and Haitian permanent deacons.

There has been little in the background and training of the average parish priest to prepare him to function collegially in such a diverse setting. Many priests and parish staffs are, however, learning how to do this by reflecting on and learning from their lived experience as they go along. As they do, they are creating new and effective ways of being Church.

The Documentation

If one were to research the official documents of the Church to find statements about the specifics of staff relationships, one would search in vain. Appropriately, the official Church documents present basic theological principles which form the context within which pastoral practice can grow and develop. The concept of the Church as the People of God is just such a principle. It implies the gradual transformation of the pre-Vatican II

hierarchial "pyramid" △ into a collegial "circle" ○

In actual practice, however, the pyramid dies a hard and reluctant death. If one were to draw a picture of a typical United States parish today,

it would probably look something like this: 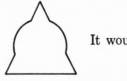 It would be

a picture of something which is not quite a pyramid and not quite a circle — a picture which leaves the viewer in doubt about which is absorbing which!

Translated into human lives at the parish level, the struggle between the pyramid and the circle makes for a lot of tension and pain as well as for growth and creativity. Thus the local Church, in the persons of parish staff members, has had quite a bit to say about staff relationships.

The most important documents about staff relationships today are the ones based on the lived experiences of local parish staffs. These are the ones which will be referred to in this chapter.

Since 1976, the staff members of the Foundation for Community Creativity (FCC) have been interviewing parish staff members to discover their lived experience of parish life at the local level. The thousands of pages of documentation collected by the FCC staff during these years form the basis for the reflections offered in this chapter.

Staff Composition

Surprisingly, one of the issues that hurts staff relationships is confusion about who make up the parish staff. In some parishes, only the full-time professionals make up the staff. In others, the parish council president and permanent deacons are included. In still others, the school principal and parish secretary are considered staff members. There does not seem to be a consensus among parishes about who is a part of the parish staff.

Interviews with parish staff members have revealed some very strong feelings about the issue. At staff meetings, some people are wondering why certain others are present, while other staff members are steaming because some people are not present. The confusion, unaired, can create unnecessary tensions among people who are expected to work together.

At the outset of a new parish year, it is important to bring together the people who contribute in a major way to parish life. There is a need to come to agreement about the criteria by which a parish staff person will be identified. In this way the decisions will not be arbitrary and will be clear to all concerned.

In effective parishes, staffs tend to be large enough to enable leadership to develop in the broader parish, yet not so large that communication and decision-making become unwieldy and even impossible. For each parish, the decision about staff composition may well be different. What is important is that a participatory decision be made, owned, and supported.

Expectations

The clear identification of the parish staff is only the beginning. Parish staffs are, ideally, pastoral teams of people who support each other even as they engage in their mission of enablement. The two elements of "support" and "mission" imply that parish staffs need to pay attention to their internal life as a group and to their external mission to and with the local Church. Staffs which spend too much time on their own internal life risk becoming narcissistic. Staffs which spend too much time on their ministerial tasks can become burnt-out contradictions to their own good news about Church-as-community.

At the outset of a parish year, it is well to engage the staff in dialogue about their expectations with respect to their own needed balance of relationship-building and task-accomplishment. It is sometimes helpful to ask staff members to represent this desired balance in visual form, perhaps on newsprint. It could look something like this:

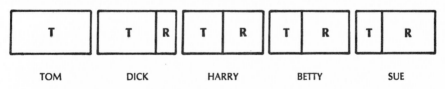

T = task-accomplishment   R = relationship-building

Pasting the newsprints on the wall can help staff members see at a glance both the similar and differing expectations. For example, Tom is not interested in building relationships. Dick, Harry, Betty, and Sue are interested in both task accomplishment and relationship-building but in different proportions. Having thus generated some data for reflection, staff members have a basis for discussion. They can proceed to sharing their reasons for the chosen balance and work toward a consensus expectation.

It should be noted here that there is no one expectation which would be ideal for every parish. Parish staffs in which most members also form an ecclesial community may place a greater emphasis on relationship-building. So may staffs which have many new members. Staffs which are very diverse may include members who are already engaged in building community with other primary people or groups. Such a staff may need to come to a different kind of expectation.

What remains important is that needs for personal support and effective ministry both be attended to. Relationships among staff members should be strong enough to nourish the individuals, encouraging them in their pastoral tasks.

Stories

There are many aspects to the relationship-building process. One of the most important ones for a parish staff is knowing something of each other's personal stories.

It is sad but true that many parish staff members who work side-by-side in ministry know virtually nothing about each other. This makes it difficult for one staff member to understand the words used by another when he or she talks about a ministerial experience. When staff members talk about their parish tasks without disclosing anything about the one doing the tasks, the messages given and received are, at best, incomplete and, at worst, incomprehensible.

On the other hand, where parish staff members have had the opportunity to share something of their lives, greater insight, understanding, and appreciation seem to follow. Where this has been done, I have heard parish staff members say things like: "I never knew that Sister Joanne worked in an office for several years before joining her congregation. That explains why she has such an interest in the working people in our parish." Or, "When Juan told us how he was trained to genuflect at the sight of a priest when he was a boy on Long Island, I could understand why he is so quiet and deferential at staff meetings."

There is no need to engage in group therapy or the kind of self-disclosure that occurs only among intimate friends for this level of sharing to happen. The use of some open-ended questions which allow people to share as much as they wish can often be helpful. Such questions might be:

• What would you like to share about the part of your life you experienced before coming to this parish and this staff?

• How did you happen to be drawn to your form of ministry in the Church?

• How do you view ministry? What were some of the events or people in your life that influenced your arrival at this conviction?

• How did you happen to find yourself here in this parish with this staff?

• What were your previous experiences of parish or parish staff life?

• How do you experience ministry in this community?

The responses to such questions can be occasionally included as part of a parish staff meeting. They would also be helpful for staff days of prayer and planning together. An environment which encourages this kind of sharing is one which communicates the message "Both the minister and the ministry are important here."

Sexuality

The sharing of personal stories is intended to deepen the levels of understanding and trust between and among parish staff members. Nowhere is this understanding more in need of being developed than in parish staffs composed of men and women in ministry. Even the readiness to share personal stories often surfaces differences between men and women staff members at the outset. For various reasons, women are often more comfortable sharing some of the dimensions of their inner life and thought, while men frequently find this difficult.

It would seem, then, that women staff members might have the edge in staff gatherings. This edge is somewhat vitiated, however, by another dynamic which often operates when men and women speak to each other in group settings. Stereotypes to the contrary, some studies of male-female group interaction show that, in mixed groups, men talk more than women. Moreover, when men speak, women tend to listen to what they say rather intently. However, when women speak, men seem to be inattentive and to disregard what is said.[1]

So it seems that men in mixed staff groups face a double challenge. They need to grow both in the ability to share out of their own personal stories and to listen sensitively to the stories of others, especially when these others are women.

Women staff members, on the other hand, need to keep growing in their belief in the validity of their experiences. They need to speak their truth with confidence and, if needed, with forcefulness. They need to give feedback to the men in the group when they feel unlistened to and unheard.

Once the personal stories are shared, it readily becomes apparent how different they are. While men and women in ministry may experience many commonalities in pastoral concerns, they differ greatly in the way they experience accountability, role expectations, access to power and information, and concept of "team."

Accountability: Often there are different accountability expectations for women on parish staffs than for their male counterparts, especially where the men are ordained. Ordained men have been accustomed to equating their parish functioning with administration of the sacraments. Once these sacramental duties have been performed, there is little expectation that they need account for the rest of their time. Women, on the other hand, lacking the sacramental function, have needed to justify their presence on a parish staff by active involvement in a number of ministries. In many cases, women on parish staffs have come from the highly structured field of education. They have been accustomed to planning and using well every minute of their time. They have been accustomed to regular supervision and evaluation.

Women members of parish staffs often perceive themselves to be as busy, if not busier than the ordained men with whom they work. They tend to resent a somewhat inequitable system of accountability. This resentment is aggravated when they become aware that they are expected to perform equivalent or greater ministerial duties while taking care of all their own personal, religious community, or family needs as well. They observe the ordained men being ministered to by housekeepers, cooks, and secretaries. This common difference in lived experience can create chasms across which it becomes difficult to communicate.

Role Expectations: For example, a young religious order priest complained at a staff meeting that his having to do the rectory food shopping and car maintenance cut into the time he had available for ministry. The women in the group were silent (unfortunately) but exchanged knowing looks which said, "We do this all the time with no questions asked. It's simply expected."

A woman staff member told of having been invited to supper in the rectory along with two other women staff members. After supper, the priests retired to the living room to watch the evening news, obviously expecting the women to clean the table and wash the dishes. Relatively small incidents such as this can contradict verbal protestations of collegiality and descriptions of the staff as a parish team.

In parishes where men and women share in the routine work, it is more likely that they are also sharing the significant aspects of ministry more equitably. This was certainly true of a parish where the pastor was found busily ironing his own laundry. Such a man could not help but have a greater understanding of the women on his staff who do this all the time.

Power and Information: Because women are relatively recent additions to parish staffs and because they do not have access to ordination, women are in positions of lesser power. The *powerlessness* of which they are already uncomfortably aware can be reinforced in some unpleasant ways.

It is lunchtime in the rectory. The priests eat a served meal together in the rectory dining room. A woman staff member eats a sandwich in her basement office. What a loss of a good opportunity to build staff relationships! This system of segregated eating isolates the woman both socially and professionally. The priests discuss parish affairs at lunch and often make decisions over the meal. Thus, the parish staff meetings become mere formalities which are nothing more than "reruns" of the lunchtime discussions.

Since women are often at the low end of the staff "pecking order" they are sometimes the recipients of anger that men on the staff are unable or unwilling to express to each other. At a staff meeting observed by FCC, a permanent deacon disagreed strongly with the pastor on an issue but was unable, out of a sense of deference, to express his feelings directly. A few minutes later, however, he verbally pounced on a woman staff member, berating her about a program he considered inadequate. In that instance, it seemed like a clear case of anger displaced from the pastor onto the "safer," less powerful woman.

Team: Men and women also differ in the internal definitions they bring to the word "team." Men, whose athletic and competitive backgrounds are often stronger than those of women, have a concept of "team" which includes a clear captain barking out orders or a quarterback calling the plays. Often pastors quite comfortably use the word "team" to describe a model which women experience as quite authoritarian. Women's experience of teamwork has included more collaboration and mutuality. When women use the word "team," therefore, they often mean something quite different from men. This is another reason why it is so important for parish staff members to share the internal meanings they bring to the words they commonly use to describe their pastoral experience and convictions.

From all that has been said, it is clear that parishes which take seriously true sharing of men and women staff members should engage in specific practices that promote mutuality. All staff members are accountable to each other for their ministerial time and responsibilities. Routine work, as well as significant ministerial tasks, is shared by all. Care is taken to see that women in ministry receive supportive services just as the men do. Men and women both have access to information and participate together in decision-making. Men and women appreciate the eucharistic significance of breaking bread together at meals.

Sexual Attraction

The possibility of sexual attraction is always present when men and women work together closely. Unfortunately, staff members sometimes refrain from any form of self-disclosure for fear of becoming vulnerable and open to a deep affective relationship.

This is not an issue for parish staffs only. It is a growing concern in the business world as well, as women move into management positions and work closely with male colleagues. A recent article in *Management Review* cautioned men and women that using sexual stereotypes as defenses precluded mutuality.

> Management should consider raising this (sexuality) topic as a legitimate issue when building teams of male/female colleagues or when dealing with bosses and subordinates who have not experienced working for or with persons of the opposite sex. Men and women often view persons of the opposite sex in roles that provide them with the greatest comfort and treat others, therefore, as their children, parents or spouses. This is easier and less threatening than learning to work together as equals.[2]

As men and women staff members learn to share their personal stories and to discuss the similarities and differences in these stories, the possibilities for "learning to work together as equals" can grow. This can only serve to enrich the local Church.

Cultural Differences

Just as the stories of men and women differ, so do the stories of staff members from a variety of ethnic and cultural backgrounds. It is important for staffs to talk to each other about their values, especially when these values have been influenced by a specific ethnic or cultural context.

There was one parish staff which struggled to be patient with a Haitian member who never seemed to meet staff deadlines. When staff members learned more about his culture, they came to realize that this staff member valued relationships over results. There had been a kind of group norm operating on the staff, a nonverbal expectation that placed a high value on American efficiency and tangible results. There was a tendency to devalue a person who had other cultural priorities. As the staff became able to dialogue about these differences, the Haitian member could better respond to the staff's need to have certain deadlines met. The staff members, on the other hand, were freed to express their deeply felt appreciation for their Haitian colleague's gifts in building warm, loving relationships in the parish.

Had the staff not been able to surface and talk about different values and arrive at a position that all could live with, the staff could have been beset with continued tension. The parish, on the other hand, could have lost the talents of a gifted staff member who "didn't quite fit."

Language

When staff members do not all speak the same language, there is an additional challenge to the building of staff relationships.

FCC has worked with a parish which had chosen to include the Hispanic permanent deacon in its definition of parish staff. There are both difficulties and benefits for all concerned. Occasionally, the deacon has to make special arrangements to leave his work place in order to participate in staff meetings. During the meeting, bilingual members of the staff take turns simultaneously translating the discussions. The staff has discovered that the benefits are worth the efforts made.

The deacon has received the benefits of being able to contribute to total parish planning and evaluation. He has been able to see his role within an overall context. The rest of the staff has also gained from the arrangement. It is no secret that some of the Hispanic parishioners share with the deacon some concerns and issues which they are too shy to relate to the priests on the staff. Staff members benefit from the deacon's special knowledge of the needs of these more reticent (and often the poorest) parishioners.

As more and more parishes become bilingual, trilingual and, indeed, multilingual, the effective parishes will be the ones which include representatives of the various cultural and ethnic groups on their staffs. They will work for creative ways to bridge differences without trying to eliminate differences. They will celebrate the giftedness of each culture as they give witness to the richness of cultural pluralism among their own members.

Role Descriptions

The expansion and diversification of parish staffs has created the need for clear and well-developed role descriptions. When parish staffs consisted totally of priests, role descriptions did not exist; it was simply assumed that everyone knew what priests did. Priests tell of simply being assigned responsibility for certain parish organizations. These, plus the administration of the sacraments, were considered sufficient. That rather informal system, however, had several weaknesses:

• The gifts of the individual often would not be taken into consideration.

• The agreement was a rather general and verbal one made with the pastor. The specifics were often unclear to the person in the role and even less clear to colleagues on the staff.

• Since the role was vague to begin with, supervision and evaluation were difficult, and accountability was weak.

• There was no link to overall parish planning. Parish jobs often revolved around maintaining organizations that had long since lost their meaning.

Coordinating a priests-only parish staff by this informal "gentlemen's agreement" method has the pitfalls described above. When this method is used with a larger and more diversified staff, it can create such an atmosphere of ambiguity and confusion that staff relationships are greatly strained.

Some good practices in parishes include the following:

• The parish has an overall parish plan from which clear role descriptions are developed.

• The role descriptions are written down. Care is taken to avoid outmoded or insensitive role descriptions.

• The entire staff, or a subcommittee of the staff, interviews new job applicants using the role descriptions as a common reference point. The interviews take care to discover what the words in the role description mean to the interviewee.

• Where some discrepancy exists between the role description and the gifts of the interviewee, changes are mutually negotiated and written down.

• All staff members have copies of each other's role descriptions. Each staff member is aware of how he/she fits into the overall parish plan.

• Periodically, the pastor or another appropriate person sits down with each staff member to evaluate the staff members' experience of the job. Again, the role description is used as the common reference point.

• Staff members are free to call each other to accountability with respect to their role. This is often done at scheduled team evaluation meetings.

• When the parish staff engages in its annual evaluation days, roles are renegotiated in the light of changes in the parish plan or in personnel.

Staff Meetings

This chapter has already mentioned the wisdom of identifying the members of the parish staff and then engaging those members in consensus decision-making regarding a desired balance between task accomplishment and relationship-building. Once this balance has been agreed upon, it is helpful to structure staff meetings to provide ways to achieve that balance.

Some things that effective parishes have built into their staff meetings to foster task accomplishment are:

• Shared responsibility for the agenda. All team members have the freedom to contribute items to the agenda. (Items relating only to the clergy, such as who has what Mass or who is in for supper at the rectory, can be settled outside of the staff meetings.)

• Rotation of leadership. This gives team members an opportunity to learn the skills of chairing. Some of the skills most needed by parish staff members who chair meetings are: (1) Introducing agenda topics in such a way as to clarify the expected or desired response from the staff (for discussion, for decision, for information). This requires careful preparation for the meeting. (2) Focusing discussion on one topic at a time. (3) Facilitating maximum participation of other staff members. (4) Summarizing each discussion once it has concluded and checking for mutual understanding of the outcome of the discussion before going to the next topic. (5) Making sure that the meeting is documented. The documentation should list the decisions made, agreed-upon follow-up, and task responsibilities.

Some things that effective parishes have built into their staff meetings to help build relationships are:

• Sharing "baggage" as the meeting begins. (Each staff member is invited to share the feelings with which he or she comes to the meeting. This helps to build staff sensitivity and mutual understanding.)

• Sharing personal stories.

• Encouraging feeling-level statements ("I" statements) during the meeting as a way of giving the team feedback about the way a person is being affected by the discussion ("I feel confused about this"; "I really appreciated the support I heard in your question"; "I find myself feeling quite angry over this unfinished task," etc.).

• Faith-sharing (more on this later).

• Evaluation of the meeting using such questions as "How am I feeling as this meeting comes to a close?"

It is important to see time as a resource and to use staff meeting time in the best possible way. When structuring the agenda, for instance, wise staffs often deal first with items needing creative thought or serious decision-making. Staff members are at their most energetic at the beginning of meetings.

After serious decision-making has been done, staff members should use some time to report on unfinished activities and to "switchboard" or tell each other what they are doing.

Unfortunately, too many staff members spend most of their meeting time in "switchboarding." They are so busy telling each other *what* they are doing that they never take time to look at *why* they are doing the *what*.

This brings up the need for reflection. So many parish staff people are so busy rushing from one activity to the next that they never have time to ask if the activity was worth doing in the first place. While many staff meetings need to look briefly at the great variety of things that are happening in the parish, it is wise to set aside some meetings on a fairly regular basis to reflect on what was learned from a single event, program, or activity. It is possible to spend an entire staff meeting, for example, responding to questions such as these:

• What was the original purpose of program X? What has been its history?

• What has actually been done as part of the program?

• By reflecting on the responses to the first two questions, what have we learned about. . .

who Jesus is for us?
our local Church?
our neighborhood?
the parishioners?
ourselves?
the mission of the parish?
this program?

• In the light of what we have learned, what seems to be the direction for the future?

• In the light of the direction for the future: What needs to be retained? What needs to be changed? What needs to be invented?

This kind of in-depth reflection can lead to important insights which then become the wellsprings of creativity for pastoral planning.

Staffs which take time at the end of each staff meeting to evaluate the meeting stand the best chance of learning from their meeting experience.

Some questions which are helpful ways of evaluating a meeting are:

Planning:

Did the agenda items reflect. . .

• my interests and concerns?

• my personal experience of the parish and its needs?

Decision-making:

1. Did I feel free to express differences of opinion and my own preferences?

2. Was consensus clear and well articulated?
3. Did my experience of this meeting make me feel more or less trust? more or less investment?
4. When conflict arose, was it avoided or dealt with in a straightforward manner?

Shared leadership:

1. Did I participate in the meeting in such a way as to. . .
   • facilitate the contributions of others?
   • promote satisfying relationships?
2. If chairing, did I feel comfortable with the role and the skills it involved?
3. If acting as secretary, how did I experience that role and its skills?

Prayer:

How did I experience the prayer as it was planned for this meeting?

Feelings:

How am I feeling as this meeting comes to a close?

Needless to say, there is rarely time after a staff meeting to share responses to all the above questions, but choosing one or two for each meeting would have a cumulative effect over the course of a year.

Some staffs have found it helpful to take turns acting as a process observer of the meeting. At the conclusion of the meeting, the observer shares with the staff what he or she noticed about the process of the meeting. Occasionally these process observations are written down and returned to the staff in addition to the minutes, which focus on the context of the meeting.

Parish staffs do not learn merely from experience but from systematically examining experience. This attitude of systematic examination should characterize both staff meetings and the more intensive efforts at planning and evaluation which occur during pastoral days.

Pastoral Days

If parish staffs regularly engage in staff meetings which provide time for personal sharing and which encourage reflection on pastoral experiences, then needs for relationship-building and task-accomplishment will be met to a great degree. However, since staff meetings are often of a relatively short duration, they are somewhat limited tools for evaluation and planning.

Some staffs with which FCC has worked take a day or more in the fall to do in-depth planning for the year. The planning is somewhat guided by the insights coming from similar days held the previous spring to evaluate the year's programs. These lengthier pastoral days have several advantages:

- They provide an opportunity for informal as well as formal sharing.
- There is time for some relaxed personal sharing and prayer.
- It is possible to engage in the lengthier process needed to seriously reflect on the totality of the parish. This includes theological reflection.

Some parishes included parishioner leaders in all or part of the pastoral days. In this way the broader parish becomes more and more involved in setting parish goals and in evaluating the significance of pastoral activities.

Both staff meetings and pastoral days are significant tools for the development of staff relationships. When well prepared for and well run, they can enhance the staff's ability to be a support group to its members. They can decrease ambiguity and confusion about roles. They can provide opportunities to forge a common vision of the parish mission and increase staff ownership of this mission.

Staff meetings and pastoral days, for all their advantages, remain somewhat formal elements of staff support. There are three other very important elements which deserve to be treated in a chapter on staff relationships. These are prayer, informal communication, and support during critical moments of life.

Prayer

Just as there are differences in personal stories and differences in expectations about staff composition and staff meetings, there are differences in meanings and expectations with respect to prayer.

To one staff member, staff prayer means a hurried Our Father at the beginning of a staff meeting. To another, it means duplicating papers with psalms and readings for all to use. To a third it means reflecting on recent pastoral experiences in the light of Scripture.

There needs to be a real listening and sensitivity on the part of all staff members when it comes to the role of prayer in each one's life. This might be an important aspect to include in the sharing of personal stories. The listening can result in the articulation of a consensus expectation which allows for the diversity within the staff. Where such listening has occurred, it has been possible for staff members to mutually enrich each other as they call each other to greater depths of prayer.

As mentioned, staff members often spend so much time doing the tasks that they do not reflect on *why* they are doing the tasks. Prayer reveals the why because prayer is a relationship with God and God is the ultimate WHY.

But relationships with God are known through relationships with other people. Therefore, it is very fruitful for staff members to reflect on their relationships with each other, with the members of the local Church, and with the broader community in the context of prayer.

It is often possible to do this by reflecting on a passage from Scripture and sharing the meaning of the passage with other staff members. Sometimes questions are helpful in encouraging staff members to reflect on their experience as staff members in the light of Scripture.

By way of an example, FCC prepared a prayerful reflection for the use of a parish staff during one of its pastoral days. Since it was a spring pastoral day, the theme was evaluation.

The passage selected was Psalm 23, "The Lord is my Shepherd." Following are some of the passages from Psalm 23 together with the reflective questions designed to motivate staff sharing and prayer.

Passage	Reflective Questions
He makes me lie down in green pastures. He leads me beside still waters.	As I think of the nourishing images of green grass and fresh water, what aspects of staff life during this past year have been nourishing for me?
He restores my soul. . . . Even though I walk through the valley of death, I fear no evil.	How has the Lord worked through the staff to give me new strength? As I think of the image of the way that goes through deepest darkness, and the prayer to not be afraid, what aspects of staff life during this year surface as painful, as in need of healing, as in need of completion?
You prepare a table before me in the presence of my enemies; you anoint my head with oil, my cup overflows.	Of what kinds of welcome am I still in need from staff members? How do I experience a need for the pouring of ointment?

The staff which used this prayerful reflection spent some time in private prayer over the questions. Then they shared their responses to the questions with each other. Finally, they shared some spontaneous prayer which arose from the thoughts and feelings they experienced while participating in the sharing.

Staffs which engage in this kind of reflective prayer and sharing open up many possibilities for growth in their relationships with each other and with God. They come to a deeper and deeper integration of the pastoral experience with their prayer life. They become more able to invite the parishioners with whom they share the life of the local Church to deeper levels of prayer and sharing as well.

Informal Relationships

Many staff members have told me in interviews that the busy day of a parish minister affords little time for "hanging around." Nevertheless, where these opportunities have occurred and where staff members have been able to interact on a one-to-one basis, solid relationships have resulted. It is in these smaller, less formal encounters, that staff members grow in feelings of belonging and of being supported. It is likewise in these more private exchanges that many conflicts can be resolved before they grow to proportions needing the attention of the entire staff.

Some things which foster the development of informal relationships are:

• A common space where staff members can gather for a coffee break or casual conversation.

• Opportunities to have meals together.

• Doing much of the preparatory work for staff meetings through small subcommittees.

• Occasional celebrations.

Critical Moments

The cultivation of both informal and formal relationships can provide a means of support that can see staff members through the most critical moments of their time on the staff. Two such moments are the first months when a new staff member is integrating into an existing staff and the last months when a staff member is terminating a relationship with an existing staff.

The existence of a clear role description can go a long way to ease confusion in a newcomer. But the role description must be accompanied by visible evidence of support and by an evaluation that is experienced as helpful and informative.

A commissioning ceremony involving the whole staff will help the parish to see the new member as part of the staff team.

Prayer with the staff can be a powerful means of grace and create opportunities to pray out of the experiences and feelings that come with adjustment.

Staff members can greatly support departing colleagues by being present to them in the internal grieving that is a part of all leave-taking. They can help to resolve unfinished issues and to participate in the good-byes. They can encourage prayer and rituals that both surface the pain of good-byes and celebrate the gifts of the departing colleagues.

If the elements of prayer, informal relationships, and ministry to colleagues at critical moments are part of the life of a parish staff, the staff members will feel nourished and supported even as they reach out to nourish and support their brothers and sisters in the parish and neighborhood.

SUMMARY

1. U.S. parishes are in the process of translating the Vatican II People of God ecclesiology into pastoral practice. The transition is difficult and complicated. For parish staff, it is a time of both pain and growth.

2. The most important Church documents on staff relationships are those coming from the local Church at the grassroots level.

3. It is important for parish staffs to come to consensus on who constitutes their membership and on the desired balance of task-accomplishment to relationship-building they will pursue.

4. The sharing of personal stories can be a powerful means of relationship building and can help staff members better understand the personal meanings each member brings to commonly used words.

5. The presence of men and women on parish staffs inevitably raises issues of differences in accountability, role expectations, access to power and information, and different internal meanings of "team." These issues, as well as those related to sexual attraction and intimacy, must be addressed directly by staffs striving for collegiality.

6. Parish staffs can be greatly enriched by members from a diversity of cultural and ethnic backgrounds. Efforts to integrate these staff members are a witness to cultural pluralism in the Church. Parishes also benefit from the special knowledge of parish needs possessed by staff members of diverse cultures.

7. The existence of clear role descriptions fosters team accountability and clarifies for staff members the context within which they are working.

8. An annual commissioning service for the pastoral staff is a way of celebrating the addition of new staff members, situating the work of the staff within the broad mission of the Church, and educating parishioners to the nature and identity of a pastoral team.

9. Staff meetings and pastoral days are important tools for staff planning and evaluation. Many parish staffs need further training in the skills needed to make the best use of staff meeting time. Staff meetings should reflect the desired balance of task-accomplishment and relationship-building agreed upon by the staff. They should be evaluated on a regular basis.

10. It is as important for staff members to reflect on what they have learned from their pastoral activities as it is to engage in those activities. The "what" should never be disengaged from the "why."

11. Staff members are quite diverse on their degree of comfort with shared prayer. However, such prayer can provide an opportunity for staff members to pray out of their lived experience of ministry to and with the parish.

12. Staff relationships benefit from opportunities to interact on a one-to-one or small group basis.

13. Staff members most in need of the support and understanding of their colleagues are newcomers who are integrating into a staff and those who are terminating their ministerial relationship with the parish.

CHAPTER NOTES

1. Gloria Steinem, "The Politics of Talking in Groups," MS. (May, 1981), pp. 43-89.

2. Jeanne Bosson Driscoll and Rosemary A. Bova, "The Sexual Side of Enterprise," *Management Review* (July, 1980), pp. 51-54.

SUGGESTED READINGS

Alban Institute. *Alban Institute Action Information about Religious Systems.* Washington, D.C. Alban Institute. This is a bimonthly publication of the Episcopal Church's research organization. It reports on parish issues based on actual research in the field. It offers an example of documentation that has been derived from the grassroots up.

Ausgburger, David. *Anger and Assertiveness in Pastoral Care.* Philadelphia: Fortress Press, 1979. This book is a short and very readable treatment of healthy ways to recognize and deal with anger and conflict.

Donnelly, Dody, CSJ. *Team Theory and Practice of Team Ministry.* New York: Paulist Press, 1977. This book combines theoretical principles about teaming with practical suggestions drawn from group dynamics resources and from experience. It could be a useful tool for parish staffs struggling with their experience of teaming.

Downs, Thomas. *The Parish as Learning Community.* New York: Paulist Press, 1979. The fifth chapter of this book offers some very practical suggestions for parish staffs who wish to move collegiality from theory to practice.

Dunnam, Maxie D., Gary J. Herbertson, and Everett L. Shistrom. *The Manipulator and the Church.* Nashville: Abingdon Press, 1968. The authors of this book have specialized in studying the phenomenon of manipulation as it surfaces among Church people. Chapters 4 and 5 could be particularly helpful to parish staffs interested in moving from manipulative to self-actualizing styles of interaction.

Flynn, Elizabeth W. *Group Discussion as Learning Process.* New York: Paulist Press, 1973. This book with its accompanying guidebook is a series of exercises designed to teach the skills of communication, mirroring, and process observation. It could be used as a self-help course by parish staffs or as a resource book.

Foundation for Community Creativity. *Newsletter.* Washington, D.C.: Foundation for Community Creativity, 1981. This quarterly publication shares what FCC is learning about the experience of Church at the local level by listening to people at the grassroots.

Hahn, Celia A. *The Minister Is Leaving.* New York: Seabury Press, 1974. This is a compilation of fourteen case studies of parishes whose pastors went on to other parishes. Although parts of this book are more applicable to Protestant congregations, the concluding reflection on congregational grieving offers valuable insights to parish staffs wishing to understand termination.

Keating, Charles J. *The Leadership Book.* New York: Paulist Press, 1978.

The value of this book is that it helps readers to identify styles of leadership which are appropriate. Because it offers options, it is a freeing book.

Management Review. Saranac Lake: American Management Association. This monthly publication of the American Management Association offers some excellent articles on issues such as staff supervision, evaluation, and the use of consultants. Many are applicable to parish staffs.

Ministries. Minneapolis: Winston Press. This monthly publication offers articles of special interest to staff members who have clear roles or who are in search of clear roles (youth minister, DRE, etc.).

NCCB Parish Project. *Parish Development: Programs and Organizations* (a directory). Washington, D.C.: U.S. Catholic Conference, 1980. This publication lists twenty-seven consultant organizations which are available to work with parishes.

Steele, Sara M. *Contemporary Approaches to Program Evaluation.* Washington, D.C.: Educational Resources Division, Capitol Publications, Inc., 1973. This monograph is designed as a reference tool. It offers a comprehensive listing of contemporary evaluation approaches together with some tips on selecting the evaluation model most appropriate for a specific need.

Today's Parish. West Mystic, Conn.: Twenty-Third Publications. This monthly magazine contains special feature articles designed for parish staffs.

Gathering
the Folks

The Rev. Thomas J. Caroluzza

Ordained for the Diocese of
Richmond, Virginia, in 1958,
Father Caroluzza taught high-
school English, was principal of
a high school, and pastor of three
parishes. Currently he is pastor
of Our Lady of Nazareth Parish
in Roanoke, Virginia. He holds a
Master of Science degree in
educational administration from
Old Dominion University in
Norfolk, Virginia, and a Doctor
of Ministry degree from St. Mary
Seminary and University in
Baltimore.

In the summer of 1967 I visited the World's Fair at Montreal. Like thousands of others, I was enthralled with the exhibits at the Czechoslovakian Pavilion. There I was bombarded with futuristic and computerized images on film and with mixed media demonstrations that delighted all the senses, rather than the limited sight and sound shows with which I had been familiar.

There was, however, something much simpler at Expo 67 which became the most memorable event of that visit for me. It began while I was looking for a gift in one of the little shops in the Belgian Village. I heard the sounds of a street band in the distance. As it drew closer to the shop, I could hear the excitement of the crowd mingling with the music. I hurried out to get a closer look, and the next thing I knew I was caught up in a parade. Everyone, adults as well as children, began following the band Pied-Piper style through the streets and into the Village Square. I was in a participative parade that ended in a festival of singing and dancing.

What was so amazing about this experience was that so many people had been gathered so quickly from so many different and private activities in that village. It is true that I love a parade and will go out of my way to watch one go by, but I never dreamed that I would get caught up in one, especially with strangers. But it happened. For a brief time in a distant city, I was celebrating with total strangers who all felt that they belonged together.

I can imagine that something similar to my Expo 67 experience might have happened that day when Jesus entered the city of Jerusalem for his

31

hour of glory. It is probable that some people merely went as spectators, and the next thing they knew they got all caught up in the event.

That must have also been true when God's people left Egypt and centuries later when the time came for them to return to Jerusalem from Babylon. The people who gathered must have experienced feelings of being together, of being caught up in the event, filled with excitement and anticipation. There is something that keeps people from doing their own private thing at times like that. It may begin with mere curiosity, but before they know it, they are in the parade or marching to the promised land or waving branches and singing Hosanna. Once it happens, they cannot wait to tell someone about it — a story generally ends with something like: "Well, you just had to be there to appreciate it."

What is it that gathers people together in parishes? How does the Church gather folks, now that people live in urban and suburban enclaves and no longer in Belgian or American villages? What has happened to the excitement and anticipation, that feeling of being caught up in something of great importance? It is true that folks will gather with that kind of exuberance whenever there's a Medieval Crusade to the Holy Land or some twentieth-century crisis. It was easy to gather immigrants into clusters in the first quarter of this century; but how does the Church gather people in ordinary times, week after week in today's U.S.A.? For a parish to work, some answers must be found to these basic questions about gathering.

The Nature and Importance of Gathering

Gathering is primarily a ministry of community building. Gathering people together is participating in the reconciling ministry of Jesus in whom "all things hold together" (Colossians 1:17). It is the ministry of linking and bonding, of harmonizing and connecting. The New Testament's favorite word for this ministry is *Koinonia,* togetherness or fellowship, literally *"sharing in partnership"* (1 John 1:7).

Basically, gathering people is a ministry of overcoming divisions, a healing and reconciling ministry, a participation in the redemptive activity of God in our world. That is why people experience a feeling of well-being, of belonging, of wholeness, of coming home, every time they are truly *gathered* in community. That is something of the feeling I experienced briefly in the Belgian Village at Expo 67. People were together. They were happy and at peace for a fleeting hour. They were no longer American and Belgian and Canadian; no longer young and old, male and female, black and white; they were gathered together as one people. Such a gathering is always a glimpse of the kingdom of God.

The kind of gathering the Church is about is not a passing or temporary experience. It is the gathering in the Lord and by the Lord. The celebration of his Word and sacrament is the enduring sign that keeps calling us to remember the original unity intended by the Lord and the lasting unity of the kingdom. The Church's celebrations of the Word and Eucharist are the focus for this ministry of gathering, when the people cluster around the Book and the Table.

If the proclamation of the Word of God puts people to sleep and the celebration of the Eucharist is boring, then the symbols, the words, the rites, and the signs that are vehicles for this divine activity of gathering have become opaque. Vatican II's "Decree on the Ministry and Life of the Priest" emphasizes this point: "The People of God is formed into one in the first place by the Word of the living God" (No. 4). The proclamation of that word needs to be such that it gathers rather than scatters.

The word God speaks is meant to be effective. The liturgy of the Eucharist becomes that effective response in Jesus Christ. The same document of Vatican Council II emphasizes the centrality of the Eucharist as the sacrament of gathering: "No Christian Community is built up which does not grow from and hinge on the celebration of the môst Holy Eucharist" (No. 6). Therefore, no matter what other Church gathering activities may be, they must always lead to the gathered community which celebrates in Word and sacrament. It is this weekly celebration that empowers people as a community gathered in the Lord to go out on mission to gather others.

Gathering: A Pastoral Image

The image suggested by the word *gathering* is a pastoral image. It is the ministry of a shepherd, or in Latin, a pastor. Jesus used the image to describe his own ministry in John 10 when he calls himself a Good Pastor who gathers his flock. In Matthew he indicates that he is even willing to go out to search for the one who is not gathered with the rest (Matthew 18:12). This gathering image has deep roots in the Hebrew tradition as an image of God's relationship with his people.

Nowhere in the Hebrew Scriptures is this image more beautifully elaborated than in Jeremiah 23 and Ezekiel 34. In those texts, Yahweh is the great gatherer of the flock that was scattered. He gathers together his people for reform and places Good Shepherds in their midst. Jesus stands in that tradition. He speaks so poignantly about this ministry of his in Matthew: "O Jerusalem . . . how often would I have gathered your children together as a hen gathers her brood under her wings, and you would not!" (Matthew 23:37). It is this same image of gathering the flock which Matthew uses to envision the end time (Matthew 25:31ff).

The ministry of gathering people is, then, a primary and essential ministry in the parish. It is a ministry which has deep roots in biblical tradition and it is something a great deal more than glad-handing fellowship. While the social sciences may give some insights concerning calling people together in groups, what the Church needs to be concerned about is something much deeper, not just good management, but good ministry.

Characteristics of the Minister Who Gathers

There is no doubt that biblically the pastor (shepherd) is the key in this ministry of gathering. In fact, some would make this ministry the defining characteristic of the role of pastor.[1] As in all ministries, this too is a ministry that is shared with all the baptized. For that reason, in the following reflections the word *pastor* is used in its broadest sense to include all those who share in the pastoral role and function, especially the parish pastoral team, but more specifically the one who has been given the responsibility of pastoring by appointment.

While an effective ministry of gathering needs to include a familiarity with the findings of the behavioral sciences, that will not be the focus here. This is not to play down the usefulness of the behavioral sciences for this ministry of gathering, but rather to see the starting point for all ministry in the scriptures.[2]

The paradigmatic text for the ministry of gathering is John 10:1-18. That text contains six basic characteristics needed in any ministry of gathering the people, namely: (1) someone who knows the people and is known by them; (2) someone who is willing to model the Christian life of faith; (3) someone who is able to give others a sense of belonging; (4) someone who is willing to make personal sacrifices; (5) someone who is a person of prayer, in touch with the scriptures; and (6) someone who is willing to reach out to those on the margins of the community.

1. *A minister is someone who knows his or her people* (John 10:3-4, 14). A pastor who is distant and aloof from the people will never have an effective ministry of gathering in the parish. The good pastor knows parishioners by name. As the Little Prince says, to know someone's name is to be responsible for that person. Adam can name the creatures and thereby become responsible for them. The knowledge of people that a good pastor needs begins with knowing their names. This is more than "knowing the cards of census and contribution" (although that may be a good starting point). There can be no real gathering of people when the pastor does not know every person by first and last name.

When parishes exceed three hundred households it becomes virtually impossible for any person to say, "I know mine and mine know me." When that happens the pastor will need to find new ways of gathering, either creating a new parish or subdividing the parish into mini-parishes. The knowledge pastors must have, of course, goes well beyond putting names with faces. "I know mine and mine know me" is a call for a deeper relationship; and this knowledge must be mutual. Some pastors may know their people, but they are not effective as gatherers because they never let their people know them.

Dr. Thomas Ambrogi summarized the process of relationships by using what he called "the four C's" of ever-deepening relationships. Applied to a mutual knowledge between pastor and people, they would be: to be an effective gatherer one must begin with *compassion*. The pastor must genuinely feel with the people, to be able to suffer with them when they suffer and be joyful with them when they're joyful. That is only the beginning of the relationship.

To know one's people means a willingness to deepen that relationship into *companionship.* The pastor must be willing to walk side by side with parishioners. A pastor never stands above people but in their midst as one who serves. A pastor does not preach *to* people but reflects on the scriptures *with* people. As an example, a pastor should never ask people to tithe unless he is also tithing in the parish. Yet how many pastors use the church envelopes they ask their people to use? To be a gatherer of people means not only being compassionate, but being willing to walk the journey with them.

This kind of mutual knowledge of each other leads to *communion,* being one with a people. Communion is the root meaning of gathering as was explored earlier in this chapter. It is the oneness in faith where people are not just walking side by side, but facing each other in the Lord. That is the goal of all ministry, to make a communion of people, one body of Christ healed of all divisions.

There is also something that tests the authenticity of communion. It is called *conviviality.* Etymologically it means the ability to live with others, but connotatively it means to live joyfully with others. It is the stance of "Zorba the Greek," that marvelous character of Nikos Kazantzakis. Even when his life's scheme-dream crumbles before the eyes of the whole community, he can dance. As the old religious hymn puts it: "Dance then wherever you may be. . . ." It goes on to say that Jesus is the Lord of the dance, even while hanging on the tree.

How many gathered communities scatter, the moment a crisis situation occurs in that community? If the pastor is to be an effective gatherer of people, he must move the community to the level of conviviality. The pastor must be willing to dance with the people, if not literally, then figuratively. The pastor must be willing to believe in hope for resurrection, even when death seems so near in the community. A good pastor must be able to say, "I know mine and mine know me." That mutual knowledge is a growing process from compassion to companionship to communion to conviviality.

2. *A minister is someone who is willing to walk out in front:* "He goes before them, and the sheep follow him" (John 10:4). This text does not sanction clericalism nor set the minister apart from the community. Rather, it sees the minister as a model for the community. In Wes Seeliger's western image, the pastor is the scout who returns to the wagon train saying, "I know you can make it; I've already tried it and I made it."[3] Much of the above discussion on the relationship of companionship would apply here. However, there is something more being suggested.

To walk out in front is to be what Jung calls a mana-person, someone who has travelled into the chaos and returned to tell it. This is not the person with all the answers, but someone who has lived life in faith, someone who has travelled the journey and even failed, someone who was not afraid to go first when everyone else was cowering. People will gather around such a person. There was an associate pastor who was a master at this. People gathered around him because he could show the way, even in little things.

When some event would come to a conclusion, he was the first one to begin cleaning up the space. Pretty soon everyone else was pitching in to make the task a simple one. If the minister gets into the practice of being the first to push the broom, that soon becomes a lifestyle in which willingness to walk out in front pervades the ministry at every level.

3. *A minister is someone who can create a space where others feel they can belong.* "If anyone enters by me, he will be saved . . ." and "I came that they may have life, and have it abundantly" (John 10:9, 10). The deeper questions people are asking in parishes are always the same questions. They are life questions: "Does it all make sense?" "How do you explain suffering, and death?" "How do I overcome my loneliness; where can I really belong?" It is these questions the gatherer of people must address. A key concern is the issue of belonging. The parish ought to image the kind of hospitality that creates a space where all kinds of people can belong. That is why parishes take steps to create an open and hospitable space where people are welcomed. Besides name tags at worship and introducing visitors before beginning liturgy, parishes try to encourage everyone to reach out to others, especially strangers.

It seems such a small thing, but it gives that sense of belonging that is so necessary in the ministry of gathering the people. For no parish can be the *ekklesia,* the assembly, the gathered people of God, if its members do not even greet one another as brothers and sisters in the Lord.

One parish had such a powerful effect on a woman that she wrote to the church about how much this chance occurrence had meant to her. She and her husband were bringing their first son to college and came to Sunday Eucharist. They were hundreds of miles from home and really felt depressed over this first experience in sending a child out of the family. As she told it, someone came up to them as soon as they got out of their car, they were welcomed by greeters at the door who made them feel at home, and the congregation welcomed them with applause as they were introduced before worship. In her letter she said: "I just knew everything was going to be all right."

To be a gatherer of people, a minister must find ways to help people feel they belong. Much of Henri Nouwen's work emphasizes this aspect of the ministry of gathering. In *Reaching Out,* he speaks of creating a free and friendly space for others so that they may move from loneliness to solitude, and from hostility to hospitality. He calls it the first and second movements in the spiritual life. That is what people must be about if they hope to be gatherers of other people. It is not gimmicks of fellowship, but creating space in our lives for others.

4. *A minister is someone who is willing to make personal sacrifices* (John 10:11). One way to phrase a question that tests that notion is: Can this community count on its pastor when the going gets rough? Hired hands are free in times of crisis; the gatherer-shepherd does not work for pay (John 10:13). He has a commitment to this people that goes beyond the rewards of his ministry. He cares for them even when they do not care if he cares.

While this may not be the place to discuss it in detail, there are some dangers in the new professionalization of the clergy. There is the danger of the pastor turning into a hired hand. When the pastor has made a commitment to the people, they will know he can be counted on in bad times as well as in good ones.

5. *A minister is someone who is a person of prayer and in touch with the scriptures* (John 10:15). While it is certain that the gatherer needs some of the qualities of the bandleader of the World's Fair Belgian experience in 1967 (some have called these the qualities of the clown), and while it is equally true that he must be a storyteller in the Dunne and Shea sense, none of these images will be effective unless his ministry is rooted in the scriptures and centered on the Lord who rules his life. This rootedness keeps gathering from being merely good showmanship. Rallying people together can only be sustained by the Lord, who is the chief gatherer. Therefore, the minister needs time for reflection and solitude, time to get a perspective on his ministry, time to deepen the quality of his ongoing relationship with this community of Christians.

6. *The minister must be willing to reach out to the alienated and the unchurched* (John 10:16). As stated earlier, God's work of reconciliation is not limited to the people gathered in church records or even at Sunday worship. All creation is groaning to be gathered into the reality God wills. People must get beyond self-nurture to fulfill the ministry of gathering. Such a move is especially difficult in the post-Vatican II days when there is so much need for reeducation. People can get caught up in programming for self-nurture to the extent that they forget what it was they were being nurtured for in the first place. The parish that is not about outreach, mission, and evangelization will soon turn in on itself with concerns for self-fulfillment. This narcissistic effect will end in the death of the community. Therefore, they must always remind themselves that they are gathered to be scattered.

The gathered community can only remain alive insofar as it is assembling those who have been on mission. They are sent out from liturgy to be called back together. The gathering ministry must always be conscious of those who have not heard and celebrated the good news. Some of those people belong to the parish and once were gathered together with it. Now, however, they are apart. Some of those people have never heard of the Church. Some are the marginals of society. Some are too busy or too lazy or too poor to have time for community. These people always need to be in the consciousness of all Christians, if one day all are to be gathered into the one flock, headed by the one shepherd, Jesus himself.

Every pastoral minister who has worked for renewal during the past fifteen years knows of the great numbers of Catholics who have been alienated from the Church because of change. They are lost, and do not feel at home in the Church anymore. While every attempt at reconciliation must be based on truth, and while there can be no compromising of the Church, it is still very important that people reach out to everyone who has been alienated by change. They are the scattered who need to be gathered again. In our parish we simply identified the inactive members and sent them a questionnaire. We asked their help in trying to identify the reasons why they felt other people were alienated. We were surprised at how few gave top priority to liturgical change. The results of that questionnaire helped us plan realistic outreach efforts in our parish for the years ahead.

Jim Dunning tells a story of a priest in San Antonio. When he arrived he decided to visit all the people. Their problems were basic: "You bring back our Jesus." They were referring to the crucifix that had been removed during the renovation of the church.[4] Many of those scattered from our parishes are scattered not because they are rigid or closed to liturgical change, but because of our insensitivities to their symbols. This is the point Urban Holmes makes so convincingly in his *Ministry and Imagination.*[5]

There are entire groups of people who are alienated from the Church and need to be gathered. One of those alienated groups that the Church rarely reaches out to are artists. In one of Pope Paul VI's talks to a group of artists in Rome, he apologized for what the Church has done in our time to cause that alienation. The great artists who gave expression to the mysteries in another age were collaborators with the Church in the ministry of proclamation. In our own time they no longer belong. Most of our congregations are satisfied with cheap reproductions and religious goods that are mass-produced. For these reasons we need to make renewed outreach, no matter how timid, to the artists of our own communities. We need to invite artists to exhibit their "secular" works in our parish buildings.

Perhaps the group that needs outreach more than anyone else is the poor, the favorites of God. As Andrew Greeley has demonstrated scientifically, the American Catholic Church has become a middle-class Church. No longer is it the Church of the poor or even the Church of the lower middle class. The good pastoral team is one that goes out in search for the poor who no longer find a home in the midst of the Church. How comfortable would the poor be in most parish churches? How do the lifestyles of ministers become the cause for that exclusion?

These are simply beginning questions the Church must face in its ministry of gathering the poor. Does the Church believe that the poor have something to teach the rest of us? Is it possible to include them without demeaning them? Are people able to work for systematic change and get beyond handouts of temporary alleviation of needs?

It is here that the question of self-nurture arises again. Many people seem to spend all their time on personal growth and self-fulfillment. They are usually fairly successful in their religious education programs, but these programs never seem to be enough. Although adult education programs have gotten better in recent years, they always seem to need to be just a little better than they are. When better ones arrive, only the best will do. The best leads to novelty, and novelty to self-destruction.

Perhaps the Church has never really asked the fundamental question: "Education for what?" Education is certainly not for its own sake. Education is for empowering people to be Catholic Christians so that they can be sent on a mission to preach the good news to all who will listen. In secular education the movement was from education for making students good ladies and gentlemen, to education for making good workers in an industrial society. John Dewey challenged that concept by calling for an education for making good citizens in a democracy. He raised the fundamental educational question: "Why are we doing this anyway?" or "Education for what?" Only when parishes begin to raise the question about religious education programs will they ever get to this last characteristic of the ministry of gathering; the willingness to reach out to the alienated, the marginal, the unchurched.

When gathering is viewed from this perspective, it becomes a ministry of evangelization. Some parishes spend too much time in kerygmatic ministry; they never get beyond self-nurture to the ministry of gathering the poor, and those who are not sharing in the good news. Harry Fagan suggests a few steps that need to be taken to get beyond self-nurture in middle-class churches. He indicates that first the parish needs to concentrate on "simplicity, on sharing, service, solidarity, and on the empowerment of poor people."[6]

John 10:16 suggests that the Church has to reach out to "the others that are not of this fold," the unchurched. So often convert-making is nothing more than rustling the sheep from other Christian congregations. It is shuffling membership from one believing Christian community to another. The *Rite of Christian Initiation of Adults* has become the most significant document of the post-Vatican II Church precisely because it focuses on the congregation's role in the ministry of evangelization. No pastoral minister will ever fulfill his or her ministry of gathering until he or she is thoroughly familiar with this document. There is no simple program that has brought about a greater renewal of parish life than the RCIA. It is here in this process that the parish can finally get out of self-nurture to reaching out to others.

Obstacles to the Ministry of Gathering

Perhaps the greatest obstacle to the ministry of gathering in today's church is the size of the parish. The average size of a Catholic parish in the United States in most dioceses far exceeds the optimal number of people for an effective ministry of gathering. As was stated earlier, anything beyond three hundred households makes it almost impossible for a pastor to know people by name, especially if that knowledge is expected to be more than knowing the names on a census card.

A second obstacle is the unwillingness of many pastoral ministers to move away from self-nurturing programs. Only when this danger is perceived as it really is will people be able to gather as they should.

Jesus gave the ministry of gathering to his disciples. He who was the chief gatherer of the flock said to them: "Feed my lambs; feed my sheep" (John 21:15). Peter and Paul took that command seriously and became good shepherds who gathered those early congregations in the Lord. That is also the ministry they handed on to others (cf. 1 Peter 2:25 and Acts 20:28). That ministry continues today for you and me in our parishes. We must be convinced that it is the Lord who is gathering his people right now where we are and live and celebrate. As James Fenhagen puts it: "The question is not *if* but *how* — the question that, by the grace of God, turns us in hope to the future, which is now."[7]

SUMMARY

1. Gathering is primarily a part of community building, a participation in the reconciling of Jesus.

2. Gathering is also a pastoral image. John 10:1-18 lists six basic characteristics for anyone engaged in the ministry of gathering people. Those characteristics are: someone who knows and is known, is willing to model the life of faith, is able to give others a sense of belonging, is willing to make personal sacrifices, is a person of prayer, and is willing to reach out to those in need.

3. The two greatest obstacles to the ministry of gathering are the large size of parishes and the unwillingness of many ministers to move away from self-nurturing programs.

CHAPTER NOTES

1. Philip Murnion, ed., *The Parish Project: What Is a Parish?* (Washington, D.C.: National Conference of Catholic Bishops, 1980).
2. For those who prefer "the good management approach" to ministry, Lyle E. Schaller has an excellent book entitled *Effective Church Planning* (see Suggested Readings at the end of this chapter). Schaller translates concepts from the behavioral sciences into terms that are useful for a more effective ministry. His caution against the common error of using small group techniques for the gathering of large groups is especially important (p. 17).
3. Mark Link, *Still Point in a Turning World,* p. 20.
4. James B. Dunning, *New Wine: New Wineskins* (Chicago: William B. Sadlier, Inc., 1981), pp. 96-97.
5. Urban T. Holmes, *Ministry and Imagination* (New York: Seabury Press, 1976), p. 198.
6. Harry Fagan, *Parish Ministry.* II (March, 1981), pp. 3-4.
7. James C. Fenhagen, *Mutual Ministry* (New York: Seabury Press, 1977), p. 140.

SUGGESTED READINGS

Dunning, James B. *Ministries: Sharing God's Gifts*. Winona: Saint Mary's Press, 1980. James Dunning focuses on the essential characteristic of ministry in our time: a variety of gifts that are shared with all the people. This book challenges the reader to discover new opportunities in the shared ministries of the Word, community-building, worship, and service-healing. A useful book for those engaged in the ministry of gathering the people.

——. *New Wine: New Wineskins*. Chicago: William H. Sadlier, Inc., 1981. This latest book by Jim Dunning is essential reading for those who are engaged in the ministry of evangelization. Not only does he fully explore the implications of the Rite of Christian Initiation of Adults with good theory and practical experiences throughout the United States, but he also gives the reader many insights into how the RCIA changes attitudes and practice in other aspects of pastoral ministry.

Fenhagen, James C. *Mutual Ministry*. New York: Seabury Press, 1977. This book is a must for anyone working in parish ministry in the 1980's. The pastoral insights he shares with the reader come from an updated theology of ministry and some good practice by the author. This is a very valuable and very readable book.

Holmes, Urban T. *Ministry and Imagination*. New York: Seabury Press, 1976. Holmes tackles the tension between transcendence and immanence which has been a common experience in the post-Vatican II Church. He argues convincingly for a rediscovery of the imaginative element in ministry as the route to mystery and meaning for the modern Christian. Especially useful are his final chapters on the priest and the congregation, where he explores the implications of his thesis for ministry today.

Murnion, Philip. *The Parish Project: What Is a Pastor?* Washington, D.C.: NCCB Publications, 1980. This booklet is a series of reflections by several pastors from parishes in different parts of the United States. Each pastor searches for an image which captures the meaning of his ministry in today's Church. One of them explores the image in this chapter, the image of Shepherd.

Schaller, Lyle E. *Effective Church Planning*. Nashville: Abingdon Press, 1979. In this book, Schaller gives seven factors for translating concepts from the behavioral sciences into useful terms for solving some parish problems: group size, place, planning models, support systems, and enabling ministry. This book is very helpful for working with groups within the parish.

The Parish as Welcoming Community

The Rev. James A. Burke

Ordained for the Archdiocese of Newark in 1956, Father Burke has been associate pastor of a large city parish and the Director of Adult Religious Education for the Archdiocese. At present he is pastor of a large suburban parish, St. Paul's, in Ramsey, New Jersey. Father Burke holds master's degrees in theology, pastoral counseling, and religious education.

The human need to be recognized as a person, to feel welcomed, to be announced as important by another's word or gesture, is an ongoing desire of every individual. The feeling that others care and want to share some of their time, words, or presence makes people respond in kind. To be in some way welcomed is to be touched by the redemptive hand of God. The challenge, then, to each Catholic Christian is to put flesh on one, simple, theological tenet: all men and women are sisters and brothers.

People Do Care

To communicate as Christians is to share and to care. The world of business invests time, money, and energy in the field of communications. Corporations make this investment to influence people for material gain. Christians do it because they care about people and wish them to share in the Good News of salvation.

As James Fenhagen has pointed out: "The Christian faith, for most people, is not communicated by doctrinal pronouncements or the solemn assembly of ecclesiastical dignitaries, but by what goes on in the Church in its most local setting. It is here, in the Church down the street, that people are caught up in the Gospel promises — or turned away. . . . The parish Church, despite its often glaring inadequacies is in a unique position to help men and women move into a new world with courage and hope."[1]

Therefore, the parish priest, the religious, and the lay person, are each called to assist people's communicating with one another as a parish community. As parish leaders, they are the initiators in creating a parish environment that has the qualities of a sharing/caring Christian community, family, and home.

Most of all, the parish must communicate a sense of love and acceptance. How to communicate this feeling is a skill and a gift, a skill that can be learned and a gift of the Spirit. Specific approaches can change a parish atmosphere from mechanical to personal, individual to communal, distant to present, non-concerned to concerned. These approaches are neither complicated nor difficult.

Liturgy

The gathering of God's people at the Eucharistic Celebration can be a natural vehicle for communicating the meaning of God's love. This time together can be enriched by creating an atmosphere that is warm, friendly, and accepting. By word and gesture, people can be encouraged to relate to one another and share their common faith experience. Some ways to create a friendly environment are:

1. Greeting: When a person visits anyone's home, the host is attentive to arranging time so that he or she is present to meet them. A friendly greeting and some small talk touches the whole personality of the invited guest and a deeper relationship begins. Shouldn't this happen on a Sunday morning as the family of God gathers to worship? Why should not priests, sisters, ushers feel an equal need to welcome the hundreds that come for Sunday Eucharist? A hearty "Good morning, how are you?" personally spoken by the pastor, associate staff member, or usher communicates in word, handshake, and smile the message "We're glad you're here — welcome!" This greeting sets the tone, creates a spirit, makes the person entering feel a little more important and helps to bring about supportive dispositions that encourage and enliven community and individual faith. It is contagious because it is a natural and human expression of belonging to a family.

2. Introductions at Mass: The congregation assembled at Mass provides an opportunity to foster deeper relationships among parishioners. To create a relaxed mood and a spirit of fellowship at Eucharistic Celebrations, some parishes have a custom that after the celebrant has reached his place and the entrance hymn has concluded, he pauses and invites those assembled to introduce themselves to one other person.

If not overdone, it works. Sharing takes place and members of the parish begin to know other members. Visitors feel welcome and parishioners feel more at home. Formality and rigidity give way to a more relaxed and comfortable feeling. The liturgy begins in a pleasant atmosphere. The effects after the liturgy are also far-reaching, extending into the parking lot and the supermarket.

3. Post-Liturgy: Sunday morning worship is a peak time of the week for most Catholics. The presence, visibility, and availability of the parish staff members (including priests) is especially needed. By parish staff members being available at different doors of the church each week, parishioners have the opportunity to speak about any of their needs.

Conversations touch every human problem: "I just heard your mother was sick. How is she?" or "Happy anniversary" or "Good luck on the Fire

Captain's exam this Friday" or "You look like a new parishioner — welcome!" The presence of parish staff members after every Mass can be a real expression of concern for parishioners.

Another way to help parishioners and visitors get to know each other is for the social activities committee to provide coffee and doughnuts after each Mass on Sunday once a month. These get-togethers can be held in the rectory or any other appropriate place on the church grounds. Gathering people after Mass is just another approach that helps the parish develop a welcoming spirit.

Parish events during the week also provide occasions when adults come together in groups. Unfortunately, some people presume that all the people in any group know each other. In many parish gatherings people do not know one another and feel less than comfortable in the group. A welcoming parish realizes that good human relationships are crucial to any human understanding and growth in Christian living. Only in a friendly, warm atmosphere can learning, teamwork, collaboration, and Christian community take place.

Visitation

"You have to know the territory," goes the line from *The Music Man*. Before companies market any product, expensive research is done to find out the needs of potential buyers. Prior to designing adult education courses, planners use different processes of personal questioning and sample surveys to assess the real needs of people. Leaders in parishes must also know the territory. Knowing comes from personal research about who the parishioners are, what their home environments are like, what their skills are and what their felt and real faith needs are.

The best way of doing research is by personal home visitation. This outreach is to old parishioners, new parishioners, unchurched parishioners, to other Christians and to non-Christians. Visitations of homes is a unique and challenging form of evangelization.

1. *Visitation by Way of Census:* Pope Paul VI wrote, "Evangelization means bringing the Good News into all the strata of humanity and through its influence, transforming humanity from within and making it new."[2] One of the most important means of evangelization is the communication of faith that is done best in a one-to-one relationship. There is simply no substitute for the parish priests' taking the census house to house.

Often, when the topic of census is voiced in priests' gatherings, there are a variety of negative feelings expressed: no time; too busy running and/or organizing this or that program; the administration and paperwork of the parish do not allow for it; takes away from sermon preparation; very few people are home; it is too mechanical. The rationalizations go on.

Certainly, home visitation is hard work and it is time-consuming. However, the spiritual and material benefits to the minister, the parish, the organizations, and the individuals visited more than compensate. There is nothing more fulfilling than the personal contact and the deepening of relationships that come from this direct meeting of parishioners.

To get personal for a moment, in our small town, the associate and I visit half the homes each year. We carry with us: (a) an attractive parish brochure, (b) a typed note, (c) census cards with registered families, (d) blank census cards for new parishioners, and (e) the prayers of a worshipping community.

Our small parish brochure contains seven goals that set forth the principles and values that guide our parish family and its growth, a listing of parish worship celebrations, names of staff persons and necessary phone numbers. This small brochure is neat, eye-catching, and informative. It is left at every Catholic home and the homes where no one answers. In the latter case, a typed note with a personal signature is also left, which reads:

> Dear Friends:
>
> I stopped by on Parish Visitation today and unfortunately did not find you in. For those families that are Catholic, I am leaving a small parish brochure. Also, for any new Catholic parishioners who are not registered, I am leaving a census card that can be filled out and returned to St. Paul's Rectory.
>
> If I have not met you personally, please introduce yourself to me after one of the Masses.
>
> If I can be of any help to you or your family, please feel free to call me at 555-1212.

When we meet new Catholic families, we fill out a new census card which calls for a minimum of information. We feel strongly that census time is a time of grace and we include prayers for it in the General Intercessions.

Home visitations are limited because of time. With sixteen hundred Catholic families, we find it important to spend more time with Catholic families who are "unchurched," "inactive," or "estranged." Namely those who other than for a wedding, funeral, Christmas or Easter, have not worshipped in any Catholic church within the previous six months.

People's stories, situations, backgrounds, and problems — spiritual, material, and emotional — are as varied as the colors in a field of wild flowers, showing every shade of the human condition.

A middle-aged man: "I've been divorced and remarried for twenty years and would love to receive the sacraments." A woman in her late thirties: "I hear a lot about Church annulments. Do you think there's any hope for me to get back to the Church? I'm bringing my children up Catholic, but I feel guilty when I can't go to communion." A senior citizen: "I've been away about forty-five years from confession, but I'm thinking about going back to church." A young housewife: "I would love to receive, but I have this problem with birth control. Can anything be done?" Another woman: "I'm Catholic and my husband is Jewish. We have two children, seven and nine, and they aren't baptized. I went to a Catholic college and I want to pass the Catholic faith on to them. I'm glad you're here. What can I do?"

Problem after problem, followed by desire after desire to be reinserted into the life of the Church. The openness and goodwill of people is disarming. There is a spiritual hunger that cries out for listening, understanding, empathy, presence, time, forgiveness, and healing.

Occasionally, in home visitations, confessions are heard, the sacrament of the sick is administered, shut-ins are discovered, and some who are interested in the Catholic Church are stimulated to be part of our catechumenate process. In all encounters, encouragement is a key attitude. People need to be affirmed. Personal contact is redemptive.

A side effect of parish visitation is the talent bank that is established. Potential ushers, lectors, catechists, and aides appear. People interested in being part of a liturgy team, and volunteers anxious to help others in service-oriented programs, come forward. We become acquainted with parishioners with various expertise: artists, electricians, financial experts, educators, carpenters, secretaries, and retired men and women willing to volunteer time. Many parishioners are willing to donate time, talent, and service to the parish and visitation-census time helps us identify them and plug them into parish life.

We knock on every door. With non-Catholic families, we identify ourselves, pass the time of day, and encourage them to worship in their religion. "I'm here to encourage you in the practice of your religion. Hang in there — it's important." Frequently, conversations will deal with members of their families who have married Catholics or have become Catholic or who were baptized and reared as Catholics and are now practicing in another faith. In the words of one non-Catholic: "Father, what you're doing in visiting the families of your Church should be done by our ministers." Ecumenically, these short encounters say and do more than many educational programs.

2. *Visitation: An Ecumenical Responsibility:* A parish does not exist in a vacuum. The parish is part of a broader community and its various religious and civic groups. A parish alive with the Spirit reaches out beyond its members. It offers signs of welcome, concern, and acceptance to the whole community. The approach should be to work together with other religious denominations on common programs and projects. This communicates a Christian spirit of caring and sharing.

One such project in our community was aptly titled: "Outreach — We Care — We Share." "Outreach" was an ecumenical visitation project planned by the Catholic, Lutheran, Presbyterian, and Episcopalian churches of our community. It was initiated by the town clergy association and quickly broadened to include the laity from the various denominations. The goal was to communicate to the entire town of forty-nine hundred families that we are a caring community and to invite them to share in the spiritual, social, and educational dimensions of the faith of their choice.

This goal was achieved by a series of sermons, training sessions, and mailings, followed by visitations of church members to all the homes of our community. Teams were comprised of two people each, and no team had more than one member of a participating denomination. This "Outreach" was to young adults and adults, and especially to those who are "unchurched," that is, those not actively involved with any faith community. Team members were trained to avoid proselytizing of any type and to concentrate on explaining the purpose of the visit, listening to the hurts, joys, and sorrows of the family, and encouraging them to worship in the church or synagogue of their choice.

Each visitor left a small brochure. This brochure gave a short explanation of the purpose of the project and identified the different churches and synagogue of our community. The success of this "Outreach" project is quantifiable only in the statistics concerning homes visited, number of participants, and in the results of follow-up visits by various congregations. The real success of "Outreach" may never be known in terms of the return of the alienated, or the new faith participation of the unchurched. However, the project can be termed ecumenically successful qualitatively. Among the identifiable results are:

• The involvement of lay people in planning, organization, and visitations created feelings of cohesion.

• The ecumenical thrust highlighted the similarities rather than the differences of various denominations.

• The simple fact that so many people were willing to give up their Sunday afternoons to witness the impact of faith in their own lives had a positive effect on the town.

• The warm reception received by the visitors was encouraging.

• The reports of the visitors concerning their personal experiences were universally enthusiastic and their personal faith was enriched.

• The reception by aged and/or the lonely was particularly gratifying.

• Although not a goal of the project, many rewarding discussions about Church and religion occurred.

When people from different religious orientations work together on a common project, good things happen. Both those personally involved and those to whom a hand of welcome is extended begin to realize in a deeper way that all are brothers and sisters under the fatherhood of God.

3. *Visitation by Way of the Sacraments:* Every year is the year of the family. We can never do enough to encourage its members, address its problems, and offer spiritual, psychological, and educational services. After a period of brainstorming by our staff, the need for more personal contact with families emerged. We decided on an outreach program that moved us away from the rectory, convent, and school into the family circle. Why not meet families on their turf, listen to their needs, and minister to them? The approach agreed upon by our staff (two priests, religious education coordinator, school principal, and pastoral minister) was to visit in the evenings

the parents of all children receiving First Communion and confirmation. The families were divided among staff members, phone calls were made, appointments set up, and home visitations took place. Approximately two hundred and fifty families were visited within a three-month period, with each staff member visiting fifty homes. Half of the families visited could be classified as "unchurched."

Our format in these visitations was simple and informal. Among the goals we set out to achieve were:

- To listen to the family story with its positives/negatives.
- To invite an expression of where parents are spiritually.
- To listen to hurts caused by Church people in the past.
- To speak of parish life, its ministries, and its celebrations.
- To encourage parents in their responsibilities as Christian parents.
- To elicit feelings and suggestions (negative/positive) about the Church and parish life.

In an informal home atmosphere, "Church" took on a richer meaning for families. Over coffee, priest/sister and family shared feelings and insights about the Church, past or present. Marital and spiritual problems were discussed. Misunderstandings were corrected and warm relationships to one of the parish ministers were initiated or deepened.

Our visitation communicated on another level that the Church cares and wants to minister to the needs of her people. The results were so beneficial that visitation by the staff members has become a top priority. All the staff agree that this is a work of evangelization and adult education.

4. *Visitation of New Parishioners:* One reason for estrangement from the Catholic Church is mobility. As Alvin Illig notes: "Twenty percent of the American people move every year. The single most common occasion for people in any Church, synagogue or temple to stop attending services is a physical move from one place to another: failure to put down religious roots. Religious function is also deeply affected by changing vacation patterns and weekends spent more and more away from home and parish."[3]

Our parish community welcomes new Catholic families in three steps. First, a personal letter is sent to the new family with a brochure on the parish and parish school. The letter reads:

> Dear Friend:
>
> Welcome to St. Paul's Parish! We are happy to have you as a part of our parish family and wish you every happiness in your new home.
>
> Enclosed are two brochures that give some information about our parish family and the parish school. We feel our parish offers meaningful religious worship, opportunities for socializing, continuous adult educational growth, and service possibilities to others.
>
> A member of the parish staff will be dropping by to greet you personally in your home. If you would like your home blessed during this visit, please call the rectory in advance.

Once again, welcome to St. Paul's — and if we can be of any help to you, or if you simply would like to become acquainted, please feel free to call upon us.

Second, to personalize our welcome, a staff member visits the family. This visit initiates a relationship with the parish and says to the family that we are glad they are part of our Christian community.

Third, approximately two months after the new family arrives, the Parish Life Committee invites them to a Sunday afternoon party at the rectory. On this occasion the whole staff is present. We make the occasion informal; new parishioners are welcomed and introduced to staff members and to one another. There is a twenty-minute slide presentation which shows various parish activities and organizations. In this way, newcomers form a direct impression of people like themselves who are participating in the life of the parish and are leaders in different areas of parish life.

SUMMARY

1. Eliciting participation in the modern parish is difficult because this is a period of fundamental change. A key to building a strong parish community is a practical, effective outreach program of welcoming.

2. Parish leaders should be present at Sunday liturgy to offer a friendly welcome. The presider should encourage parishioners to introduce themselves to one another. This warm spirit is deepened as the parish leaders are available after Mass to visit with parishioners new and old.

3. Parish meetings offer ongoing occasions for the parishioners to deepen their relationships.

4. Periodic visitation of all homes, Catholic and non-Catholic, touches lives with the gospel message in a significant way. The celebrations of the sacraments for the first time are grace-filled moments for families, and home visitation by a priest or staff member opens avenues for a deeper relationship with Christ.

5. Through an ongoing welcoming process for new parishioners, the parish community receives a continuous source of vitality and life.

CHAPTER NOTES

1. James C. Fenhagen, *Mutual Ministry* (New York: Seabury Press, 1977), p. 5.
2. Pope Paul VI, *Evangeli Nuntiandi* (December 8, 1975), No. 18.
3. Alvin A. Illig, "Getting a Handle on Evangelization in America," *The Living Light* (Spring, 1979), p. 13.

SUGGESTED READINGS

Bausch, William J. *The Christian Parish*. Notre Dame, Ind.: Fides/Claretian, 1980. This book is excellent for its practical application of renewal to parish life.

Fenhagen, James C. *Mutual Ministry*. New York: Seabury Press, 1977. This whole book is not simply a how-to book, but offers excellent insights into the Christian mission and community as they apply to the local parish.

Gallup, George, Jr. "What We Know and What We Do Not Know About Evangelizing 80 Million Unchurched Americans," *New Catholic World*. July, August 1976. This article is helpful for giving dates and statistics on religious practices of the American people.

Illig, Alvin A. "Getting A Handle on Evangelization in America," *The Living Light* (Spring, 1979). A motivating article on the need for evangelization.

Smith, Glenn C. *Evangelization Through Home Visitation*. Washington, D.C.: Office for Evangelization. A valuable manual for training parish teams to reach out to the unchurched through home visitation.

Getting People Involved and Keeping Them Happy in Service

Rosemary K. Sausen

Formerly the program director for the Catholic inner-city office in the Diocese of Wilmington, Delaware, Mrs. Sausen is currently the director of the parish outreach program for the diocese. She is also the executive secretary of the Kidney Foundation of Delaware.

In one sense there are no volunteers in the Catholic Church. By reason of baptism all people are called to help the Church fulfill its mission. While individuals have different ministries or roles within the Church, all have the same goal: to proclaim the good news of salvation in Christ Jesus. No one, then, is a part-time Christian.

From another perspective there are volunteers within the Church. Some ministries and roles demand more time than others. Some men and women are called from within the community to ordained or commissioned ministry. These people tend to spend most of their time and energy in the exercise of these ministries.

Others, while pursuing full-time occupations in other areas, give significant amounts of time and energy to the official work of the Church. In regard to Church work, these people would be popularly seen as volunteers.

The official Church is not unaware of the new situation. Recently Pope John Paul II addressed the question specifically when he wrote:

> In recent times pastors have called the laity to the service of the Church Communities more and more often. These have willingly accepted their duties and have dedicated their energies to the service of the Church on a full or part time basis. Thus, in the present day we have again taken up the practice of the early Church, when lay persons were involved in various services according to their inclination and charisms and according to the necessities and practical needs of the people of God, for the growth and vitality of the Church Community.[1]

Volunteers Are People

Recognizing, then, that in one sense there are no volunteers in the Church, and in another sense there are, it is important to look at who the volunteers are. Generally, volunteers are people who feel that they can be of service to other people and thus help improve the quality of life around them. Volunteering in any organization provides the individual with an opportunity to obtain new experiences and further develop possibly unused talents. In the United States there are millions of dollars' worth of services that volunteers can and do contribute to organizations annually. These are hours that no one can buy.

Woodrow Wilson summed up the experience best when he said:

> Nothing but what you volunteer has the essence of life, the springs of pleasure in it. These are the things you do because you want to do them. They are done with the free spirit of the adventure. They are the inviting bypaths of life into which you go for discovery, to get off the dusty roads of mere duty into cool meadows and shadowed glades where the scene is changed and the air seems full of the tonic of freedom.

Recruitment

When people talk about recruiting volunteers, they put the responsibility for their continuing in the program on the volunteers themselves. In reality the recruiters are a significant part of volunteer effectiveness. The commitment and enthusiasm the recruiter communicates to others is the key to success.

The first thing a recruiter has to do is attract the attention of the person he or she is seeking to recruit. While the parish bulletin can be an effective means, especially when it deals with a matter that is already well known in the parish, other means are usually more effective. Tasteful posters or well-designed temporary bulletin boards can serve a useful purpose, as can a volunteer request sheet that can be filled out before the person leaves church. However, the most effective way to recruit is by word of mouth. If each enthusiastic and contented volunteer expresses his satisfaction to five other people, volunteers multiply rapidly.

To recruit (and keep) volunteers, the work they are asked to do must be varied, interesting, and rewarding. There must be an attitude of flexibility built into the program, so that volunteers can fit Church activities into their regular commitments. To be a successful leader of volunteers requires direct contact in the field. Sitting at a desk just will not do it! Showing interest in volunteers with personal comments and enthusiasm lets them know others believe in the program and in them. Remembering something about the individual communicates how important each person is.

Maintenance of Volunteers

After recruiting the volunteers, the leader has a full-time job of maintenance. The successful maintenance of volunteers requires attentiveness to the individuals' needs, both personally and in regard to the task. Consider the following questions a good leader should ask:

- Have you provided a specific task?
- Is the volunteer trained for this task?
- Will you help the volunteer grow and develop full responsibility for the task?

- Will the volunteer's conscientiousness be appreciated?
- Will the volunteer be able to provide input into evaluation of the success of the task?

People who work with volunteers must be attuned to and aware of the expectations of individuals and be able to satisfy them. The leaders should try to determine what goals and rewards volunteers expect out of their volunteering. In parish work volunteers have an extra incentive — their love of God.

People who work with volunteers in a parish must be attuned to the expectations of the individual parishioners who volunteer, and be able to meet those expectations. In recruiting volunteers it is important to keep in mind that parishioners volunteer for many different reasons; for example, to get to know other parishioners, to gain experience, to grow, to feel that they are a part of the community, to help improve the quality of parish life, to get out of the house.

Parish volunteers should be treated like VIP's. In everyday contact they must know that they are valuable and important. Some of the ways of showing appreciation include:

- Certificates of appreciation.
- A special Mass for those involved in specific ministry.
- Service pins.
- Making a phone call, not to ask for anything specific, but just to chat.
- Showing interest in the volunteer as an individual.
- Soliciting the volunteers' ideas for program improvement.
- Providing individual expressions of caring; for example, by sending birthday cards.
- Being available — open-door policy.
- Being an effective listener.
- Giving the volunteer a sense of belonging.
- Showing volunteers how they can grow in their personal life through volunteering.
- Giving recognition that is appropriate to the situation.

Volunteers will stay involved only so long as they feel needed and so long as the program is moving ahead. When satisfied volunteers leave any program, they will readily tell others of their good experiences, thereby doing some unrequested recruiting for the program.

A Volunteer Program That Works

In the Diocese of Wilmington, parish social action and direct services are accomplished in parishes through a process called Parish Outreach. The process was designed to help each parish select a program to fit its unique needs. Parish Outreach is, therefore, a process rather than program. This process allows volunteers to offer their talents and abilities to their own parishes through a volunteer network, both within the parish and among other parishes. Currently seventeen parishes within the diocese have involved a total of nineteen hundred volunteers in this process.

Parish Outreach operates on some principles of recruiting and training of volunteers who work in parish communities that can be extremely helpful to parishes in other dioceses.

A major recruitment force in any parish is the parish staff. Even then, they can only expect to recruit parishioners if they have the specific programs that they can personally become excited about. It is up to them to convince people that it is worthwhile for them to give their time and energy to a specific project.

Thus, even before there are volunteers there must be some activity for the volunteers to volunteer for. Before recruiting begins, the parish council should designate a small group of interested parishioners to work on a parish needs assessment questionnaire. This questionnaire would allow parishioners to express their opinion on what they perceive to be important needs in the parish that are not being met either by the parish or by the larger community.

On a predetermined Sunday (perhaps named "Needs Assessment Sunday") the questionnaire is presented to the whole parish at the end of Sunday liturgy. It is important that these questionnaires be filled out before people leave church so that as many people as possible be heard from. (For some examples, see Appendix A at the end of this chapter.)

In most parishes the list of needs usually far exceeds the parish's capabilities of fulfilling them. Frequently mentioned needs include assistance in the areas of drugs/alcohol, stress, depression, parish visitation, elderly day care, home maintenance, family counseling, and emergency housing. The committee, in conjunction with the parish council, should have some way of putting the various needs into priorities.

Once the needs have been determined and the priorities set, the parish should have some kind of volunteer Sunday. A survey similar to the needs assessment questionnaire (see Appendix B) should again be distributed and filled out in church.

After the volunteers have been categorized according to interest, they should be called by a specially designated member of the parish to thank them for offering their services, and to assure them that they will be called in the near future. It is extremely important that people who volunteer for specific jobs be allowed to perform those jobs whenever possible, providing there has been a personal interview to ensure the individual's suitability for the ministry.

Organization is the key to a good volunteer program. Each parish needs a coordinator and a co-coordinator to work closely with all the volunteers in the parish. It is important that they recognize talents and know how to use people's talents effectively, since many of the future parish leaders come from volunteer programs.

Since the coordinators themselves are volunteers, their skills frequently come from on-the-job training. It is almost impossible to list all of the skills the coordinator needs, but the list would include the ability to discern gifts, as well as guiding, encouraging, sharing, helping, and understanding volunteers. Coordinators monitor development, share knowledge, undertake research for future programs, and help evaluate the groups when they have finished a specific task. All of this must be done with enthusiasm, imagination, patience, and love. Henri Nouwen summed it up when he wrote that the minister who cares for people is called to be skillful (but not a handyman), knowledgeable (but not an impostor), a professional (but not a manipulator).[2]

To be more specific, what happens to the volunteer who signs up for visitation work? The coordinator calls each of the volunteers and suggests that they come together for a group meeting. At the meeting, the coordinator informs people that some type of training is needed before formal visitation is done. This training may be given by the local Catholic hospital (see Appendix C).

Upon completion of the training, the group reconvenes and elects a visitation chairperson. The volunteers then decide among themselves who would like to visit the homebound of the parish, the parishioners in the hospital, and those in nursing homes. The visitation coordinator will be in direct contact with the priests of the parish who give the coordinator the names of people to be visited. It is important that someone coordinate the visitation so that everyone who is supposed to be visited is. The best way for the coordinator to keep track is through a parish visitation form (see Appendix D). While it may look like unnecessary paperwork, the number of volunteers can be such that it will be very difficult to keep track unless people actually turn in some written document.

Parish visitation volunteers tend to generate more work. During their visits they will probably see needs that can be met by other people in the parish — for example, transportation to Sunday Eucharist or to the store or the doctor. The visitor is usually not expected to do these tasks, but to report them to the coordinator who will, in turn, call the person in charge of transportation.

One way to organize volunteers is around specific tasks, with each group headed by a coordinator. These coordinator's names are published in the parish bulletin or in a booklet given to parishioners when they register for the parish.

Parishioners who volunteer do not come from one mold. They are men and women, old and young, educated and uneducated, people with nothing else to do and people with almost no extra time. Each of these people must be given the opportunity to serve, insofar as this is possible.

Another Example

One success story from a parish outreach program concerned drug and alcohol counseling. Surprised that this came up as a major need in their parish, a small group of parishioners, led by the parish coordinator, surveyed other churches in their community and found that drug/alcohol abuse was a common problem. The outreach group organized a general meeting, invited appropriate state officials, and sought their help for a community-run drug/alcohol counseling center. Because of the interest of this one parish, the State of Delaware eventually established the Open Door, a drug/alcohol counseling center with a community-based board of directors. These people cared enough to become involved, and their efforts resulted in the establishment of a very needed service.

Volunteering is reaching out to people in the parish, and the people outside of the parish. It is a giving of the self to others. What the parish has to do is not only allow parishioners' talents to be used, but to encourage and empower them. As one man said so wisely, "Empowering people is nothing less than empowering Christ."[3]

SUMMARY

1. Volunteers are ordinary people who serve those in need. They have been encouraged to volunteer by such spiritual leaders as Pope John Paul II, who has repeatedly emphasized social justice inspired by the gospel.

2. Parish volunteers may learn new skills which can later be used in providing substantial services to benefit the broader community.

3. Recruiting parish volunteers will be successful when the volunteers are offered specific opportunities for parish service. Enthusiasm projected by the recruiter, coupled with treatment of volunteers as important people, should help provide the elements for successful recruiting.

4. One example of a successful volunteer program is in the Diocese of Wilmington, which currently has volunteer programs in seventeen parishes, with a total of over nineteen hundred volunteers.

5. Recruiting principles developed include the following steps:
   • Pastor of parish council indicates interest in volunteer program.
   • Parish needs assessment survey and recruitment of volunteers to fill designated needs on "Volunteer Sunday."
   • Establishment of volunteer coordinators in the parish and training of personnel.
   • Selection of parish chairperson for each area of need.

6. Another success story concerns a parish which through its volunteer efforts established a drug/alcohol counseling center.

CHAPTER NOTES

1. Pope John Paul II, "Homily in Yankee Stadium" (October 2, 1979), as published in *Pilgrim of Peace* (Washington, D.C.: U.S. Cathlic Conference, 1979), pp. 45-46.

2. Henri J.M. Nouwen, *Creative Ministry* (Garden City, N.J.: Doubleday, 1971), pp. 110-113.
3. Unpublished comment by Harry Fagan, Director of the Commission on Catholic Community Action in the Diocese of Cleveland, Ohio.

SUGGESTED READINGS

Fisher, John. *How to Manage a Nonprofit Organization.* Toronto, Ontario: Management and Fund Raising Center, 287 MacPherson Avenue, 1978. This book gives especially good practical suggestions on how to get started with volunteers and how to follow through.

Moore, Larry F. and John C. Anderson. *Volunteer Administration: Readings for the Practitioner.* Vancouver, B.C.: The Voluntary Action Resource Center, 1625 W. 8th Avenue, 1977. This book provides self-help ideas from a rich variety of sources. Most of the ideas presented are adaptable to parish life.

The Parish Outreach Review. Washington, D.C.: The Parish Outreach Project of the National Conference of Catholic Charities, 1346 Connecticut Avenue, N.W. (20036). This review always contains articles of a practical nature.

Voluntary Action Leadership. Washington, D.C.: The National Center for Voluntary Action, 1214 16th Street, N.W. (20036). Published quarterly, this magazine deals with the question of volunteerism in a variety of settings.

Whitehead, Evelyn Eaton, ed. *The Parish in Community and Ministry.* Ramsey, N.J.: Paulist Press, 1978. Focusing on the religious mission of the parish, this book stresses community building in parish life. It is a practical guide for getting started.

Wilson, Marlene. *The Effective Management of Volunteer Programs.* Boulder, Colo.: Volunteer Management Associates, 279 South Cedar Brook Road (80302), 1976. True to the title, this book offers down-to-earth ideas on how to deal with the whole question of volunteerism.

Appendix A

_____ (NAME OF PARISH) is trying to determine the social needs of our parish community. Many of these needs are being adequately met; others are not. Please take the time to evaluate these services carefully and share with us your concern.

Name: _____ Phone: _____

Address: _____

Counseling	Needed	Not Needed
Drug and Alcohol Abuse	——	——
Family Violence	——	——
Stress and Depression	——	——
Marriage	——	——
Gambling	——	——
Pregnancy	——	——
Divorced	——	——
Widowed	——	——
Premarital	——	——

Visitation	Needed	Not Needed
Shut-in	——	——
Telephone Reassurance	——	——
Hospitals	——	——
Nursing Homes	——	——
New Parishioners	——	——
Sick and Bereaved	——	——
Elderly	——	——
Home Sharing/Parish Vine	——	——

Transportation	Needed	Not Needed
Elderly — Day Care	——	——
Parishioners to Church or Parish Activities	——	——

Youth (High School)	Needed	Not Needed
Recreation and Activities	——	——
Counseling	——	——

Young Adults (College to 35)	Needed	Not Needed
Recreation and Activities	——	——
Counseling	——	——

Elderly and Disabled	Needed	Not Needed
Home Maintenance	——	——
Recreation and Social Affairs	——	——
Parish Involvement	——	——

Nursing Help	_____	_____
Housekeeping	_____	_____
Meals on Wheels	_____	_____

Housing	*Needed*	*Not Needed*
Distressed Travellers	_____	_____
Distressed Teenagers	_____	_____
Battered Wives	_____	_____
During Pregnancy	_____	_____

Handicapped	*Needed*	*Not Needed*
Recreation and Activities	_____	_____
Transportation	_____	_____
Assistance (please state type)	_____	_____

Special Concerns	*Needed*	*Not Needed*
Home-sitting Services		
For elderly	_____	_____
For children of parishioners	_____	_____
Assistance to Needy		
Food	_____	_____
Fuel	_____	_____
Clothing	_____	_____
Emergency Financial Assistance	_____	_____

Other Services	*Needed*	*Not Needed*
Day Care Transportation	_____	_____
Police Protection	_____	_____
Day Care Center for Children	_____	_____

Thank you for your cooperation. If you know of any additional needs for yourself or others, please list below.

COMMENTS:

_____

_____

_____

_____

Appendix B
'We Are Called to Serve'

NAME: _____ PHONE: _____
ADDRESS: _____

Please Note Which Services You Could Help to Provide

1. Visitation:
    a. Nursing Home ☐   d. Bereaved ☐
    b. Sick or Shut-ins ☐   e. Elderly ☐
    c. Hospitals ☐   f. Telephone reassurance ☐
2. Provide transportation for elderly and disabled:
    a. doctor ☐   d. church activities ☐
    b. Mass ☐   e. day care ☐
    c. shopping ☐
3. Provide emergency meal for troubled persons or family ☐
4. Help organize recreation and other activities for the handicapped ☐
5. Provide emergency housing for distressed teens ☐   battered wives ☐
6. Welcome newcomers into the parish ☐
7. Help with parish food collection ☐ parish clothing collection ☐
8. Join parish youth committee (seventeen and under) ☐
9. Help disabled or elderly parishioners with the following:
    a. leaf raking ☐   d. baby-sitting: day ☐ night ☐
    b. snow removal ☐   e. housekeeping ☐
    c. home maintenance ☐   f. other ☐
10. Join young adult activities for parishioners over eighteen years of age ☐
11. Help organize a day care facility ☐
12. Organize educational programs pertaining to social concerns as the need arises ☐
13. If there is any other way in which you would be willing to help the parish, please state in the space provided: _____
    _____
    _____

Appendix C
Training Program in Pastoral Caring

Initial Core Program

1. THE WAY TO VISIT — The etiquette of effective and proper visiting. The do's and don'ts as they relate to home visiting, hospital visiting, and

nursing home visits. How to initiate and terminate a visit. What areas of conversation are more advantageous for effective visiting.

2. THE ART OF LISTENING — The art of learning how to listen. The presentation will look at listening as an active process. The program will deal with exercises on what is heard and how it is reorganized for better concentration. The participants will be able to measure their listening power and see the effects of effective listening.

3. THE LOSS/GRIEF PROCESS — Using the book *Good Grief,* by Granger Westburg, the presentation will focus on the various steps of loss and grief and the alternatives for overcoming them. This presentation will require some preparation on the part of the participants.

4. ANXIETY AND STRESS — Realizing stress and the roots of stress gives insight for overcoming it. The presentation will speak to the question of daily stress and the need for recognizing the signs of stress. Special attention will be given to the patient's stress as it is transmitted in conversation and behavior.

5. VOLUNTEERS' RESPONSE TO VISITING — A panel of active volunteers will discuss and share their experiences of visiting in a variety of settings. The various techniques of team-visiting and one-on-one visits will be explored. Parish organization and structure for visitors' support will be discussed.

Follow-up Electives

A. PRAYING WITH THE SICK — This program is designed to answer the question, "When do I pray? Should every visit be a prayer visit?" and more importantly, "How should I pray with the sick?" Discussion revolves around identifying the "hot spot" in conversations and the use of Scripture in prayer.

B. THE FAMILY: SUFFERING TOGETHER — This presentation will review the literature on family consolations — the network theory and family-centered care. The role of family in patient care will be discussed and how a volunteer can become the "enabler" in the family process. Some time will be devoted to identification of various relationships with the family unit.

C. FEELINGS: YOURS, MINE, AND OURS — This presentation will focus on feelings in a helping relationship. Discussion will center on what feelings are and are not, ways in which feelings are expressed, and learning techniques for helping people talk about their feelings. This presentation will build on past personal experience and be a valuable experience for personal growth.

D. CARING FOR THE DYING — This presentation will look at the person being visited who is in the process of dying. Evaluation of the person in the process, style of dying (acceptance, anger, letting go, etc.) will be discussed.

Materials for this presentation will be gleaned from the works of Dr. Elizabeth Kübler-Ross.

Appendix D
Visitation Form

NAME: _____ DATE: _____

DATE OF BIRTH: _____

Identifying/Background Information:

Special Needs or Characteristics

Signature _____

Date _____

Date	Length of Visit	Volunteer Comments	Follow-up

Sunday Worship

The Rev. Michael J. Henchal

A priest of the Diocese of Portland, Maine, Father Henchal received a master's degree in liturgy from the Catholic University of America in 1977. He is the executive secretary of the diocesan Liturgical Commission for the Diocese of Portland. He is the author of *Sunday Worship in Your Parish.*

The overwhelming majority of parishioners have no other contact with the Church than through Sunday worship. Most Catholics are pastorally nourished and cared for by Sunday worship or they are not nourished and cared for at all.

The centrality of the Eucharist to the life of faith is a central teaching of the Church. The Second Vatican Council said that the liturgy is "the primary and indispensable source" (No. 14), the origin, the fountain of all Church life. It is above all the Eucharist which provides the nourishment, the energy, the courage for Catholic men and women to live out the demands of their baptismal calling.

Furthermore, all the other activities and dimensions of Church life have as their ultimate goal bringing all humankind together "to praise God in the midst of this Church, to take part in the Sacrifice and to eat the Lord's Supper" (No. 10). The Eucharist is at once the source and the goal of all Church life. It is the fundamental act of the Body of Christ. It is the fulfillment, the actualization, of the Church's very nature and being. It is the privileged encounter between God and his people.

From Jesus to Vatican II

In the ministry of Jesus, table gatherings were invaluable teaching and healing moments. They were lived-out parables, acting out the meaning of the great commandment of love. Jesus gathered people of all sorts (and often all the "wrong sorts") and seated them together at one table: slave and free, Zealot and tax gatherer, male and female, rich and poor, priest and prostitute. There they had to look into one another's eyes from across the same table and their love had to become more than mere theory. Jesus' table ministry was a radical call to conversion and love for God and neighbor.

St. Paul tells us that when the early Church assembled for the Eucharist, each member of the gathering came with some contribution: a song, a

63

prayer, a word of instruction, or some other spiritual gift (1 Corinthians 14:26). The liturgy was what the very word implies etymologically, "the work of the people."

Over the course of the centuries, hand in hand with changes in the perception and operative image of the Church, all roles came to be concentrated in the clergy. Mass became something the priest did or said. Everyone else in the assembly was reduced to the role of silent spectator or mere consumer, a passivity reinforced and further conditioned by architectural developments. The people came to church for what was really private prayer, with the Mass as an environmental aid, a backdrop. They tended neither to understand, nor to take any active part in, what went on in the sanctuary; rather, they prayed their own prayers individually. This liturgical situation, of course, was simply the reflection of Church life in general, where the laity were not expected to play active roles or take responsibility for the life of the Church.

Things had come a long way from the table ministry of Jesus and the liturgical experience which Paul describes. Jesus' table ministry deliberately fostered interaction between the participants; today, other people are often thought of as a distraction in prayer. Jesus' table ministry was a radical call to conversion; today transformation often fails to take place, in that people walk out no different than when they went in. In Paul's experience, everyone was responsible and actively involved; today the vast majority are passive, silent observers.

The liturgical reforms of the Second Vatican Council attempted to restore the original meaning and power to our celebration of the Eucharist. These reforms call for that "full, conscious, and active participation" (No. 14) demanded not only by the nature of the liturgy, but by the very nature of the Church itself.

Clarifying Expectations

The problems do not come at the level of theory but at the level of performance. The people just will not sing, will not respond, do not want to sit together, much less exchange the sign of peace with one another.

People do not act in these ways out of some perverse stubbornness or willful desire to subvert renewal. They do not cooperate simply because they really do not know and understand what is expected of them. They do not know how to do the things they are being asked to do. They need an explanation not just about what has changed, but about the reasons for the change.

People operate most often out of the theology they learned as children. Furthermore, people need to be provided with a new religious experience which is as good or better than the old one. And all of this must be accomplished in a way that respects the pace and manner in which people learn and assimilate new concepts and skills, that is, in a gradual way from people they trust.

Expectations must be clear. People must be shown how. Do not presume; explain and clarify. If there is to be a vibrant liturgical assembly, someone must actively, consciously, explicitly set about forming a vibrant liturgical assembly.

Preparation

If a parish is lackluster all week long, it cannot help but be lackluster on Sunday morning. If a parish is impersonal all week long, it will not suddenly and miraculously become personally engaging on Sunday morning. Everything a parish is all week long is a preparation for Sunday liturgy. The first, essential steps must be taken at home, at work, at school, in shopping centers and bowling alleys, at the parish hall and in one-to-one encounters between believers.

Many parishes have tried to get people to come prepared for the liturgy by having read over the Sunday readings in advance. Of course the entire parish will not do it, but those who do will get considerably more out of the liturgy. Printing the scripture references for next week's liturgy in the parish bulletin is not a very effective method. Try designing handout sheets that give the scripture references for the upcoming Sunday. Suggest possibilities for family prayer or activities in very clear and nontechnical language to assist families or small groups of adults to prepare for Sunday liturgy. The prayer, discussion, and suggested activities help relate the scripture readings to the ordinary lives of people. They can then come to Sunday liturgy with something to celebrate, their lives informed by the scriptures.

Another approach is to use handout sheets not for preparation but for follow-up after the Sunday liturgy. Because it fosters spiritual growth, this follow-up is a kind of preparation.[1]

The Place Itself

From the moment a parishioner steps out of the car on Sunday and walks up the front steps of the church, what happens to that individual affects the quality of the celebration.

The place itself, the liturgical space, will speak before any minister does. Attention should be paid to the exterior of the building and special attention should be given to the vestibule or narthex of the church, if there is one. A clear, clean, uncluttered space, narthex or nave, will help create a sense of reverence and expectation. That might mean providing better lighting. It might mean applying a fresh coat of paint. It might mean getting rid of the clutter of jumbled pamphlets and lost mittens and rosaries. A little greenery, consisting of a few plants or a couple of shrubs, can significantly change the feeling of the space. Flowers are not just for the sanctuary.

Hospitality

Hospitality is everyone's job. Everyone needs to be encouraged to pay attention to those who have come to pray with them. People are not to be thought of as a distraction to good worship; they are central to the celebration. All should be encouraged to be interested in who is seated beside them. This attitude is not easy for many to develop. In fact, people have been conditioned by Church practices and by our society to remain in their own little bubble, insulated from everyone else as much as possible.

People learn best through examples. This is where the explicit ministry of hospitality comes into play. Ushers have been in our churches for a long time. But their image was more that of "bouncer" and traffic manager than of greeter or minister of hospitality. The real role of the usher is to help people feel welcome and important. They can hand out music sheets or bulletins as an excuse for making contact with others. The talking they do is more than small talk; it is a break from the anonymity and an opening to allow something to happen; something sacred. Nor is this ministry exclusive to men. Women, couples, and young people should be recruited.

In many parishes priests greet people after Mass. How much more sense it makes, naturally and liturgically, for priests to move about the congregation as the people assemble. This might mean preparing a little further in advance and/or having a lay liturgy coordinator take care of last-minute details in the sacristy. Moving the vesting area down near the main entrance helps.

Five-minute Preparation

About five minutes before Mass actually begins, it is important to have a period of preparation with the assembly. This period is not just for rehearsing new music, done only when there is a new song to learn. It is a means of emphasizing the role of the whole assembly in regard to worship. It demonstrates the importance of the assembly and calls for involvement. Someone, possibly the minister of music, goes out and explains that this or that song or this or that gesture will be part of this service and invites participation.

Unfortunately, this period of preparation sometimes annoys people instead of preparing them for worship. It becomes an annoyance when the leader approaches it without first clarifying in his or her own mind what the purpose of the preparation period is. It is easy to slip into an adversary relationship with the community. The person doing the introduction should never be condescending, arrogant, or timorous. He or she must be self-confident, affirming, gentle, and prayerful.

If people are being asked to interact with one another before the liturgy begins and also to participate in a five-minute period of preparation before Mass, some may complain that there is no time for the prayerful preparation they feel is necessary. This is a valid complaint; silence is necessary and altogether proper as part of the community's preparation. If there is a narthex of adequate size in the church, the parish can foster flexible and progressive stages of increasing silence: a lot of interaction in the narthex and outdoors but only smiles and quiet "hello's" in the nave itself. You can also ask for a period of silent prayer after the five-minute preparation period but before the actual beginning of the Mass. An even better idea would be to make fuller use of the periods of silence provided in the very structure of the introductory rites of the Mass, both at the penitential rite and at the opening prayer.

Introductory Rites

A procession is not always required. Occasionally, the ministers can simply be in their places as the service begins, having been there for the period of preparation. An opening song, however, is quite important, since it helps gather the assembly and unites them with one another. Note that the song is not so much the servant of the procession as it often appears to be. Its main purpose is simply to unite the assembly. Decisions about the kind of hymn and length of the hymn should follow from its unitive function, not from the length of time it takes for the procession to reach the chair.

The introductory rites of the Mass (sign of the cross, greeting, introductory remarks, penitential rite, Lord, have mercy, Glory to God, opening prayer) are varied and complex. Their purpose is to prepare the people to hear the Word. Sometimes they subvert the Word, instead, by being too long and wordy themselves. It is important to keep them as clean, straightforward, and brief as possible. The fewer the words the better. The two silences, as during the penitential rite and before the opening prayer, are as important as the words.

The Word

The scripture readings need to be read so effectively, with so much understanding and conviction, that people will not only be able, but will want to put down their own copies of the text and listen to the lector. A brief introduction to the reading, either by the celebrant or the lector, can help people understand it better. For example, the lector could say: "The second reading today is a continuation of the reading of St. Paul's first letter to the Church at Corinth. He's talking about the disunity he finds in the community. As he continues that discussion, he explains that how much you know doesn't make you better than someone else. After all, the foolishness of God is wiser than the wisdom of men."

After each of the readings a pause of fifteen to twenty-five seconds adds considerably to the effectiveness of the reading. The singing of the psalm and Alleluia arises from the silence and returns to the silence. And the emphasis is on the *singing* of the psalm and Alleluia. The psalm is a musical, lyrical reflection on the reading. It can be sung by a cantor or a choir straight through. It can be read with a musical background. The cantor can intone the antiphon, which the congregation repeats and then the cantor can sing the verses solo. Almost any psalm can be used — not just the one in the Lectionary. Try using the same psalm throughout a liturgical season, varying the verses but keeping the antiphon. Effective use of the psalm response will do more to improve the liturgy of the Word than any other single change you can make. The Alleluia also must be sung. In fact, if you are not able to sing it, it should be omitted.

Preaching the Word

Roman Catholic tradition has often underestimated the importance of preaching the Word. The sermon, or more correctly the homily, is often still seen as an option, which can be omitted with no damage done when you are in a hurry or on weekdays. In reality, the homily is an essential structural element of the Mass, no more to be omitted than giving Communion. In fact, the homily is a lot like distributing Communion: it breaks open and hands out the Word in manageable portions.

To read the Word and then choose to ignore it, for whatever seemingly good purpose, is more than just an odd inconsistency; it reflects an unspoken lack of faith in the importance and relevance of the Word. But if these theoretical reasons for better preaching of the Word are not enough, consider further that the quality of the homily is the principal criterion most Catholics use in evaluating the effectiveness of the liturgy.

The preaching should break open the Word and make concrete the relevance of that Word in the life of the community. For that to happen, homilists must ask how this Good News makes it easier for them to cope in their daily lives. How does it change the way they understand the world? How does it challenge them to change the way they live? Preachers must first of all preach for themselves; preach the message they themselves need to hear. Homilists who do so will never slip into the mere pieties and oversimplifications or into paternalistic and arrogant speech-making. Such homilists instead portray themselves as fellow pilgrims, moving cautiously and fearfully, at times, along the Way.

General Intercessions

After the homily, the next critical item is the prayer of the faithful or the general intercessions. Resist the temptation to have them read from a so-called "worship aid." Four or five petitions drawn from the life of the community and from the problems of the world and the Church will always be more effective than petitions prepared months in advance and hundreds of miles away. There is really no need for the heavy, pseudo-theological language that some people think adds solemnity to the petitions. A petition inviting the community to pray for peace in a particular part of the world can say just that. General intercessions should not be a series of mini-homilies. People simply need to know what they are being asked to pray for. With the petitions, less is definitely more.

Preparation of Gifts

The period of the preparation of the altar table and the gifts is really a rest period after the activity of the liturgy of the Word. Silence or maybe a little instrumental music is enough. This is a good time to use the choir. Congregational singing is not out of the question, but is not necessary at this time every week. Because this is a rest period, consider using the option of omitting the "Blessed are you, Lord, God. . . ." prayers aloud every week or even very frequently. Silence during the preparation of gifts helps prepare for the very verbal, but climactic, eucharistic prayer.

Eucharistic Prayer

The eucharistic prayer should be the sustained climax of the celebration. To enhance the eucharistic prayer, always sing the acclamations: the Holy, holy, the Memorial Acclamation, the Amen. Celebrants need to proclaim the prayer not merely recite it. It should sound almost as if it is being composed and spoken anew on each occasion. Priests should make a conscious effort to draw people into the prayer with their voices and even their body language.

Communion

Congregations need to understand the meaning of the sign of peace. It is not a greeting, not a time to introduce yourself to the person you have been sitting with for the last forty minutes. Some of the extended "gladhanding" that goes on at this time, despite all that is good about it, would really be more appropriate before Mass began.

The sign of peace is basically a gesture of reconciliation, of making up; in that sense it is even penitential. It says, "Before receiving Communion, in which we become One Body, we should show that we want to be one." Those people to whom you extend your hand and who extend their hands to you represent all those you have held yourself back from, are alienated from, and are not as open to and receptive of as you are called to be in this One Body of Christ. Making it a really religious gesture and not merely a social gesture dissipates some of the resistance of the more reserved members of our communities.

Whenever possible, Communion should be offered under both kinds, and from the cup rather than by intinction. This fullness of the sign allows a fuller experience of the Eucharist. A careful examination of your space will show you ways to make it work. You will need two ministers with cups for each minister distributing the Consecrated Bread. At first, plan to deliberately run out since consuming what is left over, if there is a lot, can be a problem.

A period of silence after Communion is very effective. Consider singing a common hymn of praise and thanksgiving at the end of this time of silence. Singing at this time may eliminate the need for a congregational recessional song. Recessionals are a problem anyway, and not just because people leave before they are over. What sense does it make to say, "Go, in the peace of Christ," and then insist that people stay and sing three verses of some hymn? Mean what you say. When you say, "Go," you should expect people to begin doing just that. Instrumental music or a choir piece or even silence can accompany the exit of the priest and ministers, which need not be a lengthy, formal affair each week.

Music

Music is one of the very significant elements in any effective celebration. In today's liturgy, music is not an option. It is essential and it affects the quality of the celebration as much as any other single element. It cannot just be taken for granted.

Much depends on good leadership from the minister of music. The first qualification for a minister of music is possession of the needed musical skills. Many parish music programs fail because the person responsible for playing, singing, and/or directing is unable to play, sing, and direct competently. Competence is, unfortunately, expensive. If your parish musician is not all that he or she should be in this area, but is willing to try, then maybe you can consider paying for lessons. Certainly you will want to make use of whatever resources your diocese can offer by way of workshops or training sessions.

Even good musicians, though, need to know that artistic competence is not enough. There are also liturgical skills to be learned. A liturgical musician must be familiar with the liturgical year and with the movement of the Mass itself. A fine musician who wants to put on a concert each weekend with no respect for the structure of the liturgy is the wrong person for the job and must either be fired or trained. A parish needs more than a musician; it needs a liturgical musician.

But a parish also needs more than a liturgical musician. It needs a *pastoral* liturgical musician. A pastoral liturgical musician is sensitive to the needs and capabilities of the particular community he or she is serving. A congregation can only learn so much new music in a given period of time, even if it is good music and liturgically appropriate. Certain styles of music will fit certain congregations better than other styles. A parish minister of music must be challenged to grow continually in all three of these areas: art, liturgy, and pastoral care.

Other Ministries

Much of what could be said about other liturgical ministers has already been said about ministers of music. Anyone performing any ministry at Sunday Mass needs practical, liturgical, and pastoral skills. It follows, then, that each person entrusted with a liturgical ministry must grow in an ongoing formation program. Perhaps three or four times a year those exercising a particular ministry should be encouraged to gather to pray and learn together. This kind of ongoing formation can help keep liturgical ministers from becoming complacent and taking their important ministries for granted. Through personal in-service training, they can be challenged to grow continually in prayer and in service to the community.

SUMMARY

1. Sunday worship is the primary pastoral care most Catholics receive with any regularity. Theologically, the Eucharist is in fact the central form of pastoral care in the Church.

2. The recent liturgical renewal has sought to recapture the spirit of the table ministry of Jesus and the liturgical experience of the early Church which was interpersonal, transforming, and actively involving for all participants.

3. Congregations need to be taught what is expected from them and shown how to take part. Much of what is mistaken for lack of cooperation is simply lack of understanding.

4. Sunday worship needs to be well prepared. All of parish life prepares for liturgy. Families and groups of adult parishioners can be assisted and encouraged to prepare for worship through the use of specially prepared aids.

5. Attention to the liturgical space helps to create a sense of reverence.

6. The hospitality of all, prompted by the ministry of hospitality exercised by greeters (ushers), opens people up to the action of God in the Eucharist.

7. A brief preparation period emphasizes the indispensable role that the congregation is expected to play.

8. Each part of the Mass should be examined to discover its meaning and purpose in relationship to the whole celebration. With that purpose in mind each part can then be executed properly and powerfully. Without such understanding the meaning of the whole can get lost in the jungle of the separate parts.

9. Music plays a significant role in effective celebration. Ministers of music ought to be artistically, liturgically, and pastorally competent.

10. Ongoing formation for all liturgical ministers overcomes the tendency of all of us to become complacent.

CHAPTER NOTES

1. One source of ideas for such handout sheets is: Sister Jean Daniel, *Our Family Prepares for Mass* (Minneapolis: Winston, 1977).

SUGGESTED READINGS

Henchal, Michael J. *Sunday Worship in Your Parish.* West Mystic, Conn.: Twenty-Third Publications, 1980. A short book, written in nontechnical language, it treats basic liturgical and sacramental theology, a brief history of the Mass, and practical suggestions for improving Sunday worship. For clergy and laity alike.

Liturgy With Style and Grace. Chicago: Liturgy Training Program, 1978. A kind of handbook for parish liturgy committees, this work attempts to deal with all the practical questions including all the ministries and the major liturgical seasons. Includes a resource list for each section as well as discussion questions.

Nowak, David E. *First, We Pray: A New Agenda for Parish Liturgy.* Kansas City: Celebration Books, 1980. Dealing with far more than just mechanics, this book forces us to examine the quality of our prayer lives as a community and as individuals. A step beyond the basics.

Sloyan, Virginia, ed. *Touchstones for Liturgical Ministers.* Washington, D.C.: The Liturgical Conference, 1978. A book for anyone engaged in any form of liturgical ministry, including the ministry of the celebrating community. Treats each ministry in a page or two of concisely worded suggestions which can serve as "touchstones" to measure a minister's effectiveness.

Walsh, Eugene A. *A Theology of Celebration.* Glendale, Ariz.: Pastoral Arts Associates, 1977. A brief digest of what is happening today in sacramental and liturgical theology as it shapes the way we celebrate Mass now. Eminently readable, like all of Father Walsh's material.

——. *The Ministry of the Celebrating Community.* Glendale, Ariz.: Pastoral Arts Associates, 1977. The second in the series, this booklet explores the role of the whole assembly and suggests ways to initiate the assembly into its task.

——. *Practical Suggestions for Celebrating Sunday Mass.* Glendale, Ariz.: Pastoral Arts Associates, 1978. The third in the series deals mostly with the ministries and the physical elements like space, vessels, the altar, etc. Like the title says, these are very practical suggestions for improving your Sunday liturgy.

——. *The Order of Mass: Guidelines.* Glendale, Ariz.: Pastoral Arts Associates, 1979. Takes us through the entire liturgy from entrance to dismissal and examines how the parts fit together and how to maintain the proper rhythm and proportions.

Celebrating the Sacraments

The Rev. Pasquale J. Apuzzo

A native of New Haven, Connecticut, Father Apuzzo completed his seminary studies at the Catholic University of America in Washington and was ordained in 1976. He has been chairperson of the diocesan Liturgical Commission and is currently director of the Office of Worship for the Diocese of Richmond, Virginia.

The vision and direction of the people of a parish will determine to a great extent the way the sacraments are celebrated in that parish. Sacraments have the power to form people, but how they are celebrated is established by those same people. The Lord is always present in the sacraments. What often needs the most attention in sacramental celebrations is anything that helps people to open themselves to recognize that presence.

Good liturgical planning helps create a total environment that enhances worship and allows people to acknowledge Christ present in his Church in the gathered community. Careful planning produces three liturgically desirable results: (1) The sacraments will be celebrated in a prayerful way; (2) people will better understand what they are celebrating and can therefore participate more completely; and (3) the celebrations will flow from the lives of people as well as from the public worship of the Church.

Vatican Council II in its "Constitution on the Sacred Liturgy" sees worship as the cornerstone of the life of the Church, "the summit toward which the activity of the Church is directed" and "the fount from which all her power flows" (No. 10). The liturgy of the Church is, however, not the entire story. As the council points out, it "does not exhaust the entire activity of the Church" (No. 9).

In the Church's understanding of the sacraments, there must be a bond between what is expressed in prayer and what is carried out in action. This interdependence is further acknowledged in the "Constitution on the Church in the Modern World" which condemns as "one of the gravest errors of our time" what it terms "the dichotomy between the faith which many profess and the practice of their daily lives" (No. 43).

Without mincing words, the same paragraph of that constitution goes on to say that people are "no less mistaken to think that we may immerse

73

ourselves in earthly activities as if those latter were utterly foreign to religion, and religion were nothing more than the fulfillment of acts of worship and the observance of a few moral obligations." In strengthening this thought, the constitution concludes: "As far back as the Old Testament, the prophets vehemently denounced this scandal, and . . . Christ himself with greater force threatened it with severe punishment" (No. 43).

Good sacramental celebrations will, then, bring together the present realities of life and the demands of faith. A good celebration will allow people to celebrate the critical moments in life — birth, love, death — as well as the daily dyings and risings that everyone experiences. Sacraments confirm people in their belief that the Lord is truly present to this people.

One of the distinctive marks of the Roman Catholic Church is its emphasis on the principle of sacramentality. The Church is a mediating force between God and people. The person does not have a relationship with God that is primarily individual, but communal, within the Church community. Vatican Council II affirmed this notion in the "Constitution on the Church in the Modern World" when it stated: "Rising from the dead [Jesus] sent his life-giving Spirit upon his disciples and through him set up his Body which is the Church as the universal sacrament of salvation" (No. 48).

The Teaching Function of Liturgy

Liturgy is worship, not primarily instruction. The sacraments do, however, present a particular vision of reality. They can change or transform the people who participate in them. St. Thomas Aquinas in his treatment of the sacraments noted that the purpose of signs is to instruct, to present people with the reality the sign signifies.[1] Because the sacraments provide an encounter with Jesus, they invite participation in a reality that has already taken flesh in him and which can take flesh again in them.

Dr. Mark Searle has written on the pedagogical function of the Church's liturgy. He presents sacraments in terms of what he calls the socializing function of worship. He explores the possibilities of "how the liturgy might be capable of exercising a critical role in the larger life and mission of the church." He sees celebrating the sacraments as a form of consciousness-raising regarding issues of immediate concern personally, communally, and globally.

The sacraments, he proposes, engage people in actions "which are consciously expressive and, more than merely expressive, which create a new 'world' of meaning." By their participation, people make "an act of hope in a genuinely alternative future," and a commitment to work "for the realization of the future which they celebrate and anticipate and the relationships which they realize in the sacramental actions."[2]

Planned Sacramental Celebrations

The celebration of the sacraments in a parish brings life to people if they are planned well. Sacramental celebrations can make a contribution to the shape and direction of life in pursuit of the future made possible by Jesus. The question that arises is whether parish liturgy planners can handle the agenda this understanding implies.

That same question, of course, applies equally to the parish community itself. Parish leaders must refrain from answering that question for planners and the community. The people of the parish have a right and an obligation to explore new possibilities, attitudes, and methods in worship according to Church norms. Open dialogue about worship and the sacraments may involve many hours of discussion, even arguments. Leaders and parishioners should not avoid these tensions, but should work together to see them through to positive results.

Sacramental theologians have never seen the sacraments as something static. Traditional theology understood sacraments in terms of their positive impact on people. The phrase from theology says, *"Sacramentum propter homines"* ("The sacraments are for people"). This understanding is restated in the Church today in the "Constitution on the Sacred Liturgy," which says: "The purpose of the sacraments is to sanctify [people], to build up the Body of Christ" (No. 59).

People who plan any parish liturgy, including Eucharist, must be willing to do a lot of praying, thinking, and talking before they approach the drawing board with pen and ritual in hand. They should begin with a discussion or a recapping of previous discussions about the purpose of the sacraments, and how they as a community can best accomplish their end. This kind of analysis demands that liturgy planners be able to articulate their own faith concerning the sacraments and compare that belief with the best and most current teachings of the Church on worship.

Liturgy planners must also be able to identify those individuals and communities who will be celebrating the sacraments. It is usually a difficult and complex task to get in touch with the need of even one person in the parish, let alone the needs of an entire community. Yet it is absolutely essential to understand how people perceive themselves and their lives if sacramental celebrations are to help transform people into the reality they celebrate.

The question is not simply whether the celebration will meet individual or community needs. A danger here would be that celebrations move toward the chaos of the merely arbitrary and the purely subjective in order to try to make sacraments personal and relevant. There is no question that sacramental celebrations need to be related to people. A more precise question, however, is whether a particular celebration responds to the need of people as they involve themselves in a conscious, daily response to the demands of faith.

The Planning Team

There are any number of approaches to the actual planning process. The ones that seem to work best are those that require the least number of people, and which use the scripture readings as the central focus for designing a celebration. A planning team of two to three people usually is sufficient.

Although they begin with the scriptures, planners will have to spend some time deciding how the different elements of the liturgy can best express or at least support the central message of the scriptures within the context of a particular sacrament. Initially this will involve dealing in concepts rather than in concrete and explicit plans. For example, a team may want a gathering song that expresses the need for confidence in order to take on a simple style of life. The team then must go to the musician to get suggestions for a particular song. The planners' job is to present the musician with the concept. Planners do not themselves come up with the final package, but will eventually work with others, including artists and musicians, to see that the end product is one in which the various parts work together to accomplish what the planners conceive as the goal.

The danger is that liturgy planners will spend their time on practical things, which are relatively easy to accomplish, rather than designing the entire celebration. Take the whole question of symbols, as an example. Sacraments are symbols which communicate the great mystery of God's love for his people through his Son. The ways these symbols are used can have a significant effect on the quality of the celebration. In some cases the symbols have become weak, poor reproductions of the real thing: hosts instead of bread; pouring instead of immersion; washing hands instead of feet; bread only instead of bread and wine; hands extended rather than laid on and touching; sacred gesture instead of liturgical dance; intinction instead of drinking.

The same symbol can be weak or strong depending on how it is used. Liturgy planners who have been trained in the Church's worship know the difference. A balloon, for example, is not a gimmick simply because someone may think it has no place in liturgy. It is a gimmick only if its use is not integrated with the central symbols of the sacrament, or when it does not aid the liturgy. Non-primary or auxiliary symbols should never distract or call undue attention to themselves. Rather they always point to the primary sacramental symbols and signs.

Principles for Planning

There are a few principles that liturgy planners should always keep in mind when they begin planning for celebrations of individual sacraments. These principles are basic:

1. Always start with the rite. There is no better explanation of what a particular sacrament means than that found in the introduction to the rite itself. For example, people who are planning a penance service would do very well to read the introduction to the *Rite of the Sacrament of Penance* in order to find the meaning of sacramental reconciliation. The sample penance services found in the rite provide planners with multiple ideas

on how to best express the Father's forgiveness and the reconciliation that comes through the Church.

2. Always concentrate on enhancing primary symbols. Sometimes planners get caught up in peripheral signs and miss opportunities that the liturgy itself provides. For example, in the sacrament of matrimony the primary symbol is the bride and groom themselves. They come to celebrate and confirm their union with one another in Jesus, and should therefore be highlighted as the central symbol.

The rite itself suggests that the bride and groom be united from the beginning to the end of the ceremony. They walk in together during the procession as their entrance into the assembly. They stay together throughout the entire ceremony. As the ministers of the sacrament, they face the congregation during the rite of marriage and pronounce their marriage promises for all to hear. They should be prepared as ministers of the sacrament to present themselves not as passive recipients but as active ministers.

3. The celebration of the sacraments should involve as many people as possible. This involvement includes the people receiving the individual sacraments as well as their families. In the case of infant baptism, for example, the parents, godparents, brothers and sisters, grandparents, aunts and uncles should have some involvement in the celebration whenever possible.

Beyond that, the parish itself should be involved in celebrating baptism. Those parishes who celebrate infant baptism at Sunday Eucharist find that it makes baptism a joyful event for the entire community. The parish begins to celebrate new birth in practical as well as symbolic ways. Simple things, like a small reception after the baptism, help move the celebration of the sacrament into daily life.

4. The celebration of the sacraments should be as personal as possible. Sacraments are essentially community events, even when only two people are present. Therefore, they should not be individualistic. They should be celebrated in the midst of the community. Even when more than one infant is being baptized, the parish is not excused from trying to make the celebration as personal as possible. The kind of preparation the parents and godparents have, the opportunities for meaningful family participation in the baptism, the way the family is welcomed by the community at the baptism — all these determine how personal and meaningful the event will be.

Another example of the need for very personal celebration is at the time of anointing of the sick. This occasion is often a tremendous opportunity for the family to pray for the sick person or to pray for someone who is dying. It is a time when the family shares in the joy of someone's love, in the tragedy of sickness, or in the reconciliation that only Jesus can bring. When the sacrament is totally individual, with just the priest and the sick person, the latter is denied the additional support and encouragement of the larger community praying with him or her. As a unifying event, the sacrament should bring those out in the hall to the bedside as the priest, patient, and community pray for physical and spiritual health.

Current Problems

Because the Church has changed the way it celebrates sacraments, it should be no surprise that there are a few problems in its current practices. The best way to begin to solve them is to name them.

1. Oversystematization. As an institution, the Church needs systems. People need to know how to get things done; they need to know the formal and informal rules about sacraments. Unfortunately, some parishes have made the system so complicated that even people of good will cannot penetrate the maze of complexities.

2. Laissez-faire. This problem is the exact opposite of oversystematization. It has no regard for the integrity of the sacraments or any interest in the faith of the participants. Whoever shows up receives sacraments, without instruction, without an opportunity to participate in the planning. Such a process, if carried on for very long, will quickly lead to ritualism.

3. Undereducation and misbelief. People in the Church, including those in ministerial roles, need continual opportunities to reflect prayerfully on the meaning of the sacraments in the life of the Church. Because they are such deep mysteries, some people treat them as if ritual alone were sufficient; others treat the sacraments with a casualness that indicates a lack of understanding. For example, some people are using the public celebration of the sacrament of penance with general absolution to the point where the undereducated are viewing the event as magic, as harsh as that sounds.

Conclusion

With the possible exception of Sunday Eucharist, people generally celebrate sacraments at critical times in their lives. They are usually times of high emotion, either deep joy or profound sorrow. These moments are prime opportunities for helping people reflect on the meaning of the Lord's love for them. They deserve the very best that the Church can give them.

SUMMARY

1. The sacraments help form people into a worshipping community and at the same time are formed by the way the community celebrates.

2. In its official documents, the Church acknowledges the interdependence between what the Church expresses in prayer and what people experience in their daily lives.

3. A person's relationship with God is not primarily individual, but communal. Thus the Church itself is the universal sacrament of salvation.

4. While they are primarily worship events, sacraments do have a teaching function in the community in that they present a particular world view and engage in that world.

5. The best kinds of celebrations of the sacraments are planned celebrations. Parishes must be willing to equip people to plan well and give them the freedom to plan. Planners have to be willing to work systematically with others to bring about the most prayerful celebrations possible.

6. Four principles for planning are: (a) Always start with the rite; (b) always concentrate on enhancing primary symbols; (c) involve as many people as possible; and (d) be as personal (not individualistic) as possible.

7. Parishes have to walk a thin line between overstructure and no structure in regard to the sacraments. In this case, virtue does walk the middle ground.

CHAPTER NOTES

1. *Summa Theologica,* III, q. 60.
2. Mark Searle, "The Pedagogical Function of the Liturgy," *Worship* (July, 1981), pp. 354-355.

SUGGESTED READINGS

Bausch, William J. *A New Look at the Sacraments.* Notre Dame, Ind.: Fides/Claretian, 1977. This book provides a clear and precise presentation of the history, theology, and recent revisions in the celebration of the sacraments. It treats the sacraments of baptism, confirmation, Eucharist, penance, and the sick, omitting marriage and ordination.

Borelli, Susan. *With Care: Reflections of a Minister to the Sick.* Chicago: Liturgy Training Publications, 1980. A practical handbook on visiting and celebrating with the sick for clergy and lay ministers. There are basic insights into the particular needs and situations of those who are ill or confined to home or institutions.

Dallen, James. *The Funeral Liturgy.* Glendale, Ariz.: Pastoral Arts Associates of North America, 1980. An excellent resource for designing and celebrating funerals with a helpful appendix of suggestions for liturgical music.

Deiss, Lucien. *The Essential Question.* Chicago: World Library Publications, Inc., 1979. A critical reflection on the question of adapting traditional liturgy to the needs and people of the present and the future.

Jones, Paul. *Rediscovering Ritual.* New York: Newman Press, 1973. After a brief introductory reflection on the nature of human ritual, this book presents practical suggestions for celebrating significant moments and events in the community.

Maxwell, John. *Worship in Action: A Parish Model of Creative Liturgy and Social Concern.* West Mystic, Conn.: Twenty-Third Publications, 1981. A collection of creative ideas for giving relevance and meaning to the celebration of the sacraments from the experiences of a parish in Oakland, California.

Ortegel, Adelaide. *A Dancing People,* West Lafayette, Ind.: The Center for Contemporary Celebration, 1976. A composite of articles with practical suggestions for incorporating dance and creative gesture into the liturgy with a useful appendix of resources for musical accompaniment.

Prayer in the Parish

The Rev. John B. Gephart

Ordained for the Archdiocese of Louisville, Kentucky, in 1946, Father Gephart taught on the secondary level both in Catholic high schools and in religious education programs before becoming pastor of a large suburban parish. He has served on various commissions and councils in the archdiocese, and is presently a member of the diocesan Liturgical Commission. He is pastor of St. Matthias Church in Louisville.

The quality of prayer for any group will depend on the personal prayer of its members. A parish that successfully nurtures the individual's receptivity and response to the Lord will be ready for vibrant communal worship. There are a variety of ways a parish can foster personal prayer.

Most often members of a parish will look to their leadership for spiritual direction. Those priests who are most remembered after they are gone are the ones whose prayer life, whose holiness, was an inspiration and example to their people. For all the administrative abilities of the priest, for all his ability to build a beautiful building, the people still look for holiness in their priests. The priest becomes more and more aware of the fact that all his learning and eloquence in the pulpit do not really make a lasting impression. What people become aware of is the holiness, the prayerfulness of their priests. It is that prayer life which uncages the Spirit to move hearts and souls. People in the pews will be moved less by the theatrical gestures of the celebrant at the altar and more by his sincerity and genuineness arising from his own personal life of prayer.

If these things are true for the parish priest, they are also true for all who minister.

Parish Staff

In their pastoral work, the parish staff (and the school staff, if there is one) have a tremendous opportunity to teach the value of prayer. In numerous counseling sessions, meetings, home and hospital visits, crisis situations, and even routine work, parish and school leaders can communicate, often powerfully, how important prayer is to the work they do. A con-

81

templative attitude toward life is easily perceived in the midst of much busyness. If a priest can pray from his heart rather than routinely "say the prayer" before a meeting, if a youth minister can authentically lead teenagers in prayer, if a school teacher can pray with a discouraged parent, if a pastoral associate or DRE regularly prays with a committee before making a decision or in the midst of tension or in gratitude for God's goodness, then those involved in these activities will become more conscious of the gift of prayer themselves.

A staff that successfully integrates prayer into its pastoral schedule provides a tremendous example to the parish. Obviously, there can be no prayer life without discipline. The example of Jesus, whose time was hardly his own, offers motivation. In reading the scriptures, it soon becomes obvious that, with all the calls upon his time, Jesus was above all a man of prayer. There is no evidence that he spent a particular period of each day in prayer; there is evidence that he felt the need to pray and, often enough, went off to pray. That his disciples were aware of this and asked him to teach them to pray was indicative of the fact that they saw him in prayer and were moved by the desire to follow him.

Following the spirit of Jesus' own discipline of prayer, one member of a parish team regularly scheduled a half hour "appointment" in the midst of a busy day for prayer. Just as in any other pastoral appointment, full time and attention could then be given without interruption. Scheduling such an "appointment" is in itself a concrete acknowledgment of the pastoral minister's need to be in touch with God in order to do his work effectively.

Parish People's Personal Prayer

If finding a time and a place to pray is difficult for priests and professional parish ministers, it seems almost impossible for everyone else. That does not have to be the case. Parishioners should be helped to realize that God speaks to them in their real-life situations. It is necessary to help people find prayer styles that are compatible with their lifestyles.

One parishioner offered the criticism that for years the only kind of help given to people to pray was modeled on the prayer life of religious orders. Prolonged periods for reflection and meditation just did not exist for most lay people regardless of good intentions. The result was frustration and guilt.

Through sermons, adult education classes, parent meetings, and one-on-one sessions, people should be encouraged to pray in those places and at those times that are natural to their lifestyles. Privacy is hard to find, but there are some natural times in a day when life seems less "peopled." It has been said that car pools, despite their obvious merit, have not caught on because drivers are reluctant to give up the only time some of them get to be by themselves.

People need to be encouraged to take advantage of those moments spent waiting for a bus or elevator; waiting in line at the bank, the supermarket, department store, or gas station; early morning time spent in the shower or with coffee cup (before the newspaper), or late at night when everyone else is in bed. The more encouragement people are given to look for God in the midst of their lives, the more joy they will experience in finding him there.

Other ways to foster personal prayer among parishioners might include distributing prayer materials, promoting good spiritual reading, and making tapes available on prayer and meditation.

Parishes can type up and run off the scripture readings for Advent (and again for Lent) with guidelines on how to use them for daily fifteen-minute prayer periods. Bibles should be made available and their purchase encouraged in each parish. There are a variety of inexpensive editions available. Some paperback editions could easily be put in the car glove compartment, pocketbook, or valise to be used during the day.

Spiritual Reading

Many have benefited from the reflective reading of a variety of contemporary spiritual authors. Most noted among these writers is Henri Nouwen, John Powell, and Thomas Green. While an increasing number of lay people are buying and reading these books, it may be a good idea to start a parish lending library. This could be a good project for someone who dislikes committee meetings but works well alone. Scripture commentaries, including the *Jerome Biblical Commentary,* should be available as well. Possibly nearby rectories, convents, or seminaries would donate some of these books.

Good spiritual reading is available in paperback. Many religious goods stores will give a parish books on consignment and often a parishioner who knows theology and is well read will volunteer to direct a bookselling project. (Run well, these can even be profitable.)

Since a proliferation of tape recorders exists in society, a parish (or several parishes) may want to set up a good cassette tape-lending library. The *National Catholic Reporter* puts out some excellent tapes on prayer and meditation. Shut-ins or older members of the parish may benefit from these. Many of the jobs around the home or apartment could be done while listening to these tapes.

Praying in Groups

Personal prayer is a gift that is meant to be shared in one form or another. It is enriched by and enriches community prayer. Community prayer helps all members of the parish to touch base with the very reason for their coming together. Parish meetings, dinners, and projects run the risk of becoming smaller versions of business ventures where minutes, memos, subcommittees, receipts, and bank statements are "the bottom line." Lavishly decorated halls, well-orchestrated passion plays, flawless record keeping and envelope systems should be only the by-products of people who gather in the name of Jesus. Prayer reminds priest and people why they have come together.

Parish committee meetings, school faculty meetings, adult education classes provide ready-made opportunities to build community through prayer. They also provide excellent vehicles for the laity to assume leadership in the area of prayer. Many parish meetings begin now with a prayer service or paraliturgy rather than a routine prayer. These serve as part of the spiritual development and growth of the people who are meeting together. Meetings can be dull, lengthy, controversial; they can also serve as occasions for the spiritual growth of those attending.

Resistance to prolonged prayer time at meetings can be expected. Religion is still a private matter for some. One parishioner remarked, at the conclusion of an opening paraliturgy, "Now that we've finished praying, we can get down to business," to which the pastor responded, "That was the business."

If a parish needs to "revive its drooping spirit" it would do well to look at the spiritual energy it invests in its liturgies and sacramental celebrations. By their nature these are *prayer-full* times. People's attention is naturally focused on God at these times. One parish planning group stated its goal this way: "It is our goal to be conscious of not getting in the way of *what is really happening* in our liturgies." Music, art, prayers, readings, as well as gesture and movement must be designed to contribute and "not get in the way."

A wake service can be a prayerful experience. Care should be taken to avoid insensitive language and awkward gestures which distract from prayer. Because people are emotionally upset on these occasions, whatever can be done to simplify the service helps. Words for prayers and songs should be provided for everyone. Directions and readings should be clear and audible.

Communal penance services can be powerful vehicles of prayer. Focus is the key to a prayerful penance service. If the community is focused on the unconditional love of the Father, if people can see the mercy of God, then they can turn away from sin. But if the readings, homily, music, and slides emphasize only sin, the penitent can become too self-conscious to pray. Real prayer is liberating and freeing, leading naturally to a change of heart.

Prayer Groups

Many people in the Church today who are looking for more personal, intimate prayer experiences are forming small prayer groups. These are not new in the Church. They have always served as a leaven in the larger parish community. Often the strength and faith nourished in these small groups is brought to the larger Sunday assembly and shared with others in different ways. The following guidelines may be helpful in setting up a prayer group.

1. Communication is vital if the group is going to be a positive factor in the parish. Care has to be taken to ensure that the group is not perceived as

a clique. Whatever means of communication works in a parish, it should be employed to get the message out that this is not an exclusive group.

2. Make it clear at the outset what kind of group it is and what it is not. For example, if the purpose of the group is to pray with Scripture, let people know that it is *not* a scripture class, parenting session, discussion club, therapy session, gripe session, or parish rumor mill. Set the parameters and stick to them. If communication within the group is open and honest it should be able to evaluate itself regularly in terms of its goals. Most groups need to be monitored from within and also from an objective outside source.

3. Establish a time limit for meetings, and stick to it.

4. Prayer groups need good leaders. Look for someone who is sensible, who makes others feel comfortable, is conscious of what is going on around and within the group, is nonthreatening, nonjudgmental or pedantic, has a good self-image, is affirming, and above all is clear about his or her role.

5. Someone on the parish staff should act as liaison to the group, providing resources and encouragement.

One of the common difficulties experienced by groups just starting out is finding a process that "works." Planning is very important. Environment, atmosphere, and timing can make the difference between a good and bad session. Sufficient materials should be on hand. Chairs should be set up ahead of time. The following process has worked very well for beginning groups who have come together to pray with Scripture.

1. Establish an atmosphere of comfortable quiet. Assure all that silence is just as valid as praying aloud. No one has to speak.

2. Read a passage from Scripture aloud slowly.

3. Read it again with pauses between phrases.

4. Go around the group and have individuals mention one phrase, word, or idea that struck them while the scripture passage was being read. No discussion should follow individual comments.

5. Read the passage reflectively one more time. Have someone else read it this time.

6. Pray. Those who wish to pray aloud may do so.

7. Conclude with a hymn that everyone knows.

The prayer life of any parish culminates in Sunday worship. According to the "Constitution on the Sacred Liturgy" from Vatican Council II, the Sunday celebration of Eucharist is the "summit toward which the activity of the church is directed" and "the fount from which all her power flows" (No. 10). There is, then, a symbiotic relationship between what people bring to Sunday Eucharist and what they take home again. The community that comes to worship with the hope and joy born of an active prayer life that goes beyond Sunday will show that in worship. The celebration of Eucharist will increase that joy and hope born of love.

In the end, a parish can be described as a praying community which unites its prayers with the risen Lord, so as to be formed by him into his sisters and brothers.

SUMMARY

1. As it has from the beginning, the Church of today carries out the mission of prayer given to it by Jesus.

2. The quality of the prayer life of any parish is directly dependent upon the prayer life of the individual members of that parish. Leadership in this area must come directly from the priest, and from the example of the members of the parish staff. People are hungry for help in learning how to pray.

3. Meaningful prayer must characterize all those moments when parish people gather.

4. The availability of good spiritual reading is essential for a healthy prayer life.

5. Every time people in the parish come together, regardless of the event, there should be some formal prayer. Particular attention should be paid to wake services and communal penance services.

6. Prayer groups within a parish can provide the necessary leaven to help the parish become a praying community. The parish must, however, provide clear guidelines for any group sponsored by the parish.

7. Since the prayer life of any parish culminates in Sunday worship, how well people pray during the week will affect the quality of Sunday Eucharist.

SUGGESTED READINGS

Brett, Lawrence, F.X. *Share the Word.* Washington, D.C.: Paulist Catholic Evangelization Center, 1980. This new monthly magazine of Bible study and sharing is published as a tool of evangelization for reaching out to the unchurched in neighborhood discussion groups. It is an excellent resource for all prayer groups. *Share the Word* provides background, commentary, and discussion ideas for each of the three Sunday readings. One attractive feature of this fine magazine is its price. It is free.

Garrotto, Alfred J. *Christians and Prayer* and *Christ in Our Lives.* Minneapolis: Winston Press, 1980. Designed for adults, these two paperbacks contain some very good material for prayer groups. Introductions list a variety of practical uses for each book. Worksheets are provided at the end of each unit.

Link, Mark, S.J. *You.* Niles, Ill.: Argus Communications, 1976. Although not a new book, this is an excellent resource for individuals and groups who are looking for a way to pray. It contains suggestions about prayer (forms, styles, places, and times). Link includes a series of prayer "experiments" that are intended for personal use but work well with groups also.

Meyer, Marty. *At Home with the Word.* Chicago: Liturgy Training Publications, 1980. This book contains the readings for each Sunday and major feasts of the year with corresponding study sheets.

Nouwen, Henri J.M. *Out of Solitude.* Notre Dame, Ind.: Ave Maria Press, 1974. Nouwen has made a tremendous contribution to American spirituality. This book provides three meditations on the Christian life. The author offers very clear and simple insights which easily inspire prayer and discussion. Other books by him which are worthy of note are *With Open Hands, Clowning in Rome, Intimacy, The Wounded Healer, Pray to Live, The Living Reminder,* and *Reaching Out.*

Oosterhuis, Huub. *Your Word Is Near.* New York: Paulist Press, 1968. This is a book of contemporary prayer that is very valuable to many parish prayer groups. It contains prayers for many occasions. Parish councils may wish to invest in copies of this book for prayer at their meetings.

Rosage, David E. *The Bread of Life.* Ann Arbor, Mich.: Servant Books, 1979. This paperback is a collection of scripture readings and reflections that focus on the celebration of the Eucharist. It is a good aid to personal and group prayer.

_____. *Speak, Lord.* Ann Arbor, Mich.: Servant Books, 1970. The purpose of this book, as stated by the author, is to help people begin to pray with Scripture by offering an outline for an entire year of daily prayer. Many have found this book to be helpful to their daily prayer. It is not limited to beginners.

van Breeman, Peter G. *As Bread That Is Broken.* Denville, N.J.: Dimension Books, 1974. This is not a how-to book on prayer. It is a very fine book about the spiritual life. Because it is contemporary and simple, readers should find it helpful in their prayer and worship. Another of his books, *Called by Name* (1976), is equally good.

'Rite of Christian Initiation of Adults' (RCIA)

The Rev. Ronald J. Lewinski

Ordained for the Archdiocese of Chicago in 1972, Father Lewinski is presently vicar for the sacraments of initiation in the Archdiocese. He is editor of *The Chicago Catehumenate* and author of *Welcoming the New Catholic* and *A Guide for Sponsors.* He is widely known throughout the country for his work in the catechumenate.

The *Rite of Christian Initiation of Adults* (RCIA) was given to the Church in 1972 and made available in English in 1974. Since that time it has had a profound effect upon the American pastoral scene. It was bound to have a deep impact upon the Church since the *Rite of Christian Initiation of Adults* has offered much more than just a revised collection of initiation rituals. It has proposed a whole new vision of what it means to become a believing Catholic Christian, what it means to celebrate the sacraments, and what all of this demands of the community of the faithful.

Taking these points seriously, catechists, laity, bishops, and priests have had to reflect upon the present status of Catholic life, worship, and service. And this in turn has led to positive changes in attitude, priorities, and pastoral planning on the parish and diocesan levels.

Not everyone, to be sure, has been so touched or convinced of the value of the RCIA. For some it is still just a complicated collection of antiquated rites better suited to mission countries. For others it is simply unnecessary. For many the RCIA is just too frightening, either because it expects too much of an already overburdened pastoral staff or else threatens to unseat all the theological principles upon which many have built their institutions and ministries.

In any event there is no turning back. The RCIA has already begun to take root in parishes and dioceses around the country. Those who have taken the challenge have discovered a freshness to the parish and its communal, sacramental, and apostolic life. They have validated the theology, process, and rituals of the RCIA through experience, while accepting the responsibility for adaptation where called for.

In those ten years since the RCIA first appeared, its development has reached a second stage. For many it is no longer a curious "new rite." Numerous parishes and dioceses now have years of experience in catechumenal ministry. New questions are beginning to emerge, especially relating to the celebration of the rites, the process of conversion, and the applicability of the RCIA to the already baptized non-Catholic as well as to the unbaptized.

There is much to learn from those already experienced in the RCIA. Their insights and reflections give us a clue to future directions. Their experience is especially valuable for those first beginning to implement the RCIA in parish and diocese. What follows here are a few of those insights and reflections on the RCIA that have surfaced around the country.

By no means are these few points, presented here as principles of the catechumenate, an exhaustive list. And of course they bear the bias of this author, who has monitored the progress of the RCIA since its birth in 1972.

1. **The RCIA Presumes Corporate Ministry and Not Solo Pastoral Direction.**

One of the most significant elements in the RCIA, which differentiate it from past efforts of welcoming new Catholics, is that initiation is clearly the responsibility of the entire community and not just the clergy. The RCIA boldly states:

> The people of God, represented by the local Church, should always understand and show that the initiation of adults is its concern and the business of all the baptized ... the community must help the candidates and catechumens throughout their whole period of initiation ... (No. 41).

It should be clear that the parish priest is not the only one responsible for initiating new Catholics. The entire community must work together to provide a suitable formation for the candidates. Of course every realist knows that an entire parish cannot relate in an intimate way with every candidate, although a community's concern, witness, and prayer should not be undermined either. What is necessary and achievable is that the direct responsibility for the catechumenate be extended beyond the rectory.

In very practical terms what this means is that, for the RCIA to be effectively integrated into parish life, the pastor must call together a number of people who will share the responsibility for the catechumenate. It may be difficult at first to assemble a catechumenate team but it is essential that the catechumenate eventually become a corporate ministry. For if the catechumenate rests solely in the hands of the parish priest, it risks becoming an enterprise not much different than former initiation practices.

The purpose then of a catechumenate pastoral team composed of laity and clergy is not just to lighten the parish priest's burden, but to become for the candidates the first of many experiential insights into the Church's identity and mission. In other words, from the outset the inquirers and candidates should recognize a Church where the laity have assumed due responsibility for the life of the Church.

While the whole assembly is responsible for the initiation of new Catholics, they will never sense this responsibility unless they are continually called to participate in this ministry. At the same time, as the catechumenate team develops, it must be careful not to become a special interest group separated from the assembly, since it is meant to represent and link the candidate to the assembly. The involvement of a good broad base of parishioners can also be the integrating link to other parish circles. Because of the mobility of the clergy and professional staff, the catechumenate needs the stability of the local lay community. Too often the parish priest has taken full charge of the RCIA as a special project. When he is suddenly transferred, the result is a dying catechumenate.

Sponsors

While the entire assembly ought to be concerned for the candidates, it is obviously impossible for a large number of people to enter into a personal relationship with the candidates. The most direct personal link from the community to the candidates is the sponsor.

At present there is some confusion in the RCIA on the distinction between sponsor and godparent. Consequently, parishes around the country have engaged sponsors and godparents in a number of different ways. In the majority of cases, parishes have called forth sponsors form the parish community to befriend and support the candidates. These sponsors are responsible for sharing their faith and serving as bridges to the larger community. Godparents are most frequently chosen by the candidates and approved by the catechumenate staff as those who participate in the final stages of the initiation process and establish a permanent spiritual relationship with the candidate.

Ideally, the godparent is the same individual as the sponsor. However, because candidates often choose godparents who may not be strong in faith or involved in the local Church community, parishes have found it wise to appoint a parish sponsor in addition to the friend or relative that the candidate proposes as godparent.

Catechumenate teams should not be alarmed by the different uses of sponsors and godparents, as those roles are still developing in this country. What matters is that the candidates are surrounded by mature Catholic women and men who are genuinely interested in welcoming and forming new Catholics. The distinction in roles will be clarified in time, although the unique needs of individuals and the circumstances of the place will probably make for variety in the role descriptions of sponsor and godparent. Sponsors and godparents perform a valuable service if they themselves are open to growth through the initiation process and are willing and unafraid to share their own experience of Catholic life. At this point, whether the Church calls these Catholics sponsors or godparents is secondary to the ministry they perform.

Parish Staff

The success of the catechumenate rests to a great extent on the parish staff. The catechumenate begins with the parish staff, who must decide if and how the program will be integrated into the parish. The parish staff must be in agreement on the value of the RCIA. They need not assume equal responsibility for the catechumenate, but they must be able to support it as a group. The parish staff may appoint a director from the parish pastoral staff or a non-staff person to coordinate the catechumenate. The parish staff, however, should always be concerned about maintaining close communication with the catechumenate director so that the staff and catechumenate are closely bonded. In turn the catechumenate director, with the help of the parish staff, should draw together a catechumenate team that will be responsible for the planning and exercise of the catechumenate, and for maintaining close and active ties between the pastoral staff and the larger assembly.

Most catechumenate teams have found that a member of the pastoral staff on the catechumenate team is essential. Many have found it to be very helpful to involve the whole pastoral staff directly during the first year so as to give every staff person an inside experience of the RCIA dynamic. Other teams have rotated the staff person to be involved so that a different staff member engages directly with the catechumenate each year.

In the future, dioceses or diocesan regions might consider pooling their resources together for training catechumenate ministers, and especially catechumenate directors.

2. New Catholics Need an Adequate Formation in Liturgical Prayer.

The formation in prayer that many Catholics remember having received at home and school was often very rigid or formalized. They recall having to memorize prayer texts and respect an unchanging stylized form of worship. As a result, many Catholics are now searching for new modes of less formal and more spontaneous prayer.

Sensitive to their own need for more personal and spontaneous prayer, Catholics engaged in catechumenate ministry have noticeably emphasized these less formal styles of prayer over the more ritualized or liturgical prayer of the Church. This is unfortunate. While helping the candidates to pray in a more personal and informal manner is commendable, catechumenate teams have frequently overlooked the value of a good formation in liturgical prayer.

The liturgy is the Church's basic source of spiritual direction. It not only includes the Mass and sacraments but the Liturgy of the Hours and the feasts and seasons of the year. Long after the candidates have completed their journey through the catechumenate, they will have the liturgy to guide them and sustain them. The Lectionary and Sacramentary are not an arbitrary collection of texts but an ordered journey through the year of grace which exposes the community to the living mystery of Christ. The liturgy is not in opposition to personal or private prayer but presupposes that an individual has already established an ongoing dialogue with the Lord in prayer. Furthermore, while the liturgy is ritualized and thus more set, it is nevertheless personal prayer, since it ought to come from the heart of the individual and community.

The current problem is that, while catechumenate teams are spending a great deal of time talking about individual free forms of prayer, there is little being done to aid candidates in praying. First of all, because the liturgy is a complex form of prayer it needs to be taught. While some of the liturgy speaks for itself, much of the structure, purpose, and meaning of the liturgical elements are not self-evident and so need a careful explanation. Catechumenate teams should not presume that the candidates will automatically "catch" what the liturgy is all about.

Second, the candidates should be helped to make the sacred liturgy their personal prayer. This is accomplished through guidance and the use of liturgical elements in informal and even private settings of prayer. For example, penitential rite "C" (from the introductory rites of the Mass) could be used in such a way that the candidates become familiarized with the pattern and helped to reflect upon the texts in light of their own lives. Then as they worship at Eucharist and encounter this penitential prayer form it can become a true prayer of the heart. Or the use of evening prayer or night prayer from the Liturgy of the Hours cannot only help the candidates pray the psalms but also expose them to the Church's Liturgy of the Hours which they may learn to adopt as a part of their regular prayer exercise.

This approach can also be applied to gesture and symbol as well as texts. The sign of the cross, a bow, incense — all of these can be incorporated into the informal prayer exercises of the catechumenate. These in turn will open the candidates to the use of these same ingredients at public worship.

The RCIA states that the catechumenate ought to be well integrated into the liturgical year. The purpose of this integration is to allow the liturgy itself to influence the formation of the candidates. By walking with the candidates through the course of the liturgical year, catecumenate teams help the candidates to draw from the richness of the Church year and to gain insight into how to celebrate and use these feasts and seasons of the calendar in the future.

The various rites of the initiation process are also significant occasions for forming candidates in liturgical prayer. Like all liturgy, the rites of the catechumenate convey and celebrate that which words alone are unable to do. They have the potential of not only touching the candidates but the assembly as well. The rites of initiation mark the gradual growth and spiritual journey of the candidates and become lessons in themselves of how liturgy and life experience are meant to entwine.

Catechumenate teams need to integrate the various rites into the full formation process, to avoid leaving these rites as an appendage to the whole. The catechesis and personal direction of candidates ought to be closely related to the rites.

From its beginning in the early twentieth century, the liturgical movement was eager to encourage the faithful to "pray the Mass." The early reformers were insistent that the baptized recognize their duty and privilege to actively pray the liturgy, to make it their own prayer. Many centuries later, even with the benefit of an ecumenical council that affirmed these early reformers, many Catholics still have not learned to pray the liturgy. (Note that it is not just a matter of understanding the liturgy, but of understanding the ministry of the assembly which every baptized shares.)

It ought to be one of the greatest concerns of the catechumenate team to ensure that new Catholics are better prepared not only to close their door and pray privately, but to join the assembly in making the prayer of the Church their own.

3. The Evangelization and Catechesis of New Catholics Ought to Be Well Balanced.

An Adult Catechesis

The Catholic Church in the United States has had a strong tradition of child-centered catechesis to which parochial schools bear witness. As the Church begins to develop more opportunities for adult catechesis and religious formation, there is a natural tendency to adapt child-centered catechetical models for catechizing adults, rather than to draw from contemporary studies on how adults learn and design appropriate new settings for adult formation.

These principles of adult learning must be applied to the catechumenate, as teams are faced with the challenge of evangelizing and catechizing adults in the faith and tradition of the Church. Adult catechists need to be trained for this ministry. There can be no presumption that someone — lay, clergy, or religious — will have the natural ability to be an adult catechist. Furthermore, it cannot be presumed that the ordained are better suited as adult catechists because of their comprehensive theological education. Without excluding the possibility of pastoral staff members serving as catechists, the agenda for the future must very definitely look to the laity as responsible adult catechists.

No doubt it will take time to find prospective catechists and train them properly. However, if the clergy continues to talk about the significant involvement of the laity but continues to exclude them as trained catechists, their importance is diminished.

The training of adult catechists might well be achieved most effectively on a diocesan level, which in turn could serve as a sign of the local Church's common concern for the initiation of new Catholics.

Content

Just as the former prayer experiences of Catholics have led catechumenate teams to emphasize spontaneous prayer forms over the liturgy and traditional piety, so too the former catechetical experiences of Catholics have led some catechumenate teams to downplay the importance of doctrine and Church teaching. It may be true that in the past faith was terribly intellectualized. One may have graduated from Catholic schools believing that to know the faith was to have the faith.

The catechumenate experience is a conversion process: it aims at forming the entire person and not just passing on a body of knowledge. It is not primarily an academic experience. At the same time, a solid foundation in the teachings and tradition of the Church is essential for new Catholics if their faith is to be informed and if they are to assume responsible roles within the Church.

There is a tendency for some to downplay the formal learning dimension in the RCIA in favor of free discussion that flows solely from personal feelings and experience. No doubt there must be room for that kind of dialogue and personal sharing. It is a very desirable element in the RCIA process; but it ought not exclude a thorough examination of Church teaching.

Furthermore, the catechesis ought to be fair and honest. In other words, it is unfair for the catechist to present everything from a personal point of view pretending that his or her point of view is the commonly held belief of the universal Church. It is far more honest to pass on the Church's teaching in a responsible manner and admit one does not understand or appreciate a particular point than to interpret it publicly to fit one's own personal taste. This does not mean that catechesis in the catechumenate should be rigid or impersonal. It only means that catechists must recognize that they are commissioned by the Church to pass on Jesus' gospel and the Church's tradition and not a personal gospel or body of doctrine.

The ministry of sponsor and godparent is invaluable in the catechumenate process because as ordinary Catholics they are able to share how they live what is taught. They take the catechesis and, in light of their own lives, make sense out of what is taught as they dialogue with candidates. Frequently, sponsors and godparents can make a contribution in this vital area of informal formation.

As far as content in the catechetical dimension, the *National Catechetical Directory* as well as many contemporary catechisms' table of contents will offer a sampling of content. Catechumenate teams should not overlook catechesis in peace and justice. The Church has spoken out loud and clear on peace and justice; and much of that preaching has gone unheard. It is just as much a part of Catholic teaching as any of the rest of doctrine is. New Catholics should be helped not only to reflect on the Church's concern for peace and justice, but be formed as ministers of peace and justice.

Ecumenical Sensitivity

Although no catechumenate team would want to offend candidates baptized in other Christian churches, they often do so unconsciously. They sometimes forget that long before men and women ask to be received into the Catholic Church they may have been educated in prayer, Scripture, and Christian theology. Candidates for reception into full communion with the Catholic Church sometimes get the impression that all their previous religious upbringing has been discredited.

Catechumenate ministers must strive to build a bridge from the candidates' present religious experience to our Catholic tradition. This demands respect and understanding for the variety of Christian spiritualities and practices. It might mean that catechumenate teams, especially the catechists, will have to take the time to study the religious roots of the candidates. There should also be a genuine openness to the prayer and tradition of the non-Catholic. Candidates should not be made to feel that they must now disown their past but find in us an eagerness to learn from their experience.

Evangelization

As it is in catechetics, so must it be in evangelization. The evangelizer ought to be a true messenger of the gospel. The message of salvation should be proclaimed with as little bias as possible. There is a tendency in the evangelization process to proclaim the message in such a way that the response is predetermined. After relating the biblical event, people are too quick to say, "This is what we must therefore do," or "This is what this means for our lives."

The proclamation of the mystery of salvation is an invitation to dialogue with the Lord. The evangelizer's purpose is to announce the good news and introduce the inquirer to the living Lord and then step back to allow enough freedom for the inquirer and the Lord to dialogue.

The scriptures, the primary resource for evangelization, have a power of their own to capture the imagination and to inspire the listener. The average American's understanding and response to the living Word has been greatly influenced by Western European theology; and it is extremely difficult now to separate the message of salvation from what theology has to say about it. This is the challenge: to present the message in all its beauty and mystery in such a way as to draw the inquirer into an encounter with the Lord and then to be patient and unprejudiced enough to allow the inquirer to respond freely.

4. The Parish Catechumenate Is Linked to the Universal Church.

As the RCIA continues to spread and develop, catechumenate teams should be cautious about becoming too congregationalist in their approach. Some communities become very complacent with their own success and view themselves as self-sufficient, forgetting their communion with the larger Church.

It is true that the candidates will find their closest support and most intimate experience of Church in the local parish. However, the local parish is only part of the full Church into which we initiate men and women. They need to see the Church in different perspectives. They ought to develop a missionary attitude, being concerned not only for their local parish's well-being but the well-being of a Church and world that extends far beyond their parish borders.

The Bishop

The role of the bishop is very significant in this regard. The bishop is the symbol of the Church's unity, a reminder to the faithful of their communion with others outside their own parish. Strictly speaking, the bishop is the principal minister of initiation since he is the chief pastor and shepherd of the local Church. In most U.S. dioceses there are either too many Catholics in one diocese or the diocese's geography is too expansive for the bishop to be as available as one might hope.

Nevertheless, the bishop can still play a significant role in the initiation process. He can propose a diocesan vision and offer guidelines for the initiation of new Catholics. He can arrange for the formation and training of catechumenate ministers. On pastoral visitations he can meet with the candidates from the parish or region. If he is traveling about the diocese during Lent, he may wish to make a formal presentation of the Our Father and the Creed, as the principal teacher and liturgist of the local Church. Because his involvement in the RCIA can be so far reaching, he may find it advantageous to appoint a diocesan director for the catechumenate.

Probably the most favorable opportunity for the bishop to meet candidates and expose them to the broader dimension of Church is in the rite of election. The RCIA clearly points to the bishop as the celebrant of the rite which is also contained in the Roman Pontifical (or Bishop's Book of Ceremonies). Numerous dioceses around the country have celebrated the rite of election at the cathedral church or in various regions of the diocese, drawing people together from diverse ethnic, cultural, and social backgrounds. The reports on the diocesan celebrations have been favorable. There is a solemnity and uniqueness to the diocesan celebration that can hardly be matched in the local parish.

There is, of course, the argument of those who feel the parish will lose something if the rite of election takes place outside the parish. However, the rite of election is only one rite of many; and while it should not be repeated in the parish, there is no reason why the local parish can not design a preparatory rite for use at Sunday Mass in the parish prior to the diocesan celebration. This would not only give the assembly the opportunity to encounter the candidates but would also move the whole assembly to think about their own ties with the larger Church.

Many dioceses have begun a practice of celebrating a Mass of Thanksgiving during the Easter season with the bishop at the cathedral church or in regional districts. This celebration, too, is a good occasion to meet the bishop and for the whole Church to celebrate the new life stimulated by the initiation of new members. Early indications show that this Eastertime Mass with the bishop is a successful occasion although it seems to call for either some particular ritual or texts to better highlight the occasion. This might well be one of the areas where a U.S. adaptation is called for.

If the RCIA is going to be more than just the latest parish "program" or "fad," the bishop's involvement will have to be more seriously regarded in the future. Both the bishop and the community have a responsibility toward each other to ensure that that involvement happens.

SUMMARY

1. The *Rite of Christian Initiation of Adults* is here to stay. But its development is far from complete. Refinement of the catechumenate process in the future will demand that the Church seriously reflect upon how well it has given the laity genuine responsibility for the initiation of new Catholics and made the catechumenate a corporate ministry in the parish.

2. The liturgical formation of new Catholics must also be more carefully attended to in the future, since the liturgy is the Church's basic source of ongoing spiritual direction and consequently of great value to the new Catholic's ongoing spiritual growth. A good liturgical formation will also help to achieve the Council's desire to bring the assembly to a full and conscious participation in the liturgy.

3. The evangelization and catechesis of new candidates ought to be well balanced. Evangelists and catechists need to be well trained to minister effectively to adults.

4. Catechumenate parishes and bishops need to work closely together so that the new Catholic will have a better appreciation of the broad dimensions of Church. As the local parish recognizes the role of the bishop in the RCIA and the bishop becomes more involved in the initiation process, there will be less chance of the RCIA's becoming the passing fad of a few parishes.

SUGGESTED READINGS

Amalorpavadass, D.S. *Adult Catechumenate and Church Renewal.* Bangalore, 560005, India: National Biblical, Catechetical and Liturgical Centre, 1973. This publication produced for the Church in India aims at giving an idea of a model catechumenate and offers guidelines to organize one. Contains good insight into the practical nature of the catechumenate.

Boyack, Kenneth. *A Parish Guide to Adult Initiation.* New York: Paulist Press, 1980. A readable and practical journey through the RCIA. This book deals with the "why" and the "how to" and shares the experience of a tested catechumenate program.

Ghilson, Richard. *The Way to Christianity*. Minneapolis: Winston Press, Inc., 1979. A guidebook to use with candidates making a spiritual journey. It offers exercises in evangelization, meditation, journal-keeping, and personal scriptural analysis.

Curtiss, Rosalie, et al. *RCIA / A Practical Approach to Christian Initiation for Adults*. Dubuque: William C. Brown Co., 1981. One of the few available resources that offers concrete catechetical suggestions. Limited as any ordered plan may be, it serves as a valuable guide for planning catechumenate sessions.

Dujarier, Michel. *A History of the Catechumenate*. New York: William H. Sadlier, Inc., 1979. A good introduction to the history of the first six centuries of catechumenate experience.

_____. *The Rites of Christian Initiation*. New York: William H. Sadlier, Inc., 1979. Based on his pastoral experience in Africa, Dujarier offers some insight into the various rites in the initiation process.

Dunning, James B. and William J. Reedy, eds. *Christian Initiation Resources*. New York: William H. Sadlier, Inc. A quarterly packet of articles helpful in understanding and implementing the RCIA.

Groome, Thomas H. *Christian Religious Education: Sharing Our Story and Vision*. San Francisco: Harper and Row, 1980. A contemporary approach to religious education that is in the spirit of the RCIA process and helpful for catechumenate ministers eager to develop a solid catechumenate methodology.

Huck, Gabe. *Teach Me To Pray: The Way of Catholic Prayer*. New York: William H. Sadlier, Inc., 1981. A book of Catholic prayers with a brief explanation of their origin and use. Very helpful in introducing new Catholics to the Catholic tradition of prayer.

Kavanagh, Aidan. *The Shape of Baptism*. New York: Pueblo Publishing Co., 1978. A popular theological and pastoral commentary on the history and reform of the rite of initiation, particularly the RCIA.

Kemp, Raymond B. *A Journey in Faith*. New York: William H. Sadlier, Inc., 1979. The story of Sts. Paul and Augustine Parish in Washington, D.C., in their use of the RCIA. Inspiring and practical — a sign of hope for those first beginning as well as the experienced.

Kramer, Geneal, O.P. *Parish Handbook for the Adult Catechumenate*. Cincinnati: Pamphlet Publications (P.O. Box 41372 A), 1980. Two books (one for candidate and one for staff) that offer concrete suggestions and catechetical outlines for a parish catechumenate.

Lewinski, Ronald J. *The Chicago Catechumenate*. Chicago: Liturgy Training Publications. A Christian initiation newsletter that serves as a forum for catechumenate ministers to share their experiences. Also includes articles and suggested resources. Published five times annually.

_____. *A Guide for Sponsors*. Chicago: Liturgy Training Publications, 1980. Booklet for sponsors that helps them understand their ministry and provides concrete suggestions for exercising their ministry.

———. *Welcoming the New Catholic.* Chicago: Liturgy Training Publications, 1978, 1980. An overview of the RCIA written for the laity. Very helpful in getting an overall picture of the spirit of the RCIA with a view toward involving the entire parish.

Lopresti, James J., S.J., ed. *Journeys.* New York: William H. Sadlier, Inc. A newsletter on the catechumenate. To be published five times annually. First issue expected in Fall, 1981.

Reedy, William H., ed. *Becoming a Catholic Christian.* New York: William H. Sadlier, Inc., 1978. Various articles on the catechumenate written by several authors gathered for a symposium in France on the catechumenate.

The Murphy Center for Liturgical Research. *Made, Not Born: New Perspectives on Christian Initiation and the Catechumenate.* Notre Dame, Ind.: University of Notre Dame Press, 1976. Eight addresses given at a liturgical conference sponsored by the Murphy Center for Liturgical Research at Notre Dame Univesity on the subject of the catechumenate.

Rite of Christian Initiation of Adults. Washington, D.C.: U.S. Catholic Conference, 1974. The official text of the RCIA.

Catholic Schools: Unique and Challenging

M. Lourdes Sheehan, RSM

A Sister of Mercy of the Union of the Province of Baltimore, Sister Lourdes has been a teacher and administrator in Catholic secondary schools. Currently she is the superintendent of schools for the Diocese of Richmond, Virginia. She recently received her doctorate in education from Virginia Polytechnic and State University.

"The most remarkable thing about Catholic schools today is not that they're doing a good job, but that the *New York Times* and the *Washington Post* think they're doing a good job. Hubert Humphrey once said: 'The appearance of power is power.' Perceptions are reality in education as in politics."

Michael O'Neill[1]

In Catholic schools the perceptions are the reality. Put another way, the Church's support, or nonsupport, of its schools is often the result of self-fulfilling prophecies. After fifteen years of significant negativity within some sections of the Church regarding schools, the challenge for today's parish is multiple: (1) to see Catholic schools — parish, interparish, diocesan, and private — as authentic and important contributors to the mission of the Church; (2) to provide structures that allow the schools to operate with responsible freedom; (3) to work toward putting the schools on a sound financial basis while dealing realistically with financial constraints.

Official Church Statements

The official statements of the American bishops on Catholic education as well as the declarations of the Vatican's Sacred Congregation on Education continue to stress the unique role which Catholic schools play in the educational mission of the Church today.[2] The National Catechetical Directory, *Sharing the Light of Faith,* adopts the position of their pastoral on education and admits that Catholic schools are the most effective means available to the Church for the education of children and young people. This directory also restates that the schools to which they are referring are those for whom building and living community is the prime, explicit goal. The twofold task of these schools, which should also provide academically excellent programs, is catechetical and evangelical.[3]

100

In March, 1981, when the bishops published a statement from their Committee on the Parish, they reaffirmed the role of the school when they said:

> The parish school is often the centerpiece of a parish's educational ministry. It offers a particularly full means for the Christian development of the young. The school complements the family's efforts to ensure formation in the fullness of Christian life and provides pupils with a sound foundation in educational skills. It is this special contribution of the parish school that earns its support from the entire parish.[4]

Historically, statements and legislation, even from bishops, do not make things happen. Obviously, the ideal of this most recent statement of the bishops will become a reality in individual parishes and dioceses only when people work together to accomplish it. The most important word is "together" — pastors, principals, parish staffs, school faculties, parish councils, school boards, and education committee members.

Parish and School

The bishops' image of the school as "centerpiece" is appropriate but must be qualified. Some would see the image as saying that the school has the central or most conspicuous position in the parish. More correctly, it is like the centerpiece which provides completeness, harmony, and distinctiveness to a correctly set table. Everyone agrees that a well-set table needs a centerpiece. Its presence indicates that the hostess or host considers the event and the guests important and significant enough to have provided an appropriately set table. While a centerpiece is distinctive in its own right, it is designed to create a total appearance of harmony and beauty in the rest of the table setting.

The Catholic school completes the total educational efforts of a parish by providing parents with an option for their children's education within a Catholic Christian atmosphere. In this understanding, a Catholic school is not an appendage to the rest of the parish; it is an integral part of the parish. Parish leaders must have this understanding of the place of the school in the total life of the parish before any further discussion of relationships can occur.

Parish and School Personnel

Because it is an institution, a school has an existence of its own. This does not mean that a parish or diocesan school can be permitted to become separated from other efforts of the parish, educational or otherwise. Rather schools must in some way contribute to the parish they are connected with and on which they depend. They must be integrated into the life of the parish.

One of the most effective ways to ensure this completeness of a parish's educational effort is to consider the school principal as a member of the parish staff, or in the case of a diocesan or regional school, as a member of the appropriate diocesan or regional body. Good organizational management dictates that roles and responsibilities of each parish staff member be clearly defined. For example, while the principal of a particular parish school may be established as administrator of the total school program, including that of religious education, and is accountable to the pastor, adequate provisions must be made for communication and cooperation between the principal and other parish staff members. The relationship between the principal and the person in the parish who serves in religious education is particularly critical.[5]

The principal and school faculty members are valuable contributors to the parish's educational efforts. Parish leaders would do well to recognize the resources which these professionally prepared teachers provide to the parish and look for opportunities to enhance their roles. Faculty members have a unique opportunity because of their positions and backgrounds to be active, participating members of the parish. In fact, many Catholic schoolteachers are active in other religious education programs of the parish. While some serve as lectors or special ministers of the Eucharist, others participate in the social ministry work of the community and in civic activities. By such involvement, faculty members not only teach what they believe, but, more importantly, they practice what they teach.

Parish and School Parents

Another way to ensure the completeness of the parish's educational mission is to structure the relationship between the parish and parent-school advisory bodies. Because of the diversity among dioceses and parishes, it is impossible to suggest one organizational model which will be applicable to all parishes. One way to deal with this diversity is for a parish to be certain that the structures which exist for participatory decision-making include representatives from all segments of the parish. Catholic school parents must participate actively in the life of the parish and be given a voice in the decision-making process. If the parish leadership recognizes the school as a vital part of the total parish, they will also recognize parents' participation in the activities of the school as a form of parish service.

It is essential that in those situations where parish school boards or boards of education exist there be some means of relating the board to other parish structures. One of the dangers in establishing separate school boards is the risk of separation of the school from the rest of the parish. The parish must work hard to see that the danger does not become a reality.

Some dioceses have mandated that there be a school committee as a part of the parish council. This model provides for the possibility of good communication between the school and other parish groups. This model, however, is not very satisfactory in parish situations where the school is large or where there are special school needs which require more concentration than an ordinary parish committee can be expected to provide.

Another disadvantage of this particular committee model is that it limits those people who like to concentrate their efforts on particular works and are not interested in committee membership as such. The schools need the concentrated expert assistance of the parishioners. One practical solution to the relationship between such a group and the parish council is to have the parish council education committee deal with broad needs and goals, and the school board concentrate on more specific school questions, keeping in mind the goals of the education committee.[6]

Another solution might be to constitute the school board as advisory to the principal, and give the principal the responsibility for communicating with the parish staff and parish council.

Problem Areas

Even when the presence of a Catholic school is recognized as the parish's centerpiece of the parish's educational efforts, there are at least three major areas which can cause problems for a parish if they are not handled properly. These three critical areas are: finances, facilities, and leadership.

The annual fights over budget approval are serious scandals in many parishes. Much of the problem stems from the fact that both schools and parishes operate out of an antiquated financial arrangement. When parish schools began in this country, they almost always received a substantial amount of financial support from the parish. When the school was the only major activity of the parish and religious women and men contributed most of their services to the school, this financial support was hardly questioned. In some places, there is still an uneven distribution of parish money going to support the school. Therefore, it is not possible to make general statements which are applicable to each parish and diocese.

There is no question that a school costs money and that the costs of school programs and other religious education programs are sometimes out of line. What is important is that the issue of parish financial support to the school be discussed rationally. The parish must make commitments so that both parish and school financial planning can extend beyond one year. It is essential that the school subsidy question be handled in an open, organized, and fair way.

For example, it may be helpful to have the parish budget include maintenance and upkeep of the school facilities since the buildings are indeed the responsibility of the total parish.

Another factor to consider is the allocation of parish funds for all education according to a formula which would take into consideration cost per pupil (participant) based on the amount of time an individual spends in the program. Some parishes have attempted to solve the financial question by separating out from the school budget those items which are strictly of a religious education and liturgical nature. This solution is frequently inappropriate since it presumes that the only parts of the school day are religious. Catholic school programs must be seen as a whole. Other approaches allocate costs based on a used-time formula, that is, according to the time the school facilities are used by other parish organizations.

One unpopular but equitable solution to the question of school finances is for a diocese to adopt a policy that the tuition charged to parents will equal the per pupil cost of operating the school with the provision that the parish will establish a scholarship fund sufficient to ensure that no child will be denied the opportunity for Catholic school education because of the parents' economic status. If this solution is adopted, it is essential that the school have some published system for determining need and that one person (who is recognized as a responsible parish leader) is designated as the administrator of such monies.

School facilities are used by many parish groups. For the sake of harmony, the parish needs a workable system for scheduling activities. Naturally, the sophistication of the system will depend on the size and use of the complex. Small irritations which grow to major conflicts can be avoided if the parish leadership determines and announces how scheduling will happen, including who is responsible for the schedule. The most sophisticated and highly organized system, however, is dependent on the informal communications which exist between and among staff members. The formal and informal systems must work together. All the good will in the parish will not be enough if someone does not assume the responsibility for coordinating activities and handling the inevitable conflicts which happen.

The other major area which can destroy a good relationship between school and parish is that of differing attitudes among people in leadership positions. Recognizing that good team ministry or cooperation does not mean that everyone thinks alike, parish leaders must have a common vision for the total parish. Where there is a school related to the parish, the common vision must include the valuable place of the school. This position does not mean that individuals cannot question or challenge those directly responsible for the operation of the school. It does mean that the very existence of the school ought not be questioned by parish leadership.

While the attitudes of each member of the parish staff are important in this regard, the pastor's is especially significant. The pastor stands in a special place within the parish community; he must be seen as a sign of unity and support for all of the parish activities. His natural interests and talents may lie outside of education, but he cannot remove himself or be distanced from the life of the school.

There are a variety of ways in which the pastor and other parish staff members can be involved in the school which do not involve actual classroom teaching. Every effort must be made to enhance the role of the pastor as the "chief teacher" of the parish. He and the other staff members should be invited to participate in all school events, especially faculty days of prayer and socials. Individual personalities are important and should be recognized and valued. However, individual proclivities and preferences cannot be allowed to dictate the future of an institution.

The School as Distinctive

The final attribute of the centerpiece is that of distinctiveness. Unless the school, like the table arrangement, contributes a certain distinctiveness to the parish, its place within the total setting needs to be questioned. That uniqueness which the school brings is expressed in the words of various statements of the bishops when they say that Catholic schools have the opportunity to proclaim the message of Christ, to foster Christian community, to offer opportunities for service, and to worship as a believing community. By fulfilling this fourfold goal, Catholic schools truly enhance and complement the family's efforts to ensure formation in the fullness of Christian life and provide pupils with a sound foundation in educational skills.

The Catholic school principal has a special responsibility to hire faculty members who believe in this fourfold goal and to provide opportunities for the faculty as adult Christians to grow in their faith. It is this adult community of faith which communicates Catholic Christian values to the children and youth of the school. It is this believing community of professional educators working in conjunction with the rest of the parish staff which makes the Catholic school unique. It is this uniqueness of the parish and diocesan school which earns support from the entire parish.

Conclusion

The Catholic Church in 1980-81 operated 9,559 elementary and secondary schools in the United States which enrolled more than 3,000,000 students.[7] Currently enrollment seems to be stabilizing, and some dioceses are reopening schools and building new facilities in growing areas of the country. Supporters of Catholic schools are making tremendous financial commitments in terms of tuition payments, parish subsidies, and fund raising. Current research has determined that attendance at Catholic schools makes a significant difference in the academic achievement as well as the religious practices and attitudes of American Catholics.[8] The facts are there. The perceptions are changing. Schools are once again being seen as integral parts of the educational mission of the Church.

SUMMARY

1. A major challenge for today's parish is to see the Catholic school as an authentic and important contributor to the mission of the Church, to provide structures that allow schools to operate with responsible freedom, and to work toward putting schools on sound financial footing.

2. The official statements of the American bishops emphasize the unique role which Catholic schools have in the educational mission of the Church. While stating that the schools are the most effective means available for the education of children and young people within the Church, they

challenge the schools to make building and living community their prime, explicit goal.

3. If schools are to achieve their ideal, they must have a common vision with the local Church. The school must be seen as something distinctive but in harmony with the complete educational effort of the parish.

4. The very nature of the Catholic school establishes its dependence on and need for integration into the life of the parish.

5. Parish and school personnel must work together to ensure that the parish's educational effort will be complete. Practically, this means that the principal is that member of the parish staff who is accountable to the pastor for the administration of the total school program. Relations with other parish staff members, especially with the religious education director, must be marked by clarity and cooperation.

6. Parish leaders would do well to recognize the valuable resource which is present in the school faculty. The faculty should serve as models for their students by contributing to the parish, by teaching, and by involving themselves in other parish and civic affairs.

7. Catholic school parents participate in the life of the parish by their services to the school. Structures for participatory decision-making in the parish should include means for all segments of parish life to be involved.

8. The issue of parish financial support for the school must be discussed rationally and decisions made so that both parish and school financial planning can extend beyond one year. These discussions must be open and organized so that adequate provisions can be made for the needs of all programs as well as for the economic status of families.

9. Parish leaders must assume responsibility for organizing and publishing a workable system for scheduling activities in facilities which are used by more than one parish organization. Even when good informal communication seems to work, someone must assume the job of scheduling the use of facilities and handling the inevitable conflicts which occur.

10. Unique personalities and differing opinions can bring strength to the team efforts of parish leaders. Nothing destroys an enterprise faster than lack of common vision. When there is a school related to the parish, the common vision must include the valuable place the school has in the parish's educational mission.

11. The pastor stands in a special place within the parish community. He cannot remove himself or be distanced from the life of the school. Individual proclivities and preferences cannot be allowed to dictate the existence of the school nor its smooth operation.

12. Catholic schools truly enhance and complement the family's effort to ensure formation in the fullness of Christian life when they fulfill their fourfold goal of message, community, service, and worship.

13. The adult professional educational community within the school communicates Catholic Christian values to the children and youth of the school. It is this believing community of faith-filled teachers, working in

conjunction with the rest of the parish staff, which makes the Catholic school unique. It is this uniqueness which earns support from the entire parish for its school.

CHAPTER NOTES

1. Michael O'Neill, "A Second Spring for American Catholic Education," *Momentum* (October, 1981), p. 34.
2. National Conference of Catholic Bishops, *To Teach As Jesus Did* (Washington, D.C.: U.S. Catholic Conference, 1973).
   The Sacred Congregation for Catholic Education, *The Catholic School* (Washington, D.C.: U.S. Catholic Conference, 1977).
3. United States Catholic Conference, *Sharing the Light of Faith:* An Official Commentary (Washington, D.C.: Department of Education, U.S. Catholic Conference, 1981), p. 95.
4. United States Bishops' Committee on the Parish, "The Parish: A People, A Mission, A Structure" (Washington, D.C.: *Origins, NC Documentary Service,* Vol. 10, No. 41, March 26, 1981), p. 645.
5. Mary Margaret Funk and James J. DeBoy, Jr., "DREs and School Principals: Partners in Ministry" (Winona, Minn.: St. Mary's Press, PACE 11, 1981).
6. Mary-Angela Harper, *Putting It All Together* (Washington, D.C.: NCEA, 1979), p. 8.
7. *Catholic Schools in America 1981* (Englewood, Colo.: Fisher Publishing Co.) in cooperation with the National Catholic Education Association, IX and XII.
8. Cf. Andrew Greeley, William C. McCready, and Kathleen McCourt, *Catholic Schools in a Declining Church* (Kansas City: Sheed and Ward, Inc., 1976) and National Center for Education Statistics, "High School and Beyond: A National Longitudinal Study for the 1980's" and "Minority Students in Catholic Secondary Schools" (1980 research projects conducted by the National Opinion Research Center under contract with the National Center for Education Statistics of the U.S. Department of Health, Education, and Welfare).

SUGGESTED READINGS

In addition to the sources cited in the footnotes, information concerning Catholic schools today, the plans and programs for pre-service and in-service of administrators and teachers, and relationships with the Church may be received from:

1. National Catholic Education Association, *Giving Form to the Vision: The Pastoral in Practice* (Washington, D.C.: The National Catholic

Education Association, 1974). This publication assists all Catholic educators to implement the message' of the bishops' pastoral on education, *To Teach As Jesus Did*. The five sections are addressed to Educational Policy-Making, Adult Education, Religious Education Outside of the School, Catholic Elementary School, and Catholic Secondary School.

2. National Conference of Directors of Religious Education, *Hear the Word, Share the Word, Guide Your People* (Washington, D.C.: National Catholic Education Association, 1978). Designed by religious education directors, this guideline offers a practical process for the spiritual formation of educational personnel.

3. Chief Administrators of Catholic Education, a department of the National Catholic Education Association, has several committees working on pre- and in-service programs for Catholic school personnel. Information concerning these and subsequent programs may be obtained from:

Rev. Msgr. Francis X. Barrett
Executive Director, CACE
National Catholic Education Association
One Dupont Circle, Suite 350
Washington, DC 20036

Adult Learning: Helping It Happen

Jane Wolford Hughes

A pioneer in adult religious education, Mrs. Hughes has been the director of the Institute for Continuing Education for the Archdiocese of Detroit since 1966. She has worked extensively with parish adult educators in her own diocese, and around the country. Her work at the United States Catholic Conference is well known. She is also a faculty member of St. John's Provincial Seminary in Plymouth, Michigan.

It's a warm evening in late June in a park on the east side of Detroit. A group of fifteen laughing adults is gathered together grilling hot dogs and eating a picnic supper. Afterward they sit intently around the tables, the laughter more subdued but still punctuating the hum of their voices. They are discussing "dealing with stress." They are from a nearby parish and, with the adult education chairperson, meet regularly in various places on chosen topics. Adult religious education? Yes.

Across the archdiocese, in a west-side suburb, a large group of people is moving from round discussion tables to an open area in the attractive room to complete their evening with a prayer ritual. They have been attending a weekly Lenten program, "We Believe — ." Together, with competent speakers, they have been struggling to understand the meaning of the articles of faith from the Apostles' Creed. In this parish all major adult education courses conclude with prayer: to take them beyond "just another class." Adult religious education? Yes.

The houses are tired and patched. Some are burned out or boarded up. People hang around waiting for something to happen. The parish here is a center for the educationally disadvantaged and offers adult basic education and preparation for a high-school certificate. It also offers care and counseling and firm support to change the life situation of God's suffering people. Adult religious education? Yes.

Success in parish adult religious education has many shapes but they are all molded with the same ten elements:

1. A caring, skilled leader.
2. Knowledge of adult learning.

3. Maintenance of a good learning climate.
4. Dedicated adult education team.
5. Understanding of needs.
6. Process of setting goals and objectives.
7. Creative design and quality content.
8. Implementing the design.
9. Meaningful publicity.
10. Evaluation of the process and the program.

For a parish just initiating adult religious education, equal attention must be given to all of the above elements. Once established, they should continue to be included in the ongoing plan. The most successful parishes in the Detroit archdiocese tell me that the following cannot be overemphasized: the caring leader working with a committee, an exciting design, and planned publicity.

For the past sixteen years, I have been part of the evolution of adult religious education. In that time it has become established as a legitimate and important part of the continuity of human development from birth to death. We now know a great deal more about how adults learn, the changes that occur in adult life stages, and to some extent the effect of life crises on faith development. I have seen the steady establishment of parish-initiated adult religious education, so that our role as the adult education office on the archdiocesan level has changed from the provider of programs to the trainer of parish leadership. In that training the Institute for Continuing Education still provides enrichment opportunities for the leaders and potential leaders, since parishes would find it hard, if not impossible, to provide such programs for themselves. On the other hand, parish leaders need to possess a high degree of motivation to participate in these unique opportunities for themselves and their people.

Church Documents

In these years of growth, the institutional Church has endorsed adult religious education with great clarity. But, as is often the case, the pronouncements have not been absorbed into total common practice. Although almost every diocese in the United States now sponsors some form of adult religious education, sustained enthusiasm for it is uneven. Nonetheless, the Church documents have set the direction and more and more parishes are following it.

In 1971, the Sacred Congregation for the Clergy said in the *General Catechetical Directory:* "They (shepherds of souls) should also remember that catechesis for adults, since it deals with persons who are capable of an adherence that is fully responsible, must be considered the chief form of catechesis. All other forms, which are indeed always necessary, are in some way oriented to it" (No. 20).

In 1973, the American bishops reaffirmed this position in their pastoral message on Catholic education, *To Teach As Jesus Did:* "Consequently the continuing education of adults is situated not at the periphery of the Church's educational mission but at its center" (No. 43). In the same document they added: "The full content of revelation can be communicated best to those able by reason of maturity and prior preparation to hear and respond to it. Religious education for adults is the culmination of the entire catechetical effort because it affords an opportunity to teach the whole Christian message" (No. 47).

The American bishops spoke again in *Sharing the Light of Faith,* the 1979 National Catechetical Directory: "Because of its importance and because all other forms of catechesis are oriented in some way to it, the catechesis of adults must have high priority at all levels of the Church. The success of programs for children and youth depends to a significant extent upon the words, attitudes and action of the adult community, especially parents, family and guardians" (No. 188).

The ten elements of successful adult religious education should be examined as they have been applied in real parish situations. Various illustrations will show that even among the elements there are nuances. The key then is adaptability to the individual situation. This brings us back again to the central and first element: the caring skilled leader.

1. A Caring, Skilled Leader

"They're 'magnet' people, your adult educators," commented a priest speaking to me at a meeting of the Archdiocesan Adult Educators Association. They do draw people to themselves. And why not! By temperament and practice, adult educators are caring, warm, enthusiastic people who work at establishing trust to enable adults to learn and to achieve their fullness as mature Christians. They are other-directed and their attitude and actions reflect it.

All effective adult religious educators I have been privileged to work with are persons of obvious faith who are committed to Jesus Christ and the Church they serve. At the same time, they are attractively human, professionally competent, bright and aware of the signs of the times. There is a ruggedness about them singular to pioneers who have known lean days and unexpected ambushes and managed somehow to stay with the work.

Listening to people in St. Ambrose Parish you catch the admiration in their voices when they talk about their adult education coordinator: "He got me involved because he was so ready to share himself and his faith. Besides, he's fun to be with." And another: "He helped me release what was in the back of my mind about religion. I just let it out, and now, with the courses he has, I'm getting myself back together. It's great!" A knowledgeable theologian, he is a great hulking size of a man, with a red beard, the eyes of a pixie, and a dedication to match his size. He is the one you will find at the east-side park gathering we talked about in the first paragraph of this chapter.

You will find an equally competent woman at Our Lady of Loretto, the parish mentioned above with the Lenten program "We Believe —." She is small, blonde, and pretty, and is an appreciated presence in her parish. She and her friend, a coordinator at Our Lady of Good Counsel, support each other's commitment to religious education; they lean on each other, ignite each other's creativity, laugh a lot, and learn together. It is seldom they are missing from a diocesan enrichment program, refreshment courses at the colleges, and occasional workshops out of town.

Their commitment to their people and their own development pay off in motivated people and successful programs. In their professional competence they have learned to affirm others who work with them collaboratively. Both are committee people who can work gracefully with others.

Another example is a religious sister working at a neighborhood center. She may not be teaching religious studies as such, but there is a lot of religious education taking place. She gets her funding from federal and state budgets and does an outstanding job helping the educationally unprepared to enter into the life stream better able to cope. Her ministry is in helping people find their own giftedness and respect for themselves. Sometimes the walls vibrate with screams. It's the beginning sessions of the communications class. As they work through and master the skills, the sounds sweeten as learners find that getting attention does not require shouting. Sister is trying to free up more and more time "to be around" rather than in teaching. It is in these one-on-one touches with her people that she can bring the presence of the Lord — without even mentioning his name.

Spread across the Detroit archdiocese there are a great many other fine examples of those bearing the title of adult religious educator. There are also well over a hundred priests who assume the role without the title. They know and support what is happening. Some of them teach on a regular basis. Some affirm a committee and work with them. Most of them are "there." "There" from the earliest pulpit announcements shared with enthusiasm. "There" . . . when the doors open on the event or the course. "There" . . . . visible, encouraging, listening, responding to their people. This leadership is important, vital, essential.

2. Understanding the Adult Learner

Knowing the difference between teaching children and adults is absolutely essential. That's not too easy for most educators trained in pedagogy. In our planning as well as in our teaching, we slip back into the methods we learned in teacher training courses and the methods used when we were taught in school or the university. Then, we wonder why the adults in our parish do not come back, or resent the sacramental preparation courses for parents. The fact is adults learn differently than children, mainly because they are no longer children! They are independent, have lived through years of experiences, and are not motivated to learn unless they can see some practical purpose or application of what is to be learned. Some may also come with the burden of unhappy classroom memories or the fear that they can no longer learn.

Scientific studies have proven that the capacity to learn continues throughout life unless impaired by ill health. Unpleasant memories can be short-circuited by learning climates that affirm the adult learner.

In 1977, the Institute for Continuing Education (ICE) sponsored three full-day workshops with Dr. Malcolm Knowles, one of the foremost adult educators in the United States. Many parish adult educators had already been in training for some time, but these sessions gave high visibility to the need for competency in working with the adult learner. Over two hundred people attended, providing a strong experiential base of adult education methodology. ICE continues to refresh that learning and continuously trains new leaders for the field. I believe we can say that today the majority of parishes have leaders who understand the adult learner.

Enthusiasm grows, as adult education leaders find that each time they work with the adult they become more comfortable about andragogy — the art and science of adult learning. They catch the enthusiasm from the adult participants themselves, who respond positively to what has happened to them. When adults have had the chance to learn some solid knowledge, reflect on it, talk about it, share their views, and go after additional knowledge on their own at their own speed, there is little chance of putting them back into the pedagogical classroom mode. It's like trying to refold a butterfly back into its cocoon!

3. Maintaining the Good Learning Climate

Think of the adult learners as your friends, visiting you in your own home, and you will have no trouble establishing a friendly, comfortable, relaxed, supportive, and attractive learning climate. We would not consider bringing guests to an undecorated basement room to huddle around a marred card table under poor lighting, or in rows of uncomfortable chairs in a barren gym that the boy's basketball team had vacated a half hour before. And yet, how often adult education events take place under such circumstances!

Good climate is psychological as well as physical. Attention to the learning environment says, "It is as important that faith growth takes place at all ages . . . so come join us as we explore the exciting prospect of getting to know Jesus better!" Good climate is communicated by the positive enthusiasm brightening the first announcements . . . in the smiling faces waiting to greet the folks on arrival and in the continual respect and encouragement affirming each participant. Fears are eased away and a sense of worth enables the person to share and grow.

It would seem that good physical arrangements would be automatic. They are not. Maybe we still think "classroom" when we think learning. It is not until planners have had a number of good experiences in ideal situations that many go home and revise. A good climate starts with a well-lighted parking lot, good directional signs, easy-to-reach rooms, adequate lavatory facilities, and well-lighted and adequately ventilated rooms. Decor of the room need not be expensive but it should be adult. Tables (preferably round) take the place of desks and, if possible, tablecloths on the tables with a pitcher of ice water and glasses on each table should be provided. Blackboards are removed. Some good art prints are hung. There are drapes on the windows and maybe carpeting on the floor. Beverages are available. The parish has done everything within its power to be hospitable, and the people come . . . and they stay. There's community being formed. The people say, "I like coming here."

At St. Lucy's Parish, the pastor and parishioners are dramatically conscious of good learning climate; they have just redesigned nine classrooms and one large room. Even though they will be used for religious education of youth as well as adults, only adult furniture is used: round tables, carpeting, drapes, artwork, lovely refreshing colors.

4. Dedicated Adult Education Team

No matter how talented or dedicated the adult education leaders are, they cannot be effective on a sustained basis working alone. They *need* other people. They need their ideas, their support, their efforts. There is an axiom in adult education that says, "The more people who take ownership of a program, the greater chance for success." The very process of the group working and praying together discovering the needs, designing, implementing, and evaluating is a learning experience.

Most adult education leaders work with education commissions or adult education committees which are part of the parish council structure. Others have less formally organized teams. Again, each parish has its own way of operating. The team should be large enough to be representative of different age levels and competencies. Each member must be an advocate of lifelong learning and understand the principles of adult education. The latter could be achieved as part of the team's first goal, but there is no substitute for the firm conviction upholding the right and need of every adult to continue to grow in faith.

In St. William's Parish, the adult education leader worked each year with a new ad hoc committee of eight or ten who gathered at the end of the year to evaluate and plan for the next. Their programs have been outstandingly successful, and part of this success has been the increasing numbers who "own" adult religious education through serving at one time or another on the ad hoc committee.

5. Knowledge of Needs

Successful programs cannot be designed apart from the people nor can they be allowed to ignore the needs of the institution or community. The team is required to use some means of finding out the answers to two questions: "Who are our people?" and "What's happening?"

The means for getting answers to these questions could be one or several of the following: a parish census, a parish survey of interests, interviews of various representative people or groups, talking to parish groups, evaluations of pat programs, reading the parish, diocesan, and community newspapers and listening, listening, listening to the signs of the times both in the parish and in the community. For instance, what is prime TV saying that touches people? Many signs are close to home — coming right into the rectory with questions, letters, comments. Listen to them!

In knowing your people you need to know age, sex, marital status, family description, location in parish, background (culturally, educationally, and economically), and where they are in their faith.

In other words, if you have people with a Baltimore Catechism understanding, plunging them into conscience formation could be like sending them down the rapids without an oar. If your population is mainly in the forties or older, a course dealing with the mid-life crisis or preparation for retirement would be more appropriate than personal stress of young parents.

Once you are able to read the signs of the times, they begin to speak to you with flashing arrows: "Go!" At the time of the heavy layoffs in the auto industry, parishes in Detroit began to offer workshops on writing personal résumés for job applications, handling stress, understanding budgeting. If there is a common problem in the community such as drug abuse, alcoholism, or racial strife, respond to it with a workshop. What affects the community affects your people.

6. Setting Goals and Objectives

Once the team has some grasp of the needs, the next step is to set general overall goals to give direction. A goal is a statement of the desirable situation you want to achieve in answer to the need. An example of a statement of a goal could be: "To help the people develop a closer relationship with Jesus." Write as many goals — broad statements — to cover the needs you discovered. However, be realistic. Prioritize them and limit yourselves to those you feel you can accomplish within a specific length of time.

Objectives are specific actions that must be taken to achieve your goals. You may have several objectives for one goal. For example, on the goal above dealing with the relationship with Jesus, the objectives could be: (1) to offer a New Testament scripture course in the fall and spring; (2) to celebrate as a parish the birth of Jesus with special rituals during Advent; (3) to have a Lenten series on Wednesday nights on the passion of Jesus; and (4) to have a faith-sharing parish retreat in June.

For you to work with your objectives and have others in the parish understand your plans (and therefore support them), objectives must be clear, specific, measurable, and realistic.

A final suggestion: collaborate as much as possible with other parish groups and other parishes. Referring again to the goal on the relationship with Jesus, it could be a total parish goal under which various group objectives would fit. The Family Life Committee could write an objective such as, "To foster family scripture reading and sharing," or the Justice and Peace Committee could state, "To offer a study program on the Gospel of Matthew and the social teachings of Jesus."

We must remember to serve the diversity within our parishes. While one overall encompassing goal might apply to everyone, the narrow objectives may not touch everyone's interests. Collaboration makes possible a full, healthy plan.

7. Creative Design and Quality Content

The design part of planning can be the most fun. This is the time when creativity frolics with your thoughts as you address the objectives. You dream a little. Sentences begin with "What if we . . ." as the team enters into the creation of a plan. You will follow the rules about adult learners but these will not inhibit the free flow of ideas. The best program designs have variety as well as unity, rhythm, and color. Another adult education axiom is that if you enjoy designing the program, most likely the participants will be caught up in that spirit.

It is a basic assumption of good planning that there is no settling for less than the best in quality and authenticity of the content being offered. Careless or shallow scholarship is insulting. Experimental thinking — unless clearly labeled — is dangerous. There should be no doubt in the minds of the team members about the knowledge, ability, and integrity of each presenter.

Our Lady of Sorrows Parish is large, pulsing with a vibrancy of interest and activity that is fed by scores of parishioners. The particularly talented staff members are gifted at enabling others and building community. Consequently, many people "own" the programs. Each year the parish has an overall theme, and both regular and new events fold their objectives into the theme. They have ongoing scripture study through two types of programs, Lenten and Advent programs. They have sessions on stress, social issues, personal spirituality, various forms of ministry, collaborative efforts on family life, retreats, prayer days. Social events add their particular zest to the year: St. Patrick's Dance, picnics, golf days, bridge tournaments, bike trips, kite flying days, etc., and a strong Christian service program testifies to the witness of their belief.

Educational opportunities weave through the months tying people into a growth pattern that becomes a habit. The people anticipate the events both regular and new, because they recall with pleasure good experiences of the past. When they receive their calendar for the year in early fall, people talk about it and begin planning to attend.

One of the high points of interest is the "Bright Lights" weekend or week. The title refers to bringing in nationally or internationally known scholars. Two years ago Rosemary Haughton came to speak at the liturgies on Sunday, a principal lecture on Sunday evening, sessions with individual groups during the week as well as a continuing workshop through the week. Last year, Rev. John Shea spoke at the Sunday liturgies and again at a late Sunday afternoon lecture/dialogue meeting. This exposure to scholars to the greatest possible audiences provokes the parish adults and young adults to examine their own faith more deeply, to grow . . . and ask for more. More is continually supplied, formally in programs and the excellent homilies and informally by an excellent parish paperback rack and the availability of the staff.

At St. Lucy's, a talented woman directs a rich and balanced set of learning opportunities with a good proportion on spiritual development. The days of recollection scheduled for eight months on the first Friday of each month have been so popular that a shorter time span of Ignatian exercises will be offered in the evenings. They are also promoting self-directed "Retreats While You Work," again using Ignatian exercises as the basis. This past year St. Lucy's had a number of workshops on stress management for specific groups: women, families, and senior citizens. Another popular series dealt with the feminine dimension in Scripture and a five-week series on "Masculine/Feminine" which recognized how both attributes contribute to the wholeness of each person.

In a small farming city in the southern part of the archdiocese, one sister reports that all ages entered into a learning experience last year at St. Joseph's Parish. Almost the whole year was devoted to preparing for what they called "Times of Jesus Museum." They realized that when reading the scriptures it is important to understand the times and setting in which Jesus lived; so they set about to provide an opportunity for people of the community to *experience,* by way of a museum-type setting, the times of Jesus. In the year of getting ready, people were sent scurrying into libraries and museums to study tools, geography, houses, crafts, clothing, customs, and symbols that were part of the daily lives of those who lived in Jesus' times. The museum was a great success and those attending had a clearer view of how Jesus lived, but certainly the greatest learning was in the process of getting ready, as is often the case!

8. Implementing the Design

This phase of programming *demands* close attention to detail. In this period the team will limit its free-flowing creativity to an orderly precision of making budgets, checklists, time schedules, and the assignment of responsibilities. Nothing should be left to chance! Even the obvious should be listed: like who is picking up the speaker at the airport and who is in charge of the sound system. It may be that in this phase some adjustments in the design will be made. Certain plans are too expensive. Some resources or presenters are not available. Concentration on all the details will expose the impractical or the impossible. These problems need to surface early, when you have enough time for alternative plans.

Once the doors are open and the program is in progress, it still isn't time for the team members to kick off their shoes and completely relax. The tendency to do so is human but a mistake. The job is not finished. The learning climate of hospitality must be maintained. There should be ongoing monitoring of the presenter to be sure he or she is supporting the adult education methodology with special regard to affirming the adult learner. At least one team member should be around at all sessions representing the parish, keeping the pulse, quietly evaluating, and being ready to meet the emergencies which so often arise.

When it comes time for implementation, it is obvious why a team effort is indispensable and why carefully following orderly procedures is necessary for peace of mind as well as effective programs.

9. Effective Publicity

If your program is positively dazzling, but no one knows about it — you can guess what will happen: it fizzles! Why then is getting the news out so often the weakest element in planning for adult religious education programming? Perhaps because it is so alien to the training of those in religious studies. No one even suggests that they take a course in graphic arts or a workshop in copywriting, or that they save samples of intriguing direct mail and attention-getting advertising. Full courses might not be necessary, but they would do wonders for your self-confidence. At least get some books from the library, make friends with a good and trusted printer, and plunge in and try!

Before you write a news release or design a brochure, there are a few rules you need to know about the whole concept of publicity:

a. Planning for publicity should be integral to the total planning and not left for the last couple of weeks before the event, when someone says, "Don't you think we should get something in the paper about this?"

b. Make a list of all the groups of people who might be interested in the program.

c. Make a list of all the different forms of publicity/promotion you will need to reach the people on the above list, such as an overall calendar, brochure, news release for parish papers — community and civic organizations, pulpit announcements, posters, flyers, letters, radio, TV.

d. Make a calendar that will show the schedule for whatever forms of publicity you intend to use. This must include preparation time, printing time, mailing dates for each. (This requires you to have contacted the papers to know their deadlines for your copy and a printer — if one is to be used — to know how much time is needed to meet your mailing date.)

In your preparation of the actual releases or brochures, consider these three suggestions:

a. Check costs. Here is where your relationship with a printer is necessary. He can advise you on good buys in paper and what shape, size, and color to use in your brochure. He can teach you tricks on cutting costs. With his help you can produce an attractive piece at almost the same cost as a mimeographed one but with more selling power.

b. Be truthful. Do not promise what you cannot deliver. If you say your session is "the best ever" it had better be the best ever, or people will be wary of your promises the second time around.

c. Be simple in style and short in length of copy and layout. Make a first draft. Eliminate the unnecessary. Make a second draft. Eliminate. One of the major pitfalls of the beginner is to say too much; too many doodads, arrows, lines, and curlicues confuse the eye. Lots of clean, uncluttered white space is a lovely virtue. So is tight, strong copy with short sentences and few adjectives.

All of the parishes mentioned in this chapter are absolutely sure that good promotion has been part of their success. One woman says, "Choose attractive titles that provoke interest." At St. Joseph's, they make it a point to encourage the participants to tell their friends about their happy reactions. Word of mouth is a potent way of advertising. A sister maintains that a good marketing principle is to offer one new and different exciting event each year, such as the theme "Celebrate God's Gifts and Our Giftedness," which related artistic competencies to prayer. It featured six artists, including a potter who showed the group how to work with clay. Pull out the promotion stops for major programs. Be sure copy and art indicate that everyone is welcome.

10. Evaluation of the Process and the Program

Evaluation is vital to growth in the planners and the programs, and yet, it is often treated lightly and its benefits diluted. Being serious about evaluation means being willing to listen and to change throughout the entire planning and implementing process. It calls for a conscious, probing mentality, needling into the heart of what the process was to accomplish and the objectives of the design. This is not easy, but lesser efforts are almost like playing games and give you back little helpful information.

The record of evaluation should contain two things: (1) facts — title of event, presenter, date, time, place, number attending each session, and (2) reactions. The reactions should come from the participants, the presenter, and the planners. Reactions can be obtained through the sensitivity of the planner. (How often have you been at a meeting where things just were not coming together? You knew it in your bones and did not need to read an evaluation form.) Reactions should be obtained both orally and in writing (through the use of evaluation forms or questionnaires). Combined, they can give you a fairly accurate picture of whether or not you achieved the mark.

Evaluation forms should not be long but must be designed to provoke the people answering to reflect on the experience and do some analyzing of the situation. This will do them a service and is a *very* important spin-off from the evaluation process. It helps the learners deepen their awareness of what was learned.

Questions on the evaluation should be grouped according to category, such as general attitude about the experience, specific learning questions, process, climate, comments, and suggestions. The answers mean more if you have asked questions about the person's identity, such as role or ministry, sex, and age group. If you do not need all this information, do not ask for it. By the amount of space allotted, you indicate the kind of answers you expect.

When your people see that you have listened to their comments, they will cooperate in using the evaluation form and accept it as a contributing part of the planning and learning process.

SUMMARY

1. *A Caring, Skillful Leader.* The leader is central to the success of adult religious education. Such a leader will utilize and adapt the elements of adult religious education to meet the needs of his or her people and be a personal sign to growth in faith.

2. *Knowledge of Adult Learning.* Most studies on adult learning agree that adults learn differently than children. Adults are more independent, self-directing, want immediate application of their learning, and retain more of what they learn, if they can articulate in interaction situations.

3. *Maintaining a Good Learning Climate.* Adult learning takes place more readily in an atmosphere that is friendly, supportive, and respectful of the person's adulthood: physically, psychologically, and intellectually. The lack of this element alone can cause failure in programming.

4. *Dedicated Adult Education Team.* A group of interested, dedicated people to work with the leader will assure an on-target balanced program and acceptance of adult religious education. They should be representative of the diversity of the parish in age and background.

5. *Knowledge of Needs.* The team should know how to discover and interpret the interests and needs of the people *before* planning takes place. Consideration should be given to the needs of the parish, the Church, and the community to integrate them effectively into the overall plan.

6. *Setting Goals and Objectives.* Once the learning needs are assessed the team should define them through the statement of an overall goal and prioritize the means to achieve the goal through a list of objectives or learning opportunities.

7. *Creative Design and Quality in Content.* Through skill, experience, and observation the team should design a year's series of adult learning experiences that vary in format yet respond to the goals and objectives and respect the principles of adult education methodology. There should be a basic assumption that the best in quality and authenticity of content are being offered.

8. *Implementing the Design.* Careful attention to detail, following orderly guidelines, and listing all procedures and responsibilities on a time table will enable the program to take place successfully and with peace of mind for the team.

9. *Meaningful Publicity.* The planning for publicity must be integral to the total *early* planning. It should be intelligently timed and use the best possible skills and means available to get the information to the potential clientele for proper motivation.

10. *Evaluation of the Process and Program.* Questioning and analyzing both the process and program all the way through the ten elements of adult religious education leads to growth in the planner and improvement of future programs.

SUGGESTED READINGS

DeBoy, James J., Jr. *Getting Started in Adult Religious Education.* New York: Paulist Press, 1979. Understandable general text to be first used by parish adult education planning teams.

Downs, Thomas. *The Parish as Learning Community.* New York: Paulist Press, 1979. Clear, usable examination of the parish as the place where much adult religious learning takes place.

Girzaitis, Loretta. *Church as Reflecting Community: Adult Learning Models.* West Mystic, Conn.: Twenty-Third Publications, 1977. Especially helpful in charting adult growth in faith: where, when, and how it takes place.

Hughes, Jane Wolford, ed. *Ministry to Adult Learners: A Workbook for Professional Development.* Washington, D.C.: U.S. Catholic Conference, 1981. The first major guide and workbook of competencies required of those who work with adult learners.

_____. *Parish Adult Educators Development Clinic Handbook.* Institute for Continuing Education, Archdiocese of Detroit, 1977. Compilation in loose-leaf notebook form of reprints, instruments, and models covering steps to successful programming.

Knowles, Malcolm. *Modern Practice of Adult Education,* New York: Association Press, 1970. The principal source text produced on adult education. Used for continual referral by *all* practitioners. Recently revised to incorporate latest findings.

McKenzie, Leon. *Adult Religious Education: The 20th Century Challenge.* West Mystic, Conn.: Twenty-Third Publications, 1975. Proven theories and techniques in adult education applied to the parish situation.

Moran, Gabriel. *Education Toward Adulthood.* New York: Paulist Press, 1979. A rich understanding of adulthood, education, and lifelong learning.

Young Adults: Their Challenge and Their Gift

The Rev. Michael G. Foley

Ordained for the Diocese of Worcester, Massachusetts, in 1971, Father Foley received his licentiate in sacred theology from the Gregorian University in Rome. As Coordinator of Youth Ministry for the Diocese of Worcester, he has worked for many years with the United States Catholic Conference reviewing, developing, and implementing pastoral strategies for young adult ministry. In 1979 he was named one of the top ten outstanding leaders in young adult ministry in the United States.

Back in the late sixties, the haunting sounds of Peter, Paul, and Mary's "Where Have All The Flowers Gone" lamented the absence of so many young adults lost in war. Today many parents and pastors echo a similarly wistful sentiment as they experience the notable absence of so many young adults from their parish gatherings. For, indeed, during the period from the late sixties to the mid-seventies, the average church attendance of young adults for a typical Sunday liturgy fell dramatically to about thirty-eight percent. Although this decline has apparently leveled off[1] perhaps no other group in the parish is the focus of so much pain and concern.

Young adults are those members of the parish community, usually between the ages of eighteen and thirty-five, who are involved in the transition from adolescence to adulthood. It is a period in which a person's ideals begin to be translated into a committed way of life and critical decisions concerning career, lifestyle, and choice of partner are being worked out. It is unfortunate that in such an important period of life, a young person is likely to have only peripheral involvement with the parish, if they have any involvement at all with organized religion.

In 1971, the *General Catechetical Directory* recognized that this time of life was often full of problems and yet had not been sufficiently studied and investigated.[2] Much has been learned since then. The Church has come to appreciate how young adulthood is a period marked by experimentation with lifestyle, relationships, vocation, educational goals, and even spirituality. It is a time when personal freedoms and individuality are primary, while responsibility seems of secondary importance. Another characteristic is frequent, spontaneous (and, at times, idiosyncratic) change. Flexibility and openness to new options and opportunities are constantly sought.

Moreover, the Church has come to appreciate how critical its effectiveness with this group is for the overall health of the entire community. They are not a small isolated group. The total number is large, almost fifty-seven million people between the ages of eighteen and thirty-five. They have real impact, especially economically, on the values and trends of American culture. What people can buy in our department stores, supermarkets, and specialty shops is profoundly influenced by the fact that young adults control almost fifty percent of the general merchandise market. Finally, perhaps as no other group, they reflect the extraordinary pluralism and diversity of American society.

Many of the most crucial dimensions of young adult lives are defined, not by a general psychology or a broad sociology, but by very special needs arising within small subgroups. These subgroups are strongly influenced by the fact that they fall into one or more of these categories: single, Hispanic, divorced, out of work, a woman, a Vietnam veteran. It is difficult to develop broad plans to handle such diversity.

In recent years the Church has spoken more and more vigorously about her concern for young adults. The American bishops' *Call to Action,* the *National Catechetical Directory,* the *Secundo Encuentro,* the *Plan for Pastoral Action for Family Life,* among others, have emphasized the needs in this area of ministry. Just recently the Department of Education of the United States Catholic Conference published its long awaited *Plan for Pastoral Action for Single Young Adult Ministry.*

However, there is no stronger advocate and spokesperson for both the challenge and possibilities of young adult ministry than Pope John Paul II. He has made it a point to speak directly to young adults in his many travels throughout the world, recognizing and calling for the responsible use of their gifts in the Church.

> Never try to ignore the irresistible force that is driving you toward the future. The Church is not frightened at the intensity of your feelings. It is a sign of vitality. It indicates pent-up energy, which is itself neither good nor bad, but can be used for good causes or for bad . . . And I am positive that you can meet this challenge [to work for the good], that you are willing to assume this responsibility. Above all that you are ready to prepare yourselves, now, today.[3]

The confidence in the basic goodness and ability of young adults and respect for them as persons that characterizes so much of Pope John Paul II's message is perhaps the real key for unlocking this ministry in the parish.

It is so easy to be turned off and even scandalized by much of what takes place in young adult lives. Often their lifestyles and relationships seem at odds with our own secure values and the teachings of the Church. The exuberant and questioning stylė of the searcher can be viewed as an aggressive attack on dearly held truths. People trying to work through many confusing personal life choices are often seen as inattentive and uncaring of the broader concerns of the community.

An attitude of confidence and personal respect can help leaders work through such initial concerns and fears and introduce an opportunity where change and growth might take place. In such an atmosphere they become much more likely to proclaim the mysteries of faith in language young adults can understand. Such a stance invites young adults to share in a community where people can grow in intimacy and commitment. It encourages their probing of spiritual depths through worship and prayer, and calls and motivates them to use their skills and gifts in compassionate service to others.

Principles for Developing a Young Adult Ministry

1. *Solid parish renewal, rather than simply developing another new specialized ministry, is more important for bringing young adults into the heart of parish life.*

In theory, the Church has much of what young adults are searching for. Unfortunately what the Church is in theory and what actually takes place in practice often vary widely. Parish communities that capture the spirit and practice of Vatican II tend to attract more than their share of young adults. Basic foundations of sound, life-centered liturgical celebrations and preaching and a collaborative spirit and process for decision-making contribute to a healthy environment for young adults. A sense of personal care for members of the community and of compassion for those beyond the parish, offers a spirit of welcome and hospitality. An acceptance of the many skills and gifts found within the parish, thus encouraging participation in shared ministry efforts, provides a setting where challenge and accountability can be fostered.

2. *Within such a setting young adults must be specifically recognized and welcomed as essential and creative participants in a parish's life.*

It is a fact that young adults often feel excluded from the mainstream of parish life. In the midst of so much activity, there is often little to which they can directly relate. Archbishop Jean Jadot, former apostolic delegate to the United States, while addressing the American bishops, put it quite simply: "[Young adults] make up one of the most abandoned groups from the religious point of view. They are part of the 'anawim' of our time."[4] It is not that parishes do not want them. It is simply that parish people often do not have time for them. They are busy about so many other things.

In preaching and programs the parish needs to make conscious recognition of the presence of young people and deal more directly with the issues that are important in their lives. There is seldom a sensitive homily given on sexuality, work, or loneliness that does not elicit a personal response by way of thanks or question from young adults in the congregation. Many pastoral leaders have sensitized themselves to such concerns by gathering small groups of young adults for conversation and a meal. Such an informal occasion provides a time and setting where quality listening can take place. The very act of listening already communicates real care and concern. (The *Plan of Pastoral Action for Single Young Adult Ministry* is a rich resource for developing an appreciation of young adult concerns and needs.)

Admittedly, involvement of young adults can be somewhat unsettling to the secure and the sedentary. They will usually bring new ways and new excitement to long-enduring projects and organizations such as a St. Vincent de Paul Society, a religious education program, or a parish council. Often the "old guard," while realizing that somehow young adults are necessary for the future of their activity, resent the intrusion and challenge of fresh perspectives and new ideas. It is, however, precisely in the exchange between the "tried and true" and the "new and creative" that the possibility for real growth emerges for all concerned. Dialogue and mutual responsibility are essential ingredients to any young adult involvement.

3. *If the parish takes advantage of those special occasions when young adults living on the periphery are present, there can be meaningful contact for future involvement in the parish.*

While there is surely a place for a specific outreach ministry to young adults, people already have at their disposal a variety of opportunities to reach young adults. Although it is true that only thirty-eight percent of the young adults who consider themselves Catholic might be present at any given Sunday liturgy, it is usually not the same thirty-eight percent. Often they will just keep in touch with the Church so that in the course of a month or two a majority of young adults will have entered a particular parish church.

Moreover, there are a number of occasions when young adults seem to arrive in hordes. Special feasts like Christmas and Easter are truly evangelical moments when the invitation of the Gospel can be extended with power and beauty. When such profound life experiences such as marriages, funerals, and the birth and baptism of a child are treated both in their preparation and celebration as precious and personal encounters between a forgiving and loving God and his people, even jaded young adults are often moved. However, when such events are treated routinely, they not only fail to build a bridge to young adults, but often reinforce negative attitudes toward the Church.

When nonpracticing young adults present themselves for marriage or bring their child to be baptized, these are special occasions, not for berating or chastising, but for helping them unravel the meaning of these events. Here they might experience in a profoundly personal way an invitation to real Christian community. The development of support ministries by lay people to assist in these preparations provides a personal pastoral touch that is bearing much fruit. These volunteers often have more time to spend with the young adults and bring with them the practical wisdom gained from similar experiences. When properly trained, they can have an extraordinary influence on the spiritual development of these young people.

4. *If lifelong religious learning is sincerely valued and implemented in a parish, young adults are more likely to participate in it.*

The gap between theory and practice in parishes is seldom more evident than within the educational apostolate. While much of our language speaks of lifelong, "womb to tomb" religious education, most of the Church's time, money, and personnel is still centered on the education of children. Learning is too often experienced as a "childish" task. It is no wonder that young people, as they grow through their middle teens and try to put aside the things of childhood, include religious education among the discards.

The participation of youth and young adults in parish religious education programs seems to be in almost direct proportion to the involvement of adults in similar programs. Where adults are actually involved in formal learning, youth and young adults tend to participate along with them or in their own programs.

Where parishes have known success, the religious learning seems to have certain characteristics. First, it is life-centered and is concerned with teaching and sharing a very practical faith. Young adults are often involved in a great deal of experimentation, most of which is directed at finding new possibilities for lifestyle and relationships. The teachings of Scripture and the Church should be approached within the context of issues such as these. It is not so much a question of preparing for life issues but of dealing with situations in which they are already involved. There is a real urgency to such learning.

Life-centered learning takes place best within an atmosphere of shared learning. All participants, including the leader, see themselves as learners. It is important that leaders have personalized the authentic teachings of the Church in their own lives and have the capacity to help others to do so.

Second, effective religious learning in the parish is prophetic, at least in the sense that it challenges complacency in lifestyle and lack of responsibility in the world community. Our heritage of working for peace and justice, both personal and communal, within a framework of eschatological hope gives the Church an immense prophetic strength. Young adults have much to learn and gain from this heritage.

The enticements of a materialistic society which seeks happiness through security and affluence are proving to be both hollow and destructive. Many young adults are ready for something else. As their minds expand to see themselves in the context of a world community, so too do their hearts often grow in response to the needs they encounter.

Third, effective religious learning is truly revelatory in that it opens the broad meaning of life and human destiny to people as they change and grow. Each stage of growth has its own problems and strengths, its own tasks and responsibilities. Sometimes people become so immersed in their own particular stage, they lose perspective on their full life journey. Such isolation can breed strange consequences.

No matter what stage a person is in, the good news of Jesus Christ offers a clear and profound meaning for life and participation in an awesome destiny. Within the context of a rich community of faith, people can begin to locate themselves within their own full life experience: past, present, and future. They can lay claim to their heritage as a member of a Communion of Saints that encompasses all dimensions of space and time. Change comes to be seen within the framework of continuity and commitment. Crises of transition are given a context of support and vision.

When young adults are given an opportunity to encounter a mature presentation of the faith, they very often respond with enthusiasm and surprise. Revealed truths do make sense and do have practical consequences. They also help people to appreciate their own personal value and share more fully in the great adventure of salvation history.

4. *Outreach to young adults beyond the parish is best done by young adults themselves.*

Young adult ministry need not lay an added burden upon the community. As more young adults become involved, they share in the burden of ministry and support. There is, however, a need to develop means of reaching beyond the parish to other young adults in the community. This task is best accomplished by young adults themselves.

Effective programs, such as retreats or action groups, usually prosper because young adults support them and tell others about them. A community that is cordial to young adults will soon have a reputation for welcome and hospitality. This community will be known as a place where anyone can visit and be treated with care and respect. The pastor must take the lead in treating people that way. This kind of reputation will be noticed by young adults many miles away.

Parishes, however, need not depend on the grapevine to do outreach. More and more parishes (or, more accurately, clusters of parishes) are seeing the value of, and therefore providing the resources for, young adults to actively and directly perform a variety of ministries with their peers. With reasonable training very dedicated and spiritually mature young adults are reaching people who would not be touched in any other way. The "Aura" training program of the United States Catholic Conference has been a pioneer in developing both professional and volunteer resource people for this ministry.

It is critical that those young adults who have both the capacity and inclination to do this ministry be called forward by the community, be properly trained, and adequately supported. The forms that their ministry will take will depend greatly upon their own particular skills and the unique needs of young adults locally. Their training must equip them with the proper relational and organizational skills to assess these local needs sensitively and to develop creatively a pastoral response, by bringing others into the sharing of this work.

A real danger in initiating such a ministry is to expect it to fall within the form of a highly traditional program. A young adult ministry that is merely an extended youth group is doomed to failure. In fact, the "club" idea is seldom successful. It tends to attract the least mature young adults and quickly becomes a closed corporation with little inclination to transcend personal concerns.

The most successful ministries seem to take the form of a network, where a number of individual programs and services in a region pool their resources and talents. They might be coordinated at some central location but the services reach into a variety of local situations. The young adult population is highly diverse and very mobile. If a service they want is found within a reasonable distance they show no hesitation in traveling to it. Outreach ministries will have impact where young adults actually live. They will also gather people with similar concerns and interests.

Often such ministries will take place far outside the experience of the parish community. Many of the issues emerging in the young adult culture are provocative and threatening. Yet this is often the area where the gospel is needed most. If a parish is blessed enough to have people who have the ability to represent the gospel and the Church in such areas, they must be willing to give them hard, enduring support and respect their judgment.

Perhaps some will view this idea of outreach as an unnecessary headache. Why should the parish launch itself into such muddy waters? There is enough to do within the parish itself with those already involved. Such statements evoke sympathy. Yet the very nature of a Christian community challenges people to go beyond the comfortable and secure and to penetrate the world with the good news. The parish is by far the best setting from which to extend such an effort. The communal setting of worship, learning, and service provides a solid base on which young adult ministers can find enrichment, encouragement, and accountability for their extremely challenging task.

The process of making contact, providing opportunities for care and growth for young adults, and inviting them to a fuller way of Christian living will only be accomplished by those who have the courage to step out into their confusing and uncomfortable world. The long-term benefits to a community that is willing to take risks and be transformed in the name of Jesus Christ is well worth the effort.

SUMMARY

1. The term "young adults" refers to those people usually between the ages of eighteen and thirty-five involved in the transition from adolescence to adulthood.

2. Ministry with this group is important because it is a period of life-

forming decisions that will have great impact on their future spiritual development.

3. In recent years the Church has been calling for a concerted effort in the development of this area of ministry.

4. Confidence in the basic goodness and ability of young adults and respect for them as persons is the key for unlocking this ministry in the parish.

5. Solid parish renewal, rather than simply developing a new specialized ministry, is more important for bringing young adults into the heart of parish life.

6. Young adults must be specifically recognized and welcomed as essential and creative participants in a parish's life.

7. The parish should take advantage of the special occasions when young adults are present to build a bridge for possible future involvement.

8. If lifelong religious education is sincerely valued and implemented in a parish, young adults are more likely to participate in it. Effective religious education is usually life-centered, prophetic, and revelatory.

9. Outreach to young adults beyond the parish is best done by young adults themselves.

CHAPTER NOTES

1. George Gallup, *Religion in America: The Gallup Opinion Index 1977-78* (Princeton, N.J.: The American Institute of Public Opinion, 1979,) p. 5.
2. Sacred Congregation for the Clergy, *General Catechetical Directory* (Washington, D.C.: U.S. Catholic Conference, Publications Office, 1971), p. 67.
3. Pope John Paul II, "The Irresistible Force of Youth," *Origins,* Vol. 10, No. 38 (March 5, 1981,) p. 595.
4. Archbishop Jean Jadot, "1979 Address to the U.S. Bishops," *Planning for Single Young Adult Ministry* (Washington, D.C.: U.S. Catholic Conference, Publications Office, 1981), p. 62.

SUGGESTED READINGS

Boelen, Bernard J. *Personal Maturity: The Existential Dimension.* New York: Seabury Press, 1978. This perceptive presentation of the developmental process by a fine philosopher/psychologist is particularly rich in its insights into some of the deeper dimensions of young adult life.

Carrier, Hervé. *The Sociology of Religious Belonging.* New York: Herder and Herder, 1965. This classic analysis of the issues of religious need and communal living provides a sound background for enriching parish life.

Department of Education, U.S. Catholic Conference. *Planning for Single*

Young Adult Ministry: Directions for Ministerial Outreach. Washington, D.C.: U.S. Catholic Conference, Publications Office, 1981. A product of three years of collaboration, this booklet provides both a theoretical and programmatic framework out of which young adult ministry, especially with singles, can be developed.

_____. *Position Papers and Recommendations from the Symposium on the Parish and the Educational Mission of the Church.* Washington, D.C.: U.S. Catholic Conference, Publications Office, 1978. A broad range of parish educational issues is presented with specific pastoral suggestions.

_____. *The Single Experience: A Resource (Reflections and Models for Single Young Adulthood).* Washington, D.C.: U.S. Catholic Conference, Publications Office, 1979. Both general background papers and specific program models are presented in this concluding document of this interdisciplinary symposium.

Groome, Thomas H. *Christian Religious Education: Sharing Our Story and Vision.* San Francisco: Harper and Row, 1980. A significant model for pastoral education is introduced along with very practical examples for implementation.

Murphy, Elly, ed. *Reflections on a Changing Church: Young Adult Women in Ministry.* North Andover, Mass.: The Center for Single and Young Adult Ministry, Merrimack College, 1980. The results of a national symposium on women in the Church are compiled in this straightforward and perceptive review of young adult issues as they relate to women.

O'Neill, Patrick H. *The Single Adult.* New York: Paulist Press, 1980. One of the real pioneers in young adult ministry shares very practical insights into the lives of single young adults.

Potvin, Hoge Nelsen. *Religion and American Youth: With Emphasis on Catholic Adolescents and Young Adults.* Washington, D.C.: U.S. Catholic Conference, Publications Office, 1976. The research team from the Boys Town Center at Catholic University presents the results of their studies and makes projections for pastoral trends.

Yankelovich, Daniel. *The New Morality: A Profile of American Youth in the 70's.* New York: McGraw-Hill, 1974. One of America's foremost sociologists of young adult lifestyle presents the results of his research in the area of moral behavior.

_____. "New Rules in American Life: Searching for Self-Fulfillment in a World Turned Upside Down." *Psychology Today* (April, 1981), pp. 35-91. This long article, which will be expanded into book form, presents the latest findings and projections for changes in young adult behavior and values.

Youth: Transition to Adulthood (Report of the Panel on Youth of the President's Science Advisory Committee). Washington, D.C.: U.S. Government Printing Office, 1973. This is one of the most comprehensive reviews of the processes of becoming adult in an American setting. This multidisciplinary approach is rich in insight.

Integrated Youth Ministry

Gloria Reinhardt, RSM

A member of the Sisters of Mercy of Merion, Pennsylvania, Sister Gloria has worked with youth for seventeen years in various parishes and high schools in different dioceses. She is presently Coordinator of Youth Ministry in the Diocese of Richmond, Virginia.

"We'll have two hundred youths show for a social event but less than fifty for a religious education class."

"Our young people would rather go to a nondenominational youth meeting than be at their own church."

"We offer things for our young people and only a 'few of the old faithful' will show."

"After confirmation, we don't see our youth again."

"Our young people just don't seem to be able to articulate their religious values. They don't seem to buy into the traditional ones either."

"Many of our youth go to the Catholic school and, except for Sunday Mass, they are not part of parish life."

Do these statements sound familiar? Most people could probably add a few more to this litany. Youth work can be frustrating. Yet in recent years the Church has made considerable strides in: raising adult awareness to the needs of youth; perceiving youth ministry as broader than CYO, religious education/CCD, and the Catholic high school; educating parish leadership to realize that their future depends on involving today's youth in the community's life. Still, in spite of all these accomplishments, there is definitely something wrong. Young people are seen as a vital part of the parish, but they are not yet integrated members of the parish community. They often form, within the community, a ghetto that is grossly uninformed. The challenge of youth ministry lies in the development of a ministry that fosters an informed, integrated member of the parish community.

Rootedness of Integration

The year 1976 was more than just a national bicentennial event. Within the Church setting, it produced the document "A Vision of Youth Ministry." Commissioned by the United States Catholic bishops because many youth needs were not being met by existing programs, the document moved from the dual approach to youth, that is, CCD/religious education and

131

CYO, to a multifaceted entity comprising seven components. "A Vision of Youth Ministry" set forth the goals of "fostering the total personal and spiritual growth of each young person, and drawing young people to responsible participation in the life, mission, and work of the faith community."[1]

These goals were based on the model of ministry found in the New Testament. There was no concept of youth ministry in the early Christian Church; yet, there were four basic thrusts that colored those times. They were: the ministry of the Word, the ministry of the community, the ministry of serving/healing, and the ministry of celebrating.

Youth ministry first broadened those New Testament foundations as it identified these distinctive aspects: Word, Worship, Creating Community, Guidance and Healing, Justice and Service, Enablement and Advocacy. The document then asks the parish community to examine where young people are in the scheme of psychological, physiological, sociological, and spiritual development.

The youth scene has changed somewhat since 1976. The conclusions of descriptive, empirical research, such as "Boys' Town Study of Youth Development" and the Princeton Religion Research have shed some new light on the adolescent. ". . . Our youth have a definite prayer life and hold serious religious beliefs."[2] At first glance it seems that they develop these qualities divorced from the institutional Church. However, further insights from these studies "suggest our youth's non-participation actually is manifesting an alienation from *self* and *others,* not specifically or explicitly from religious institutions."[3] The institutional Church is probably the only vestige of authority left to adolescents on which they can vent their rebellion and hostility. Family, society, and government have lost credibility as authority structures.

Adolescence is a transition from the dependency and immaturity of childhood to the physical, psychological, and social independence of adulthood. The adolescent is affected by the interplay of cultural and biological factors, with cultural determinants playing the dominant role. Adolescence is a wonderful process of transformation, but it must be rooted in strong ethical and moral values. It is a time when new possibilities of thinking, behaving, and feeling appear only gradually through the developmental period. Parish and parents must grow with the young person and help them clarify their experiences, giving meaning and direction to their lives. Parents need the parish community's assistance in the process of identifying values. With the reemergence of the "preppy generation," young people need the parish to challenge their values, conformity, and behavioral patterns. If every youth needed a parish based ministry, it is *now.*

The parish has within its community the resources to help youth articulate their story. It must take the time to hear that story and help them recognize both a pattern and a hope even when embarrassing experiences must be confronted.[4] If vital experiences are to be shared only within a ghetto of peers, there is little hope for a transformation and growth. Young people need the varied experiences of adult models from the parish to develop fuller adulthood.

If the birth rate continues on its downward trend, the parish of the nineties will be largely comprised of people over forty. Who will do the ministering to the needs of the young people? It will fall to the youth of today who will be the young adults of tomorrow.

A principle of youth ministry states: "True ministry duplicates itself."[5] Youth ghettoes do not grow; rather they stagnate and become visionless places of boredom and self-centeredness. The sociological, historical, and theological foundations of youth ministry challenge the Church to a ministry that is based on a collaborating model of integrating youth into the parish community. It is a job for the *whole parish.*

Integrating Leadership

The setting is a parish with young people numbering less than 20, 100, 500, or 1,000. The numbers matter little; it is largely the attitudes and approach that are crucial to youth work. In the beginning process of integrating youth into the parish, the makeup of the group must mirror the parish's concept of total parish integration. This leadership group must consist of youth, young adults, parents, interested adults, and senior citizens. To have a member of the parish staff as part of the nucleus is important. However, with increasing demands upon Church personnel, there is little possibility of someone from the staff having that much time. This group may seem too large, but it is inevitable that it will subdivide into a core group and subsequently, an advisory group.

There is still the perennial problem of how to get other people to assist so that the core group will not experience "burn out." The method is simple. Solicit involvement under certain rules. First, ask people directly; the early Church never used a bulletin for communication. Second, ask them for a specific role, such as advising the junior-high students on community building; taking the youth to a concert; or giving three hours of chaperoning duties at a lock-in. Third, affirm them by asking both parish staff and the youth to express their gratitude. Finally, ask them only periodically. If the above rules are followed, no one will be accused of "working the people to death" and volunteerism will flourish.

It is important to remember that whatever the core group devises or the advisory board suggests, there are specific indicators of youth participation which herald success.[6] And while some may say that this structure is too organized and institutionalized, it must be remembered that the Church is an "institutionalized servant-community."[7] If integration is the thrust, then youth ministry must mirror the total parish, even in the core group and advisory board.

Laying the Foundation of Integration

Michael Warren calls it the ministry of welcome,[8] Merton Strommen the ministry of friendship.[9] Whatever the title, they all indicate a basic presupposition to all Church ministry, namely that there first must be a period of trust building, or what youth ministers call "relational ministry"[10] — pre-evangelization. Ideally this process means going out where the youth are and getting to know them on a one-to-one basis. This approach has been the keystone of many successful nondenominational youth groups. If a parish is fortunate enough to have a full-time professional, this might be a suitable beginning point. But how does a parish without the services of a full-time professional accomplish this relational ministry? A different approach is in order.

Parish integration is closely aligned to faith development. Faith is "a way of thinking which involves knowing, being, and willing,"[11] and religion is the articulation of that faith in the parish community. As people internalize faith, so also must they deepen their involvement in the base community that assists them in the relational dynamics of that faith. John Westerhoff presents the dynamic of pre-evangelization when he writes about the experience style of faith. Those good experiences which make a person feel wanted, needed, and important are vital to future internalization and articulation of faith. Youth need a pre-evangelization stage which offers them experiences that are not necessarily aligned with some great doctrinal concept, but are attached to the importance of the person. It is in these experiences that the relational ties are developed and deepened.

Summer is often the best time for these events. Parishes should offer events such as swim parties, barbecues, trips to amusement parks, and bike trips. Schedule these events at different times to meet the needs of all groups, especially those who work. In the beginning, it will be necessary to make phone calls asking people to come (this is a great place for retired people to help). If the events are well planned and well publicized, the youth will be there.

Do not plan from one event to another or make each event unique and spectacular. During the post-Easter period, the core leadership group should develop a plan, presenting the details on Pentecost Sunday to the parish and the youth. To help with the workload, parish leaders can be called upon during the summer. Remember, young people need to see the parish staff, as well as the parish community, present at events beyond Sunday liturgies. The many goals in all of these endeavors include the central goal of involving both the youth and the community in personal encounters.

Integration Through Proclamation

After the adolescent is made to feel important and welcomed by the community, expect a greater involvement in the community. This entry-level involvement is a faith expression primarily through association on the part of the young person. Through these associations young people develop feelings of trust in the group. It is in this context that the community can issue a challenge to the young people to transcend feelings of pleasure and rise to a new level of spirituality which allows them to respond more sensitively to the invitation of the Lord Jesus. Their response must be totally free, but there will be no response unless the challenge is issued.

This evangelizing approach has been reinstated in the adult community through the *Rite of Christian Initiation of Adults,* where the message is proclaimed and a response is solicited. However, many adults who are bold in challenging other adults are afraid to challenge youth. The Church, for example, seems to challenge youth only in the areas of sexual involvement and Mass attendance, while the more evangelistic churches have issued a broader challenge. Their youth, and many Catholic youth as well, will respond to this challenge.

Young people are not less religious than their elders; surveys indicate otherwise. Most teenagers are hungry for something or someone to believe in; according to James deGiacomo, "Though they may shy away in fear from long-term commitments, they yearn for values or causes that might deserve their loyalty."[12] The problem is not the youth, but the adult community which seems to be unable to articulate the challenge well. Perhaps they have not formed an adequate philosophy of life for themselves, thus hindering their ability to pass it on. Here, young people challenge the total parish, for as youth formulate questions about the meaning of life they are asking them on behalf of the entire faith community.

These questions need to be posed in a reflective setting, if a response is to be effective. Retreats offer this setting. In the last fifteen years, numerous successful retreat models have been developed nationally to satisfy this need. One obvious deficiency is that they provide an evangelistic setting in a widely based community rather than among a close and intimate parish community where the young person will return to live out his or her new commitments and insights. This statement is not to condemn TEC, Encounter, Quest, Discovery, or Christian Awakenings. But they should not provide the initial and only challenge to our parish youth. The initial experience of evangelism is the parish's responsibility. After that initial experience, the young people are more open to an area or diocesan retreat challenging them to deepen their faith and give service to the wider community.

Many parishes do not provide these evangelistic experiences for their youth because they lack facilities or experienced personnel, and otherwise feel inadequate to conduct retreats. Consequently, they often "water down" one of the national models and thereby frequently do a disservice to their youth and/or the model. To be challenged, young people do not need large groups, the emotions produced, and the depth reached. They need a setting where the community's message and experience can be proclaimed and experienced.

The parish retreat may not bring about an obvious conversion moment that is sometimes apparent in the more sophisticated models. However, many of the emotional conversions in diocesan and national models are experiences which do not last. Conversion, which is part of this evangelization moment, is not an immediate enlightenment or recognition; it is, according to Richard McBrien, "rather a gradual and continual movement to a higher quantum level of human consciousness."[13] There will be many conversion moments in a person's life which appropriately should be stimulated by the "home" community which supports, nurtures, and challenges the young person.

The catechetical component of youth ministry is one of the most exciting, yet one of the most feared. Catechesis explores the faith that unifies the community. The task has a dual purpose. One job of the parish community is "to lead its members to adopt its symbols and to internalize its meaning."[14] It should bring about socialization into the community's way of thinking. Youth need to be involved in the community's search for meaning in the gospel message.

In the past, youth ministry seemed to stop at the pre-evangelization and evangelization stages. Often, because the adults and youth were at the same level of faith development and shared many of the same feelings, young people were left unchallenged, inarticulate, and ignorant of the richness of their faith.

Young people are looking for some sort of guidelines to unite the fragments of their lives. If the Church does not have detailed and unified catechesis as part of youth ministry, it has failed to proclaim the message. As Pope John Paul has written: "There is no separation or opposition between catechesis and evangelization. The specific character of catechesis, as distinct from the initial conversion-proclamation, is maturing the initial faith and educating the true disciple of Christ by means of a deeper and more systematic knowledge of His person and message."[15]

Catechesis, and more specifically religious education, has the challenge of redefining and deepening youth conversion. Programs must be designed to meet the needs of young people who are experiencing all levels of conversion. As Richard McBrien says, "We do not educate to faith; we educate from faith and out of faith."[16] Many of them will need to see the relationship of the message to their everyday experiences, that is, in terms of "religious socialization."[17]

Religious education needs to share the message as it takes place and is influenced by the culture of young people. Francis Kelly points out some specific characteristics inherent in a proper catechetical component:

• "It must be systematic . . . not impoverished, but programmed to reach a precise goal.

• "It must deal with essentials without any claim to tackle all disputed questions or transform itself into theological research.

• "It must, nevertheless, be sufficiently complete — not stopping short of the initial proclamation.

• "It must be an integral, Christian initiation — opening all to the factors of Christian life."[18]

Youth need to deal with life-and-death questions. Adults who intervene in their religious lives have to give them the gift of religious language. Also they need to provide youth with the reasons for the faith that is in them. If young people are to own their faith, then a proper catechetical setting is imperative. Shown below is a developmental model of catechesis in a parish setting. This catechesis exists on three levels:

1. Catechesis that is based on religious and cultural life experiences.
2. Catechesis that involves the moving internalization of faith.
3. Catechesis and ministerial development that witness an owned faith.

Evangelization of Youth in Faith

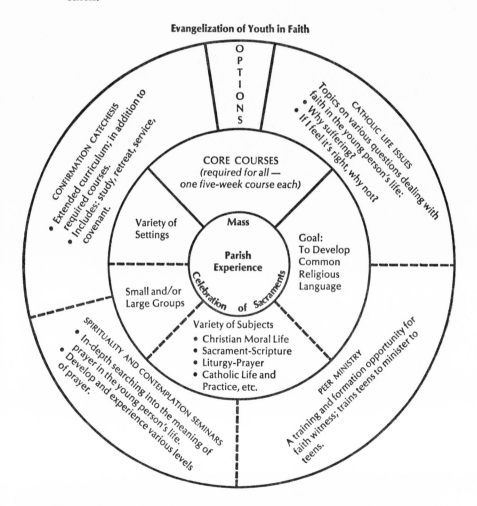

Obviously there are deficiencies in every model. The parish should in any case be sensitive to the various styles of faith and intensity of conversion.

Integration Through Empowerment

The adult community's greatest service to youth would be to tap their energy and prevent them from falling into complacency. Training them to minister to alienated youth is the best way to accomplish this goal. A systematic approach to "peer ministry" enables youth to reach out with a skill and sensitivity that can powerfully reveal the true meaning and efficacy of our faith. It brings the possibility of a real experience of the Lord Jesus through other people. As the parish begins the process of empowerment, the youth witness to their faith and challenge the parish community to a greater sense of its own mission. Following is an outline of one peer ministry program in the Diocese of Richmond.

Peers

PEERS (Peers Enriching Each Other by Reaching Out Successfully) is a program helping young people to articulate their beliefs while teaching them to express a caring attitude for others. This simple goal statement contains the scope, sequence, and the emphasis of this particular program.

The basic intent of this approach is:

1. Identifying those young people who possess leadership ability and a sincere faith level.

2. Developing among the peer ministers the ministerial skills that are needed to express a caring, loving attitude.

3. Developing a support community for the peer ministers.

4. Reaching alienated, disenchanted Catholic youth by means of a one-to-one ministry.

5. Helping the peer ministers to realize their rightful place in the evangelization mission of the parish and the broader Church.

6. Enriching the faith life of the peer minister.

The program offers instruction and practice in those ministerial skills which invoke a caring attitude among peer ministers. It has a sequence of formation, information, and transformation. Peer ministry seeks to educate the heart as well as the mind, so that peer ministers will develop sensitivity for others. The program enriches the peer minister's own faith while teaching him or her how to show love to others as the gospel demands.

The PEERS program is divided into four phases. First, there is a retreat experience where prospective peer ministers are called to listen to the Lord, others, and to themselves. In this phase the emphasis is on community building and the supportive aspects of group involvement.

Second, theoretical foundations are explained and horizons expanded as the youth are challenged to reflect on the Lord, his community, and his mission.

Third, the participants are helped to develop ministerial skills that would be needed when ministering in an alienated youth community. Relational and leadership skills, such as questioning, listening, nonverbal communication, decision-making, observational skills, guidelines for starting coversation, and assertiveness guidelines are presented, along with a reflection on the ministry of the Lord.

Fourth, there is a recollection period in which the young people are asked to reflect on their ministry as it is celebrated by the community. Implementation of the ministry is begun and monthly evaluative meetings are scheduled.

These four phases cover approximately six months; timing is at the discretion of the individual peer minister trainer and local parish community.

The PEERS program provides young people with an opportunity and a challenge to assume some responsibility for the growth of faith in others. Such a program involves them in sharing and witnessing their faith-vision with other youth, and in the process allows them to strengthen and affirm their own faith. PEERS develops the skills needed in religious leadership, the ability to work effectively with groups, to direct group discussions, to plan and conduct religious events, and to reach out to others who are hurting and in need. Many young people are craving authentic religious experiences. They are looking for involvement and opportunities for service. They are yearning to deepen and share their faith. The PEERS program will do exactly that.

The primary challenge today is for the parish community to develop an awareness of its own responsibility to integrate youth into fuller membership in the community and to call them to a maturity of faith.

SUMMARY

1. In spite of advancements, a void exists in the field of youth ministry, both for the parish and young people. Various surveys reveal the depth of the desire adolescents have for membership in the adult parish community. Leaders of a parish should strive for total parish integration, adults and youth complementing one another, challenging one another, teaching one another.

2. The parish community should be conscious of the steps of faith development, realizing it is an injustice to expect maturity without development. Pre-evangelization and evangelization experiences are the responsibility of the parish community. This community is the place for young people's initial experiences of faith. The challenge to become fuller members of the Church is first given in this community.

3. Empowerment is the real point of integration, since it gives youth a level of confidence and integrates them into the adult community. Peer ministry brings to the youth community a one-to-one experience of the Lord Jesus. Through this process, both youth and parish are challenged to a greater sense of mission and commitment.

CHAPTER NOTES

1. "A Vision of Youth Ministry" (Washington, D.C.: U.S. Catholic Conference, 1976), p. 4.
2. "Religion in America" (Princeton, N.J.: Princeton Religion Research Center, 1980), p. 63.
3. Andrew D. Thompson, "Alienation and Adolescents," *Living Light* (Fall, 1979), p. 311.
4. Michael Warren, "The Stories of Young People," *New Catholic World* (March/April, 1979), p. 89.
5. "A Vision of Youth Ministry," op. cit., p. 5.
6. Young people will engage in those activities: (1) that have been part of their planning; (2) that develop relationship with peers and adults; (3) that make a difference or are perceived as fulfilling some definite goal; (4) that allow some form of evaluation in growth; and (5) that fit into and are viewed as part of a larger entity.
7. Richard McBrien, "Models of Conversion, An Ecclesiological Reflection," *Living Light* (Spring, 1981), p. 14.
8. Michael Warren, "Youth Catechesis in the '80's," *Origins* (April 10, 1980), p. 690.
9. Merton Strommen. *Five Cries of Youth* (New York: Harper and Row, 1974), p. 27.
10. Thomas Zanzig, "Youth Ministry: Reflections and Directions," *Pace*, No. 11 (1981), p. 3.
11. John H. Westerhoff, III, *Will Our Children Have Faith?* (New York: Seabury Press, 1976), p. 90.
12. James J. DiGiacomo, S.J., "Will My Child Keep the Faith? Today's Faith in Focus," *Catholic Update* (August, 1980), p. 4.
13. McBrien, op. cit., p. 7.
14. A. Roger Gobbel, "Christian Education With 'Adolescents': An Invitation to Thinking," *Living Light* (Summer, 1980), p. 134.
15. John Paul II, "Catechesi Tradendae," *Origins* (November 8, 1979), p. 334.
16. McBrien, op. cit., p. 15.
17. A. Roger Gobbel, op. cit., p. 135.
18. Rev. Francis Kelly, "Catechesis for the 1980's," *America* (June 21, 1980), p. 517.

SUGGESTED READINGS

Corbett, Jan, et. al. *Creative Youth Leadership: For Adults Who Work with Youth.* Valley Forge, Pa.: Judson Press, 1977. A step-by-step plan that assists in training local volunteer adult leaders in youth ministry.

Fletcher, Kenneth R., et. al. *Extend: Youth Reaching Youth.* Minneapolis:

Augsburg Publishing House, 1974. This work explores the concept of peer ministry. It offers a detailed program of youth reaching youth.

Harris, Maria. *Portrait of Youth Ministry.* Ramsey, N.J.: Paulist Press, 1981. This book explains the traditional areas of ministry in light of its contemporary setting. It includes exercises and suggested activities which bring the theoretical to practical terms.

Hope for the Decade: A Look at the Issues Facing Catholic Youth Ministry. Washington, D.C.: U.S. Catholic Conference, 1980. This compilation research paper offers various developmental models and an extensive and most updated bibliography published in youth ministry.

Resources for Youth Ministry. St. Louis: The Lutheran Church's Missouri Synod. A periodical published four times a year, which focuses primarily on creative material dealing with youth ministry in the context of the local Church.

Samuels, Mimi and Don. *Peer Counseling.* Miami: Fiesta Publishing Corp., Educational Books Division, 1975. An authoritative guide for the organization, training, implementation, and evaluation of a peer counseling program.

Children Are People

Mary Jane Gorman

Ms. Gorman has been an elementary and secondary school teacher in Catholic schools for four different dioceses, and has worked extensively with parish religious education programs. As Minister of Liturgy and Adult Education at St. Rose of Lima Church in Gaithersburg, Maryland, she was instrumental in developing small community learning within that parish.

"Let the children come to me, and do not hinder them; for to such belongs the kingdom of heaven."

Matthew 19:14

A Problem

In the past, the Church focused much of its attention on children. The hope of the future, the Church's resources were directed toward their education. Recently, the focus has shifted to adults and their formation. This shift has caused conflict in many parishes. Perhaps some of the energy of this conflict could be used more constructively if parishioners would think in terms of collaboration rather than competition.

Parishioners should examine the nature of children and the responsibility of the Christian community to its children within the context of the whole community and its growth. The following questions would be a start: What do Church documents say about children and the responsibility of the community? How does the parish vision or model affect its children? Who is a child? Who has the responsibility for the child and how can this responsibility be fulfilled? Can religious education happen without faith community?

The Church

It is impossible to develop ministry to children without including the family and the total community. *To Teach As Jesus Did* acknowledges that good religious education for children takes place within the context of the experience of community. Whether a child is in Catholic school or not, the responsibility to nurture remains the same.[1]

"The Declaration on Christian Education" from Vatican Council II

142

makes it quite clear that the primary responsibility for children lies with the parents (No. 3). This responsibility does not change when the child reaches school age. The community, on the other hand, has the responsibility to support the parents in this task. The Church, along with parents, has the responsibility of passing on the faith in an *appropriate* manner (No. 4).

The documents emphasize the role of parents in determining the readiness of children for the reception of the sacraments and in being part of that preparation. This participation in preparation builds a special kind of intimacy between the parent and child as they relate to God and to each other. The process also necessitates the parents' evaluating their relationship to God in faith.

It is the parent who first shares faith with the child, who plows the ground and plants the seeds of early prayer and ritual, who begins to shape the child's concept of God. But it is the parish community which nurtures these seeds along with the parents. In watering and fertilizing the faith-growth of the child, the parish helps determine whether God becomes the old man who judges and punishes or the loving God who saves. This process of formation is generally called religious education.

Religious education has to do with communication, but it is more than that. It is an attempt to understand theology in conjunction with the human sciences and then to determine the means to communicate this understanding.[2] Religious education is the focal point where theology, sociology, psychology, and education meet. Catechesis is a particular form of religious education[3] and, as such, draws on the use of the sacred and human sciences.

Recognizing the contribution of modern psychology, the *National Catechetical Directory* (No. 32), *To Teach As Jesus Did* (No. 131), and "The Declaration on Christian Education" (No. 217) emphasize the necessity of presenting appropriate catechesis to children at the appropriate times. People who work with children must have an understanding of the stages of human development and the capabilities of children within these stages.

These contemporary insights into human development have once again focused attention on the question of methodology in catechesis. There is no one, best methodology for teaching any age level. There are, however, some criteria that apply to all learning situations involving the Church. For example, in a secular world, every person needs a degree of religious literacy according to his or her age.

Everyone who calls himself or herself a Roman Catholic Christian needs to understand some very important things. These understandings include a knowledge of the teachings and traditions of the Church, including Scripture. They also include prayers and practices that people generally consider important in the Catholic tradition. To be meaningful to the individual, all of these things must be reflected upon in the light of the individual's experiences. Revelation is always understood in reference to personal experience. At the same time, personal experience becomes more meaningful in the light of revelation.[4]

Before doing specific tasks with children, those involved in religious education need to reflect on the parish itself. Children grow and develop according to the models set forth for them by their parents and the larger society. The particular society at issue here is the parish.

First, the parish needs to reflect on questions such as: What kind of model or structure do we follow? Do we have a parish vision? Is the vision shared with parishioners? How is the vision stated in the goals and objectives of the parish? Is the parish totally dependent on the parish priests or staff? Could we, in the unforeseen future, remain together as community without a priest? Recent educational and organizational research shows that the more clearly an organization's vision is communicated and accepted, the more successful the organization.

These are not trivial questions, for it is the responses to these questions which determine who the parish is and who the children will become. It determines what kind of knowledge the parish wishes to impart, the kinds of experiences it wishes them to have, the skills it wants developed, the kinds of memories retained. The responses also show whether the parish is a pilgrim People of God, a Faith Community, a Herald, Sacramental or Servant Church, a Base Community, a circle, a circle of circles, or a pyramid.

The second step is to look at the educational programs as they are or as the parish would like them to be. This may be done in an extensive discernment process such as the *Growth In Faith Together* program by Father James R. Schaefer (Paulist Press), or a weekend "town meeting" processed by an outside facilitator. Both staff and parishioners should be involved in this discernment process. Some questions to address may be: Does the parish have a school? Do the parents or the parish expect the school to do more than it can? Does the parish have a school-model CCD, peer groups in parish homes, peer groups in a parish center, or family education? Do these strucures use class model, individual instruction learning centers, or a combination of these? Is sacramental preparation a part of, or separate from, these groupings? Are children or families included in the rite of Christian initiation of adults in the parish? Which of these educational models best fulfills the three aspects of Christian formation: the message, celebration, and service?[5] How is the model communicated to the parents?

Only after determining its position should a parish look at various tested educational or parish models. These can be investigated, studied, and even adopted with adaptations. If the parish decides to remain with a school or school-model CCD, it must provide a faith community which includes adults. Educational and socialization systems which always segregate children for instruction deprives them of adult role models and adult/child relationships.

Parents: First Role Models

As the primary educators of their children, parents must be consulted when a parish determines its direction in regard to religious education. The staff will find that listening to them can save some unnecessary steps. Parents know what they want in simple terms.

One example of parental participation was a small group which gathered to examine the problem of ministry to children. They developed a set of goals based on the value classifications of Dr. Harold Lasswell in his *Pre-View of Policy-Sciences.* The values used were power, enlightenment, wealth, well-being, skills, affection, respect, and rectitude.

Among the goals they stated were: (a) to assure parents of their rights to make decisions concerning their children and to support them in this responsibility; (b) to empower children to make decisions by including them in specific goal-setting in family life, education courses, fun activities; (c) to develop in children a sense of membership in the Christian family; (d) to gain some service skills by participating in parish activities; and (e) to provide an atmosphere during peer group sessions where children experience the love and affection of peers and adult figures other than parents.

The group really felt that the best thing that could happen to children would be for the adults to decide who *they* want to be and then the parish should offer lots of supportive and educational help to parents. Some of the models and programs will be given in the sections on adult and family education.

The Child: A Person

The child is, first of all, a miracle of creation. No longer thought of as a miniature adult, the child is a thinking, growing, developing individual who belongs to a particular family, with a particular place in that family, a particular culture, and a particular faith community. There are a few other givens as well. The child is at a particular age, a particular stage of physical, emotional, faith, and moral development, who stands in need of guidance, structure, well-being, security, acceptance, and understanding.

It is not possible to explain here all of the theories which have been researched and developed. The names and theories of Jean Piaget, Erick Erickson, Lawrence Kohlberg, James Fowler, Ronald Goldman, John Westerhoff, Thomas Groome, and Iris Cully should be familiar to those working in religious education for children.

It is important to realize that the six-year-old child is just completing the preoperational stage when things happen by magic and is entering the operational/concrete stage when effect follows cause — at least with concrete causes. This realization helps determine not only the *who* but also the *what* and *how* of religious eduction. The use (or non-use) of Scripture, the use of recited prayers, the content issues — all of these begin to fall into place when the child of this age is understood. Operational thinking in the seven- to nine- or ten-year-old deals only with very concrete concepts. Being able to say words does not mean that the child understands them. Words used by adults may be given an unexpected meaning by the child.

By the time the child is ten, a memory and sense of time, a sense of history and chronology, develop. It is a time to begin autobiographies because these help children to form identities and they now have enough material with which to work. Beginning to tell one's own story is quite a challenge at this stage.

Fifth and sixth graders are very exciting to work with as they question, argue, and make insightful discoveries. Their sense of fairness is very straightforward and this leads to arguing. John McCall, in his *Growing Up,* describes this stage as the age of lawyers when children will argue about anything.[6] Finally, as the child is preparing for junior high or its equivalent, his or her development of abstract thinking is becoming more and more apparent.

Not only must religious educators know what kind of content can be used at the various age levels and stages, but any ministers working with liturgies, sacraments, homilies must do so as well. When children pray or play it is time to listen, for at those times they reveal themselves best. It is also in prayer and play that children can best integrate Bible, liturgy, service into their individual faith development. It is in listening that one learns that children hate to be talked down to or to have their very real experiences made light of. Children prefer a short, well-structured homily to a long, drawn-out "dialogue" homily which some adults tend to think is cute. It is in listening that one becomes convinced that children have minds of their own — that they are people.

Understanding what kinds of processes are appropriate to the age level can mean the difference between getting a message across and talking to yourself. Curriculum scope charts are developed with these stages in mind. Manuals for the various texts not only describe these stages in some detail but show what can be taught, when and how. Familiarity with the materials used in the parish is important to give the ministers a sense of continuity, a commonality of language, and easier lines of communication for all concerned.

Faith: A Living Growth

No one can give faith to another. One can only share his or her life and experience of faith. Each person must "write his or her own story." The story of faith begins first with a perception based on a sense experience. For a child it means such simple things as a beautiful flower, the sun, a cloud, a candle, a dip in the pool, a picnic. The experience of sitting in the dark with a flickering candle, having picnic breakfast during Easter week, or searching for the Alleluia egg provides images, smells, sounds, and feelings. As the experience is reflected upon, insight begins to take place. The poem, the song, the prayer, the picture which follows is the concrete result of reflection.

Reflection at this age is generally new to children. They must be helped to do it. In the lower grades, reflection must be kept very simple, based upon very concrete experiences. Sometimes it takes the form of games;

sometimes the process is reflective prayer. Upon reflection, when the heart is ready, the insight develops and demands a response of some kind — an action. The response must then be celebrated in some way. It may be sung, acted out, talked about, played about. It is the perfect time for prayer.

Holiday hysteria can be diverted with half-day retreats on that crucial last day of school before Christmas or Easter. This can be done with children as young as third graders. It sounds very threatening to catechists, but with well-paced activities, and silence laced with lots of singing and music it works like a charm.

A warning must be repeated. Children are children. They are *not* adults contained in little bodies. Children have great potential, but they are not finished products. Neither, however, are they just potentialities. Children are real people who contain the seeds of faith life. They learn their religious rites and traditions by imitation, gathering affective experiences which eventually make them feel like they belong to a loving group which espouses a special person — Jesus. As a result, they do special actions in his name and gain the insights which become living, expanding faith.

In *Will Our Children Have Faith?*, Dr. John Westerhoff compares faith to a tree which, growing in the proper environment, expands ring by ring. The tree never diminishes but continually adds to that which has already grown.[7]

Faith growth, according to Westerhoff, is experienced in four stages which he calls experienced, affiliative, searching, and owned faith. The child in the EXPERIENCED FAITH stage obtains experiences of faith by listening, watching, and imitating adults. The community provides experiences of trust, love, and acceptance upon which the children reflect. As a result, the children grow. Word and deed are never separated.[8]

In AFFILIATIVE FAITH the sense of belonging develops from participating in parish or small community activities. In Sunday First Communions and parish fiestas, the child sees everyone sharing special moments of which they are a part.

Another characteristic of affiliative faith is the development of religious affections. Feelings of affection come before acts of thinking. Children need many opportunities to experience awe, wonder, and mystery as well as opportunities to sing, dance, paint, read, and act. Watching the first snowfall of the season in silence or the flood of the river in Spring can be the kindling wood of reflective prayer. Children understand Advent, Christmas, Holy Week because the feasts and celebrations touch the heart more than the head.[9] Feasts deal with babies, donkeys, banquets, crosses, a suffering man. These are things which happen within their experience so children can relate to them.

A sense of authority is the third characteristic of the second stage. It marks the community's affirmation of a story and a way of life that judges and inspires the actions of that community. Children need to be aware of the community's story. It is essential for faith, for it is from the community that the child develops a sense of tradition. Children and early adolescents need to belong to and participate in an identity-conscious community of faith. This is how the story is internalized, rehearsed, and eventually owned by the person.[10] Parents can tell this story as can aunts and uncles. In fact, unless it is heard at home, the story is liable to fall on deaf ears when the children are in church.

Toward the end of adolescence, a person enters the stage of SEARCHING FAITH. Adults usually recognize this stage in the psychological development of the young person but sometimes fail to see it as a stage in faith development. The characteristics of searching faith are doubt and/or critical judgment, experimentation, and the first endeavors at commitment. Finally, as adults, a person enters the stage of OWNED FAITH. The adult generally experiences some kind of conversion, whether slow or sudden, which leads him or her to witness to this faith in word and lifestyle.[11]

The main concern here is that these last two stages be recognized as stages beyond the capabilities of the elementary-school child. It does not mean that the child cannot have some kind of emotional religious experience; it simply means that the experience must be recognized for what it is, a part of growing. Like any growth cycle, growth in faith cannot be left to any one style of educational input. It is a family effort. It is a community effort. No family is expected to stand alone to meet all of the faith needs of its children.

The Bible: The Story

As the basic library for the Christian faith, the Bible is in an ironic situation, at least as far as children are concerned. It contains the story the community wishes to tell, the prayers they wish to say, the life lesson they want the children to learn. Yet, it is written in a way that contains symbols, abstractions that children simply cannot grasp. The Bible was written for adults, not children.

Because there is so much material in the Bible, Dr. Iris Cully in her book, *Christian Child Development,* cautions educators not to hurry in trying to introduce all of it to young children.[12] Rather, as they grow in maturity and begin to understand the forms of writings, new material can be used. In the meantime, the stories of Jesus and the Apostles are always readable, full of images and drama suitable for the children to use and enjoy. As children listen to the reading of the plagues, around the seder table with the family or community, the Exodus takes on a real meaning.

The story of Bartimaeus or Joseph appeals to the literal mind of the child and it taps his or her own life experiences. When children role-play Joseph discussing his coat with Reuben the eldest, or the prodigal son discussing his party with his older brother, they gain many insights into sibling relationships. The very *process* of this discovery helps the children to deal with meaning and helps them integrate these insights. To be told is not necessarily to know.[13]

As children grow older, different methods can be used. The class can become local newspaper reporters who interview the Apostles as they struggle with the early communities, or Mary Magdalene as the primary witness to the Resurrection. They can use puppets in role-playing or reenacting a scriptural event. Using puppets relieves some of the threat of disclosure which this age group begins to experience. With proper preparation, children can read passages for prayer services or narrate the mime of others, which is not only fun but develops needed reading and liturgical skills.

Liturgy: Prayer and Play

A Christian community is one in which, by definition, people pray and worship together. This coming together in liturgy is the main vehicle used to "tell our story," to offer those experiences of the heart upon which faith is built. Liturgy is the common tie which binds all aspects of the community together into a whole. The Church helps the community tell its story through the celebration of the liturgical year. It helps the individual tell his or her story, as well as the community's, through the celebration of the sacraments. *The National Catechetical Directory* (No. 112) states explicitly: "Faith and worship are intimately related. Faith brings the community together to worship; and in worship faith is renewed. . . ."

Children have a natural affinity for celebration. They deal with the concrete readily. What could be more concrete than candles, books, incense, bread, and music? They may not understand the meaning of the symbolism involved, but they take great pleasure in the liturgical sights, sounds, and movements.

There is a wealth of books and materials which suggest how to do liturgy with children. First on any list is the *Directory for Masses with Children.* This book describes many of the liturgical principles which must be kept in mind when planning Masses with children. The guidelines allow great creativity of form and adaptation.

Liturgical activities should not, however, be saved for Eucharistic Liturgies only. In fact, Eucharist should be a culminating experience rather than the common means of prayer. It is in praying and doing liturgical actions in the family, the classroom, and the home of the catechist that children gain liturgical skills and learn to feel comfortable with group or public prayer.

Children love ritual, especially familiar ritual. The supper table becomes the reconciliation room. Birthdays and farewells have special rituals at the breakfast or supper table. Sunday dinners celebrate the Sabbath which makes the Sunday liturgy more understandable. Special glasses or dishes are used and the cloth is spread. The Advent wreath lights the winter darkness and the family paschal candle retains the sense of Easter. These events teach far better than words. Banners can be carried in procession around the classroom or hung in the recreation room. The banner and the making of it are the experience, the prayer. The trip to the sacristy to see the vestments and sacred vessels becomes an event worthy of dinnertime conversation, especially if one of the priests or the parish religious educator conducts the tour.

Singing and music-making are joys in themselves. Making homemade rhythm instruments to accompany the hymns or songs is part of the fun. Melody, rhythm, movement, and a feeling of joy are the important factors. The use of particular songs becomes ingrained in the heart. These moments are transformed into meaning and memory at a later time. A well-known short psalm or song brings delight to younger children. The use of good music as a background during art or drama activities helps to instill a love for good and enduring church music. Chant makes wonderful background music for movies. Why do modern teachers and liturgists fear using that which has passed the test of time? Music is also a wonderful mood-setter for storytelling and prayer, whether reflective or recited.

When the word "liturgy" is used, one usually thinks of music, ritual, and lots of words. Children are used to having their senses bombarded. One of the gifts that catechists can give to children is the gift of silence. Children respond very well to silence if it is structured well and does not last too long. Silence can be built into every scripture reading, paraliturgy, class session, and evening meal. It is during silence that reflection can happen, an insight can be gained, a response can be prepared. It is then that the spoken prayer can come from the heart and liturgical silences take on more meaning.

Life Crises: Times of Grief and Pain

Liturgy, in the broad sense, celebrates everyday life. This everyday life sometimes includes personal, family, or national crises. Ministers working with children should use these teachable moments rather than deny them. Crises become a part of children's prayer, the telling of their story. Coping with grief, anxiety, and fear is sometimes more painful for children than adults, for children do not have the same resources available for coping. Having some songs, proverbs, and class or family sayings which are used fairly regularly are a help in confronting these situations. Sometimes children will use them so spontaneously they will shock adults.

Long ago, a sixth-grade class had learned the English version of *In Paradisium* or "Go Forth To Paradise." They had learned it for the feast of All Souls. The day that John Kennedy was shot, the children went to the chapel with other grades to say the Rosary for his recovery. When the prayers were finished, they returned to their classroom to await further news. They bent silently over their art work rather stunned by the situation. The teacher saw the flag keeper walk through the yard toward the flagpole. She called it to the attention of the children who stood silently at attention to watch him lower the flag. Suddenly, one of the children began to softly sing, "Go forth to paradise. . . ." With one voice they all picked up the hymn and sang it to the end as the flag was lowered. The teacher stood bathed in tears of grief and utter awe at what her children had done. Children do have a sense of the appropriate. If they have been given the tools, they know how to use them at the appropriate time.

Illness can be a time of growth or desperation. The child suffering severe or terminal illness may become isolated by adults who do not know how to cope with death in the young. The threatened, frightened child, whose psychological space is invaded hour after hour to care for the body, is left stranded with his or her spiritual and psychological needs unrecognized. Helping these children and parents takes a special gift of understanding.

Montessori methods can be of great help in preparing sick children for the sacraments, talking with them about death, and just praying with them. Montessori methods can be used in many areas of teaching about faith. They need not be dropped when children leave the primary grades. The principles still hold for older children and can be valuable in the classroom and in the home.

At this age, social concerns activities are usually done best at home or within the small community. Crisis times, however, do offer moments for helping children to reflect on the needs and sorrows of others. Third and fourth graders begin to be inspired by stories of the missions, the poor children of the world, the sick children in hospitals. However, children who live with poverty, sickness, and neglect every day are not inspired by stories of it; rather they need to be given hope. This comes from watching adults work, pray, and play together.

More and more, divorce, death, loss of a friend, and moving have become common crisis experiences for children. The commonness of the event does not change the trauma or grief which ensues. Besides the use of ordinary means to deal with these times, the parish may need to consider such things as counseling, support groups, and special workshops for parents to help them help their children.

One resource which is often overlooked is right down the street at the local public library. Many values connected with morality, social justice, personal sorrow, and growing up are treated in beautiful ways in children's literature. The children's librarian can supply lists of materials on various grade levels which pertain to the everyday problems that children have to face. She or he can also give the child or adult individual help in selecting materials.

The books cover the gamut of needs. There are fiction books and there are "tell it like it is" books, such as Eda LeShan's *Learning to Say Goodby: When a Parent Dies.* Although written for children, any adult would do well to read it. Both fiction and nonfiction treat handicaps, the ache of preadolescence, and now the latest problem — ageism. The library even has books on the primary level which can be read to or read by children.

Every minister working with children on any level should have access to the world in which children live. Besides listening to and playing with children, one of the best ways to get that contact is by taking a trip to the children's section of the library. Look at the Caldecott Award winners (an award for illustrations) and the Newberry Award winners (literary excellence). They are wonderful tools for vicariously listening to children. One evening with children's books will be a real eye-opener and a heart-opener as well. It will also relieve the reader to know that adults are still needed by children who are growing up and growing in faith.

SUMMARY

1. Both the Gospels and the documents of the Church specify the responsibility of the community for the welfare of its children and its duty to pass on the good news in a manner appropriate to the ages of the children.

2. The religious formation of the children in a parish will depend to a large extent on the way in which the parish perceives itself as Church. A pilgrim people of God will function quite differently from an autocratic pyramid-styled structure.

3. Parents are the primary educators and role models for the children, but parents must be supported in this role by the Church in its fellowship, educational programs, social services, and continuing spiritual formation.

4. The child is not an adult, but a person who develops slowly in predictable patterns of perception, cognition, emotions, and, to some extent, behavior. These stages must be respected when working with children whether educationally, liturgically, or socially. The child's greatest asset is caring adults who welcome him or her and help in the development of his or her own story.

5. Faith is not a body of belief, but an ongoing experience of God which, if properly nourished, develops throughout life. Only the early stages of faith are attainable by children.

6. The Bible, the basic library of the Christian religion, is an adult book. Whereas caution is advised for its use with children, there is much concrete biblical material which can be used advantageously in music, drama, liturgy, and prayer.

7. Liturgy is essential to any kind of educational program for children. Almost purely experiential, it is through liturgy that children learn to pray in common, come to an understanding of sacraments, a sense of an identity-community. Children learn to worship by worshipping.

8. Life crises happen in every child's life. Early childhood is a time for great learning and insight. Both parents and teachers need resources to help them support children during such stressful times.

CHAPTER NOTES

1. National Conference of Catholic Bishops, *To Teach As Jesus Did* (Washington, D.C.: U.S. Catholic Conference, 1973), articles 14, 83, 84.

2. National Conference of Catholic Bishops, *Sharing the Light of Faith: National Catechetical Directory for Catholics of the United States,* (Washington, D.C.: U.S. Catholic Conference, 1979), article 26.
3. Richard P. McBrien, *Catholicism,* Vol. 1 (New York: Winston Press, 1980), p. 29.
4. *Sharing the Light of Faith,* op. cit., No. 176.
5. Ibid., No. 37.
6. John R. McCall, *Growing Up* (New York: Paulist Press, 1972), p. 37.
7. John H. Westerhoff, III, *Will Our Children Have Faith?* (New York: Seabury Press, 1976), p. 90.
8. Ibid., p. 94.
9. Ibid., p. 95.
10. Ibid.
11. Ibid., pp. 96-99.
12. Iris V. Cully, *Christian Child Development* (New York: Harper and Row, 1979), p. 147.
13. Dorothy Jean Furnish, *Exploring the Bible With Children* (Nashville: Abingdon, 1975), pp. 14-17.

SUGGESTED READINGS

Berryman, Jerome. "A Gift of Healing Stories for a Child Who is Ill." *Liturgy,* pp. 15-20, 38-42, July-August, 1979. Out of his hospital experience, Dr. Berryman uses Montessori methods to bring help to the sick child.

_____, "Being In Parables With Children." *Religious Education,* pp. 271-285, May-June, 1979. Using concrete materials, even small children can begin to deal with literary forms and parables.

Bucher, Janet Marie, C.D.P. *Run With Him.* Cincinnati: North American Liturgy Resources, 1974. A practical source book for planning liturgies with children in primary and intermediate grades.

Furnish, Dorothy Jean. *Exploring the Bible With Children.* Nashville: Abingdon, 1975. Dr. Furnish develops basic principles concerning the use of Scripture in education, prayer, and liturgy.

_____. *Living the Bible With Children.* Nashville: Abingdon, 1979. Activities for children based on specific principles developed in *Exploring.* . . .

Gesell, Arnold, Frances L. Ilg, and Louise B. Ames. *Youth: The Years From Ten to Sixteen.* New York: Harper and Row, 1956. A reference book which has not gone out of date, *Youth* describes the physical, mental, and emotional development which can be expected at each level. Part of a series.

Griggs, Donald L. *Translating the Good News Through Teaching Activities.* Livermore, Calif.: Griggs Educational Service, 1973. A treasure of scriptural activities to use with children.

Groome, Thomas H. *Christian Religious Education: Sharing Our Story and Vision.* San Francisco: Harper and Row, 1980. A whole section of this book is devoted to the growth and development of children as it relates to religious education.

McCall, John R. *Growing Up*. New York: Paulist Press, 1972. A gem which describes children and adult reactions to them.

Shea, John. *Stories of Faith*. Chicago: Thomas More Press, 1980. A portrayal of one's self-identity and faith growth in terms of each person's own story.

Sloyan, Virginia, ed. *Signs, Songs and Stories*. Washington: Liturgical Conference, 1974. Basic liturgical principles with a wealth of ideas and helps for doing liturgy with children.

Westerhoff, John H., III. *Will Our Children Have Faith?* New York: Seabury Press, 1976. Faith is analyzed and educational principles applied to the stages of development.

The Youngest Parishioners

Elaine McCarron, SCN

A Sister of Charity of Nazareth who recently completed a Master of Divinity degree at the Toronto School of Theology, Sister Elaine is the Minister of Religious Education at Holy Spirit Parish in Virginia Beach, Virginia. A former elementary teacher, principal, and diocesan staff member, she is actively engaged in the educational and liturgical dimensions of the religious formation of young children.

Theological Reflection on Childhood

Though a subject of controversy within the Church, the centuries-old practice of infant baptism inserts young children, not long after birth, into the Christian community. What to do with them between baptism and the reception of First Eucharist/first penance is a challenging question for the Church in general and the parish in particular.

The Church, responding to criticism of being too child-centered in the past, is intensifying its approach to adults. It must continue, however, to focus love and attention on its youngest children, acknowledging their presence within the faith community. It is not merely a question of caring or providing for young children while preaching and teaching for the adults. It is not just waiting patiently for the children to grow up and join the adults, able then to begin the real work of knowing God and what Church is all about. Rather, mindful of its children from birth, growing in faith together with them, a parish shares in the richness of this stage of human life, acknowledging it as a gift of the Creator.

Christians look first to Jesus and his words and actions in the New Testament for direction in regard to young children. Jesus did not ignore children. He was aware of their presence (Matthew 11:16-19); he had personal contact with them (Mark 10:13-16); and he had a dynamic, new way of interpreting childhood (Matthew 18:1-5). Most of the biblical references concerning Jesus and children end with Jesus speaking to his disciples, presenting them, through the child, with his message.[1]

One example of how Jesus behaved with children is Matthew 18:1-5 (Mark 9:33-37; Luke 9:46-48). According to Weber, the Greco-Roman world at the time of Jesus regarded the child as a blank mind to be educated and formed into a member of the human race. To the Jews, the child was a member of God's chosen people to be disciplined and formed by knowledge of God and his Law. Jesus reversed both of these ideas in response to a question by his disciples as to who among them was the greatest.[2] Jesus responded by taking a child, in his culture the learner, and making the little one the focal point of his message. Weber explains:

> Consequently, a reversal in the teaching/learning situation occurs, which indicates at the same time a reversal of being: the first must be last, the least one is great, the person who humbles him- or herself like a child is the greatest in the Kingdom of heaven.[3]

This brief look at one text indicates the radical interpretation of childhood by Jesus. The New Testament study of other texts relating to Jesus and children also sheds light on the child's place and role within the Christian community.

The scriptures abound with references to people as children of God. Thus children give the parish an opportunity to reflect on the nature of childhood, which continues in every person even in maturity. Childlikeness is the basic attitude of everyone's continuing relationship with God. The trust, openness, expectation, and dependence of the child become those conditions in each person's life that enable him or her to become more fully children of God. The child, then, becomes a symbol for all Christians in their basic affiliation with the Creator.[4]

To be operative, to attempt to grasp the reality of salvation, symbols must be present and visible in some form or other. If children are left at home while the community worships or are secluded in a room out of sight of the rest of the congregation, only with great difficulty will people grasp the full meaning of being called children of God.

Childhood was not, however, created for the purpose of being merely a symbol for the rest of humanity. It is, in itself, a fullness of life, a value that finds its purpose not just in the maturity that is to come but also in its present state of living and loving.[5]

What the Church Says

The Church in its Vatican II document "Declaration on Christian Education" states that it is the right of every Christian to receive formal faith formation. In doing so it expresses the sentiments of papal encyclicals relating to catechesis, both before and after its time, right up to the recent *Catechesi Tradendae* of John Paul II. Conscious of human development, the Pope speaks of people being "gradually introduced" into the Christian mysteries. So that they may ". . .become daily more appreciative of the gift of faith" (No. 2).

Perhaps the most important statement in this document and one that has had the most influence on Christian education today, was the acknowledgement that parents are "primary and principally responsible for the education of their children" (No. 3). It is this statement that has radically changed the preparation and celebration of the sacraments of initiation and reconciliation by giving parents an active role in the direct catechesis of their children. The effect of this document, however, on preschool religious education has been minimal.

Perhaps the most practical Church document relating to young children is the *Directory for Masses with Children* from the Sacred Congregation for Divine Worship. It describes in detail the possibilities for the participation of children in liturgical worship. From a base of sound pedagogy and child psychology, the directory addresses the issues and problems involved, expressing the desire and concern of the Church to "follow its Master, who put his arms around the children . . . and blessed them (Mark 10:16). It [the Church] cannot leave children to themselves."[6]

This brief document has had far-reaching effects on the liturgical life of young children. It gave Church approval to timid parishes who had done nothing with children at liturgy, and it gave encouragement and new insights to those brave parishes who had experimented in this area long before its publication.

Sharing the Light of Faith: National Catechetical Directory for Catholics in the United States gives specific attention to preschool catechetics, especially in the section "The Stages of Human Development." With strong emphasis on the role of the family, it encourages parishes to assure that the religious formation of young children happens and that it is in the hands of competent people. It mentions the good effect that can come from coordinated family programs that help parents "become active, confident, and competent in encouraging their children's emerging faith" (No. 177).

In the same section, a brief paragraph devoted specifically to catechesis for preschool children, while encouraging parish programs for the children themselves, states that the main focus should be on parents, helping them to "deepen their faith and become more adept at helping their children." The directory echoes the strong emphasis on parents by Vatican II.

A Brief Look at Some Theories

Two points need emphasis before moving to practical things. First, it is important to recognize the manner in which development takes place. What the child learns comes from interaction with the environment. The early acquisition of knowledge depends on activities such as sensorimotor play and imitation. This fact should be remembered when planning a program for the preschool child.

Likewise, the strong egocentricity of the child places limitations on the development of communication and cooperation so important to the formation of community.[7] In addition, the very openness and dependence praised by Jesus make the child impressionable, cautioning those involved to prepare with care the manner in which they present the Christian message. The amount presented is of utmost importance; too much information at too early an age will hinder, not help, the child's faith formation. People should always tell the child the truth, but nothing that will have to be negated later. Do not overload. The child is not capable, nor interested, in receiving the message with all the theological ramifications or spiritual insights adults are capable of understanding.

In their religious world, children are concerned with essentials. When people convey the essentials of Jesus' message and when they do so with few words, many materials, and assorted activities that recognize the manner in which a child learns, the child will receive the teaching with joy and enthusiasm. The child shares with the rest of the human race a sense of the transcendent God. The particulars of the Christian message are, however, unknown to a child.[8] But if the right person using the right method conveys the right insights, the child will welcome what is taught. It is toward the reception of such truths that nature tends and the faith of baptism assists.

Second, research in the area of preschool catechesis has resulted in several theories that can serve the parish well. Space and the scope of this chapter permit only a brief mention of these theories.

The recapitulation theory holds that the child retraces the religious development of humanity in general, going from the primitive, through various stages, to a meaningful faith. The parental projection theory states, in essence, that the child's personal religion is representative of the child/parent relationship. In other words, the parents are God for the child until their limitations are realized.

Piaget's theory of intellectual development has greatly influenced theories of early religious development, especially seen in the work of Elkind, Godin, and Goldman. They propose that the child passes through stages of religious development that correspond to intellectual development. Consequently, what is taught should relate to what can be understood. James Fowler has added the affective realm to Piaget's cognition theory and presents six stages through which he believes one's faith progresses.[9]

Though not widely known, religious development was at the heart of Maria Montessori's method of education. She had great respect for the interior life of the child, advocated a sensorial environment at the beginning of religious development, upheld the value of deeds over words, and encouraged the teacher to a special humility and patience when introducing the child to the Christian message.[10] Her method came from observing and listening to children, something those involved with the preschool age would do well to imitate.

Montessori's vocabulary may appear outdated but her perceptions are worthy of study. Her method continues today through the work of Sofia Cavalletti, an Italian religious educator of international reputation, whose insights regarding the religious potential of the young child and creative materials to assist development have influenced not only Montessori proponents but many other catechists as well.

A study of theories and experts will unearth contradictions which may confuse and bewilder as to the proper path to take. After prayerful study, parents, catechists, and parish staff must trust their own insights and the Spirit within for direction. Those who know and love particular children can best prepare a religious environment for them. As Rosemary Haughton has pointed out:

> The child who has been baptized has been "taken on" by the Church, and the Church, in the concrete, turns out to be particular people — parents, relations, teachers, friends.[11]

Maria Montessori and Sofia Cavalletti child-tested approaches and materials. If they failed to engage the child they were discarded. Though experimentation is not a word people like to associate with children, it is in reality the path a parish must take in regard to its formational endeavors. What is worse is to provide no guidance or programs for the parents and children of this age group.

Some Practical Suggestions

An initial opportunity for the parish to minister in the area of religious formation for young children is baptismal preparation. Many of these programs do an excellent job of discussing the important issues of faith through a discussion of the theology of baptism and the ceremony. Many of these same programs are weak in preparing parents for the task of forming their child in faith.

Realistically, such a component would take place prior to the baptism. Ideally, it could happen after the baptism, relating it to the mystagogia stage of the *Rite of Christian Initiation of Adults*. Such sessions may be spaced at intervals and a correspondence set up between the age of the child and the information presented. They could be general sessions to which all parents of preschool-age children would be invited. Conducted by parish staff, experienced parents, and occasionally, imported experts, they might begin by encouraging parents, praying with them, and making known the desire of the Christian community to assist them and welcome their children into its midst.

Next, information regarding when and how to introduce the child to prayer, liturgy, and Scripture would be helpful. Emphasis should be given to religious practices in the home and programs in the parish relating to young children. There is no lack of resources available to assist parishes in designing a faith formation component for a baptismal preparation program.

Most parishes have nurseries where parents may leave their children while they worship. A nursery needs to be clean, attractive, and spacious, equipped with safe furniture, toys, and materials for play and learning. In parishes where this is not the case, one wonders at the bravery and trust of parents who leave their children in them.

Christians, through the centuries, have been noted for their care of children. One of the criteria as to how well they care may be seen by touring the parish nursery while it is in session.

The nursery need not be staffed only by parents. Senior citizens, youth, and parish members who have no children may enjoy assisting in the nursery if they are given the opportunity. It is important that men as well as women take a turn with this ministry. Staff members should frequently visit the nursery and talk with the children. If all this is done, the parish community will give witness to its concern and love for its youngest members.

In some parishes it is a custom to bring the children from the nursery for the last blessing and dismissal rite. It seems obvious from what was said in the beginning pages of this chapter that such an action would benefit the entire community.

The *Directory for Masses with Children* states:

> Sometimes, moreover, it will perhaps be appropriate, if the physical arrangements and the circumstances of the community permit, to celebrate the liturgy of the word, including a homily, with the children in a separate area that is not too far removed. Then before the eucharistic liturgy begins, the children are led to the place where the adults have meanwhile been celebrating their own liturgy of the word.[12]

Such services have become very popular in some parishes and often include four- and five-year-olds. In one parish, those who lead the liturgy of the Word for children are in the entrance procession with the lectors, eucharistic ministers, and the celebrant. This gives evidence to the importance this parish places on this part of its worship life.

It is ideal for children to come to church, take their places with their families, and be called to this service by the presiding priest. If this happens, children will situate their own service within the context of the total liturgy with greater ease than if, when coming to church, they go immediately to a room apart from the main worship area.

The service itself should reflect the adult liturgy of the Word, using the readings (or at least the Gospel) as the basis of the service. Drama, dance, mime, children's literature, films, music, and other creative avenues may be used to interpret the reading. Each service should include prayer, song, and Scripture to ensure its worship character.

Some parishes with large numbers of children cannot always provide liturgy of the Word for its children every Sunday but manage to do so at least once a month. Even those parishes which can logistically manage a service every week might consider three Sundays a month so that the children will know the experience of worshipping with the entire community.

On special feasts, or on a Sunday when the Gospel is especially appropriate, the community together with the children may celebrate a liturgy commonly termed a "children's" or "family" liturgy. These are familiar events in most parishes, particularly at Christmas and Easter. Often they appeal as much to the adults as they do to the children, not because they touch the child in all of us but because they touch the affective part of our nature. They are creative, artistic, and celebrated with feeling which may be missing factors in some adult worship.

A parish may include in its regular catechetical program weekly classes for preschool children. Such classes could supplement the religious environment of the home and be a source of additional spiritual growth for the child. Also, family programs that take place at the church, with classes for various age groups and a culminating activity for the family in a community setting, provide enrichment for the entire family. The preschool child in such a program widens his or her horizons and experiences Church within the security of the family. Sunday worship may give a similar experience but the family program provides an additional opportunity.

A parish may provide a time for young children to come to the church, perhaps on a Saturday morning, to become familiar with the surroundings, the vestments, vessels, and especially the gestures of the liturgy. The gestures, simply explained with an invitation to imitation, are for young children the most effective way to introduce and teach the liturgy. This is evidenced in the joyful participation of children at the gesture of peace.

The parish staff should make an effort to acknowledge children as they enter and leave the church with their family. Sometimes they are forgotten in this ritual and it becomes a greeting among adults. Sometimes children, in the arms of their parents are blessed, or touched, or in some other way noticed by the priest or special eucharistic ministers as the parents approach to receive the Eucharist. Both of these are simple things but they extend to the children the recognition of the community.

Because they are alive, young children move, talk, laugh, and cry. At a given liturgy on a Sunday, the presence of many children doing all these things may interrupt the atmosphere in which adults like to celebrate. Patience on the part of the community and consideration on the part of parents is necessary. There is one parish that was created (as its name, "Sandbox Community," implies), because the adults believed their children were not welcomed graciously in their former parishes. During the liturgy of this community, children move about freely or play on the floor with other children. The effect is not bedlam but a surprisingly quiet atmosphere. Most likely the relaxing, accepting environment reduces tensions in adults and children, resulting in peaceful, quiet behavior by the children.

To form a parish community around the children may seem like a radical solution. Each parish, however, needs to deal with the same situation that created the "Sandbox Community." Possibly one liturgy during a weekend could be announced as a "family" liturgy at which parents would realize their children are expected and most certainly welcomed. One may question why this discussion is necessary if a nursery is provided. A parish must respect the wishes of parents who may not desire to use the nursery for quite legitimate reasons.

There are two groups of children toward whom the parish should show special concern. First, the children of single parents or families only marginally involved in the parish community need to be noticed. Identifying such children and reaching out to them will be a challenge for any parish. If everything revolves around family participation they will surely be neglected.

Second, children with serious or long-term illnesses or handicaps are entitled to the care, presence, and prayers of the Christian community. They are sometimes overlooked and it is well to remember that the ministry of the Church to those who are sick is a universal one and not subjected to age barriers.

SUMMARY

1. Children are a gift of the Creator. As with all gifts from God, they require from those who receive them care, love, attention, respect, and prayerful contemplation of the Creator's intention in putting them in our midst.

2. Parishes planning the faith formation of its youngest members must take into consideration the intellectual, physical, and emotional stages of development of the child and should study some of the literature available in the area of religious development of the child.

3. Any programs for this age group must put special emphasis on encouraging and assisting parents in their task of forming their children in faith.

4. Parishes should make families with young children feel comfortable and welcome by providing clean, safe, well-staffed nurseries, well-planned and separate liturgies of the Word, and occasional "family" or "children's" liturgies.

5. The children of single parents and chronically ill or handicapped children must be given special concern and support.

CHAPTER NOTES

1. Hans-Reudi Weber, *Jesus and the Children* (Atlanta: John Knox Press, 1979), pp. ix-x.
2. Ibid., p. 43.
3. Ibid.
4. Karl Rahner, "Ideas for a Theology of Childhood," *Theological Investigations,* Vol. VIII (London: Darton, Longman and Todd, 1971), pp. 46-47.
5. Ibid., pp. 33-35.
6. Sacred Congregation for Divine Worship, *Directory for Masses with Children* (Washington, D.C.: U.S. Catholic Conference, 1974), p. 1.

7. Jean Piaget, *Play, Dreams and Imitation in Childhood* (New York: W.W. Norton, 1962), pp. 289-90.
8. Sofia Cavalletti, "Cathechetics for Children Under Six," An address given at the North American College of Rome, May 1972.
9. Hart M. Nelsen, Raymond H. Potvin, and Joseph Shields, *The Religion of Children* (Washington, D.C.: U.S. Catholic Conference, 1977), pp. 2-4.
10. Maria Montessori, *The Child in the Church* (London: Sands and Co., 1929), pp. 2-4.
11. Rosemary Haughton, *Beginning Life in Christ* (Westminster, Md.: Newman Press, 1966), p. 11.
12. *Directory for Masses with Children*, op. cit., p. 6.

SUGGESTED READINGS

Brusselmans, Christiane with Edward Wakin. *Religion for Little Children.* Huntington, Ind.: Our Sunday Visitor, 1970. A helpful book for parents that deals in part with the many and difficult questions children ask about religious matters.

Cavalletti, Sofia. *Il Potenziale Religioso Del Bambino: Descrizione di Un 'Esperiencza Con Bambini da 3 a 6 Anni.* Roma: Citta Nuovo Editrice, 1979. (This book is scheduled for an English edition by Paulist Press under the title: *The Religious Potential of the Child.)*

——, and Gianni Gobbi. *Teaching Doctrine and Liturgy: The Montessori Approach.* New York: Alba House, 1964. Dr. Cavalletti's works offer both theory and practice to assist parish staff in the faith formation of young children.

Curran, Dolores. *Who, Me Teach My Child Religion?* Minneapolis: Winston Press, 1974. A book that will encourage parents in their task of religious formation of their children.

Groome, Thomas H. *Christian Religious Education: Sharing Our Story and Vision.* San Francisco: Harper and Row, 1980. A scholarly but practical treatment of religious education. Groome does not deal with the faith formation of children under six, but educators of very young children will find this book valuable in realizing where the children are heading. He proposes a shared praxis approach involving the interaction of the Church's story and vision with the individual's personal story and vision. With young children it seems we are privileged to help shape their story and vision.

Haughton, Rosemary. *The Dawn of the Christian Life.* New York: Paulist Press, 1970. A mother as well as a scholar, the author traces the beginning of faith in the life of a child. Also discusses theories of religious development.

Nelson, Hart M., Raymond H. Potvin, and Joseph Shields. *The Religion of*

Children. Washington, D.C.: U.S. Catholic Conference, 1977. Research into the religious development of children that gives a brief accounting of theories and studies in this area.

Weber, Hans-Reudi. *Jesus and the Children.* Atlanta: John Knox Press, 1979. This book presents biblical resources in relation to young children for study and preaching. The appendix contains helpful study sheets for parish groups.

Westerhoff, John H., III. *Bringing Up Children in the Christian Faith.* Minneapolis: Winston Press, 1980. The author, pastor, parent, and religious educator shares personal reflections and offers practical suggestions to aid in faithful Christian parenting.

Is Family Religious Education Possible?

Maureen Gallagher

Ms. Gallagher's background includes teaching and administration on the elementary-school level, work as a parish religious education director, dean of students on the college level, and teaching in various universities. She holds a Master of Theology degree from the University of Notre Dame and a Master of Art History degree from Rosary College. Currently she is a Ph.D. candidate in adult education at the University of Wisconsin.

Family Catechesis: Fact or Fantasy?

Some people think of family religious education as an idyllic concept; it happens around a peaceful supper table with much enthusiasm. Others see red flashing lights at those words, coupled with a whole list of defenses as to why it cannot work in "our" parish.

The first thing a discussion of family religious education needs is a definition of the topic. Family catechesis, the more accurate name for family religious education, is an approach to catechesis which focuses on the growth in faith of the family as a unit, as well as the growth in faith of each individual within the family. The task of the family catechist is: (1) to help the family grow in faith by providing opportunities for a family to understand and live the message of the gospel; (2) to help strengthen the bonds within the family and with other families; (3) to enable families to pray and worship together; and (4) to motivate families to serve, care for, and nurture others.[1]

The goal and tasks of family catechesis are no different from those for child- or adult-centered catechesis. It is the setting and emphasis which is different. If those are the only differences, why bother with family catechesis? The answer to this question can be approached from three directions: historical, sociological, and theological.

Historical Reasons

Historically the Judeo-Christian tradition has placed a strong emphasis on the family in terms of passing on the faith. For the Hebrews the primary catechists were parents — with the prophets, sages, and poets all providing support services. Controlling a child's conduct, passing on the stories of God in an imaginative way, and celebrating the deeds of God were the main way the faith was passed on. The father had the primary responsibility of presenting religious ideas to his household. To do this effectively he had to reevaluate the meaning of his faith and interpret it in his own life experience. There was no such thing as passing on bare facts. What was shared was a living faith. To excite the imaginations of his wide-eyed children, a father used vivid, concrete detail, thus nurturing the internal faith growth of his children.

For the early Christians, parents too were the primary educators of their children. During the first five centuries of the Church there were three major educational influences on children: the family, the liturgy, and the community. This was more or less the case until the Reformation in the sixteenth century. At that time Martin Luther admitted that parents had the first duty to educate their children, but he found them to have "hollow-piety and selfish aims." To correct this situation, he set up schools for children and wrote the first catechism.

Following the Council of Trent the Roman Catholic Church also began to tackle many of the problems Luther addressed. New orders of religious were formed to run schools for children, a new phenomenon in the Church. Previously the religious orders, especially the Dominicans and Franciscans, worked mainly with adults. The general practice in the Church today of putting major educational emphasis on children dates back to the late sixteenth and early seventeenth centuries. Therefore, from a historical perspective there is a long tradition of family catechesis, even though that tradition has not been generally maintained during the last four hundred years.

Sociological Reasons

Major sociological research coming out of the National Opinion Research Center (NORC) points to the importance of the family in terms of predicting religious performance of children. Dr. William C. McCready's research indicates that two factors primarily influence children's religious behavior: (1) the religious behavior of parents, particularly fathers, and (2) the quality of relationship between mothers and fathers.

Further research by McCready indicates that in single-parent homes the child picks up the parent's own self-perception regarding faith.[2] So if the single parent is a well-adjusted, faith-filled person, a child will absorb this and be nurtured in his or her religious behavior.

The point McCready is making is that religious behavior is influenced by the perception children have of their parents. McCready goes so far as to say the popular bumper sticker "Have you hugged your child today?" might well be revised to "Has your child seen you hug your spouse today?"[3]

It should be further noted that while some sociologists point to the demise of the family, some of the best work (such as that done by Kenneth Keniston[4]) indicates that the family is not collapsing. Rather it is still the best solution for transmitting systems of meaning from one generation to the next. Keniston's research concludes that in order to mature, children need at least one parent who is "hooked" on them. Thus from a sociological perspective parents fulfill an important role in transmitting religious values to their children. In this context parents are religious educators by being parents. They intentionally and unintentionally pass on religious values to their children.

Theological Reasons

From a theological perspective two major approaches can be taken with regard to family catechesis. One is a scriptural approach; the other relates to Church documents.

One of the objectives of family catechesis is to enable families to discover that spirituality is inherent in family life. Spirituality in this context refers to the discovery and lived experience that there is more to life than meets the eye. It is a recognition of the extraordinary in the ordinary, the presence of God, the risen Jesus, the Spirit. Spirituality refers to helping people *see* differently. Teilhard de Chardin says it appropriately: "By reason of creation and even more the incarnation nothing is profane for those who know how to see."[5]

From a theological viewpoint family catechesis seeks to give people insights into their lives which will help them see things in a way that brings meaning to existence. Insight can be defined as primarily pattern recognition.[6] By helping people see the connections between the patterns in Scripture and their own lives, they are led to discover and nurture a vital faith. They begin to see the interconnectedness between their lives and the lives of the scriptural heroes. This gives them a sense of confidence that their life has meaning and that the thrust of their lives is in the right direction.

Examples from Scripture abound in family imagery. One senses that the scripture writers could not think of a better way to tell people of their intimate relationship with God than to use family imagery. Excerpts from Hosea illustrate the point: "When Israel was a child, I loved him, and out of Egypt I called my son. . . . Yet it was I who taught Ephraim to walk. . . . I took them up in my arms . . . and I bent down to them and fed them" (Hosea 11:1-5). God is also symbolized as a mother. Isaiah states: "Can a woman forget her sucking child, that she should have no compassion on the son of her womb? Even these may forget, yet I will not forget you" (Isaiah 49:15).

Reflections on such passages affirm parents and enable them to see patterns in their lives reminiscent of the scripture writers.

The scriptures constantly point to the God-life in the family. Jesus himself faced many problems similar to what parents face today. Who would want to deal with a blustery, impulsive Peter, or a Thomas who had to try everything out for himself, or a Philip who often missed the point? Many of Jesus' characteristics and actions are very much like those which are seen in healthy family life. Jesus constantly affirmed people; he made friends rather easily; he shared many meals; he experienced confusion; he studied the scriptures and understood the patterns in them; he used a lot of common sense; he trusted and was betrayed. This is the stuff of family life. This is where holiness is found.

Therefore, from studying the scriptures it is possible to see how family life fosters growth in faith. It certainly is the natural place to begin. The creative use of Scripture can help families discover God in their everyday lives because the most powerful images of God in Scripture are couched in family settings.

The Church recognizes the importance of the family and points to parents as the primary educators of their children. In one way or another three documents from Vatican II allude to the sacredness of the family and parents' roles in the education of their children.[7] More recently the *National Catechetical Directory* states:

> God's love is communicated to infants and young children primarily through parents. (Parents') faith, their confidence in human potential and their loving and trusting attitude toward God and human beings strongly influences the child's faith.[8]

The directory goes on to explain that the foundations of faith, of the human capacity for relating to God, rests on the ability to accept self, relate to others, and respond effectively to the environment. These abilities are developed through a child's relationship to his or her parents. Family relationships are the most powerful models for fostering or hindering Christian growth. This may not be surprising when talking about very young children, but the directory in reference to children between the ages of six and ten states: "The immediate environment, normally the home, remains the principal setting in which children experience a relationship with God."[9]

How Does a Parish Initiate Family Catechesis?

Assuming that there is some interest in family catechesis, what are the steps to be taken to get a family program functioning? The success of any family program depends upon the quality of planning that goes into it. It is not out of the question that it will take a full year to plan a program to be implemented the following year. The following are basic planning steps that anyone can use:

Step I. Create a task force to study the issue of family catechesis. The task force should be representative of the parish decision-makers (priest, council members, director of religious education, school principal) as well as potential participants. The ideal number for such a group is about seven people. The number should not exceed ten. At a later date the group may wish to break up into subgroups and add more members to the subgroups.

Step II. Define the area of concern, in this case, family catechesis. Be sure all have a sense of the broad meaning of family so that programs will not be planned for the "Waltons"! A good resource for understanding the scope of family ministry is the National Conference of Catholic Bishops' Plan of Pastoral Action for Family Ministry.[10]

This document has broken family ministry into six areas: ministry for pre-marrieds; ministry for married couples; ministry for parents; ministry for developing families; ministry for hurting families; and ministry for leadership. This does not mean that the task force has to deal with all these areas, but it will do a better job if it is aware of the large scope of family ministry. Besides having a good understanding of family ministry, the task force should have a basic understanding of what catechesis is about. The definition given earlier in this chapter provides a good starting point for discussion. It is important to understand all dimensions of catechesis and not equate it only with transmitting information about religion.

Step III. Identify the needs. Once the basic concept of family catechesis is understood, the task force needs to begin to assess the needs of the parish in regard to family catechesis. This assessment can be done informally, initially within the group by asking some basic questions. Do any of our present catechetical programs focus on the family? (Perhaps; sacramental programs do.) Could any of the present programs be expanded to include the family? Should more emphasis be placed on family involvement? If so, why? Are there parent needs which are not being met? Do we do anything to support single parents? Are our liturgies designed for family participation? Does the Catholic school involve families? Are there activities for senior citizen families? Are there service opportunities for families? Recreational opportunities? Such a discussion should begin to generate some possibilities.

After the group has explored the question, and presuming it has come up with apparent needs concerning family catechesis, it is *very* important that as many parishioners as possible be consulted to get their input and help them identify their own needs. Broad participation at this stage will add to the success of any program that develops because the program is more apt to be targeted to the felt needs of the participants. Consequently, they will feel more ownership for the program and more responsibility to make it work.

There are several effective ways to do needs assessments. One way is to prepare a well-structured questionnaire of not more than one page and to distribute it in church, allowing time for it be completed and collected after the liturgy. A high return will result from this method but the responses are often superficial. A second way is to mail the questionnaire and request that it be mailed back or dropped off at church. With this method there will be fewer responses but the quality will probably be better.

A third way to assess needs is to do a telephone survey of people in the

parish and tabulate the results. A fourth way (and one which is very effective but takes more time to organize) is to have block or area "coffees" and
through informal discussion assess needs.

Too many programs have been planned based on what administrators
saw as needs. These programs have failed because they did not meet the felt
needs of the intended participants. Two resources are particularly helpful
on the subject of needs assessments: *Sounds of the Family*[11] and *Family-
Centered Catechesis.*[12]

Step IV. Analyze the needs. The needs which surfaced should be
analyzed to discover which surfaced more than once in different ways and
which are most urgent. (For example, support groups for single parents, or
support groups for parents of adolescents.) Which needs are most basic?
Note that the catechetical dimension of family life is broad according to the
tasks delineated at the beginning of this chapter. This means that at times
family catechesis can just focus on parent needs in terms of who comes to a
program.

Step V. Set goals. After needs are analyzed, goals must be set to meet
these needs. Goal-setting always includes long-range and short-range goals.
Short-range goals focus on what can be done relatively soon, or what should
be accomplished immediately. Long-range goals incorporate things which
definitely should happen, but for one reason or another cannot happen at
present.

To be effective, goals need to be specific. One way to write a specific
goal is to be sure it answers the following questions: Who? What? How?
When? The following are examples: By January 1 the chairperson of the
task force will have contacted the diocesan office for resources on family
catechesis and ask that someone speak to the task force. By April 1 Maria
Sanchez will have met with parents of adolescents to come to a clearer understanding of how their needs can be met. By May 1 Larry Olson will have
assembled a group of divorced and separated parents to encourage them to
begin their own support group. By April 1 of the following year John
Callahan will have explored with the director of religious education the possibility of starting a family program to supplement the regular CCD program. By making goals this specific, there is a better chance that they will
be accomplished because it is very clear who is to do what, by when.

Step VI. Implement the goals. During this stage of planning (depending upon what goals were set up), it is helpful to be aware of the various resources available to meet needs, especially if the needs involve the formation of new programs. Programs should always meet goals which are
based on real needs. Programs should never be implemented just because
they look like exciting programs.

At this point in the planning process the task force should examine programs being implemented in other parishes, as well as published programs,
to see if they meet the needs which surfaced in the assessment and goal-setting process. If there are things which others have done which are helpful,

use them. There is no sense in reinventing the wheel! Some programs which may be helpful and bear examination include the following:

1. Family Clusters. Although there are many ways to do family clusters, one of the most successful was developed by Dr. Margaret Sawin.[13] A Family Cluster is a group of four or five complete family units which contract to meet together over an extended period of time for shared experiences. The groups provide mutual support for each other, learn skills which enhance family life, and celebrate their beliefs.

2. Family Learning Teams. The program consists of a more formal approach to religious education with the curriculum planned by leaders in various family groupings. The program founders stress that the program is adult-centered and community structured. The community is seen as the co-educator of the child along with the individual instructor. Normally, professional help should be used to get the program started. Dr. Joseph and Mercedes Iannone are the founders of this program.[14]

3. Family: A Parish Religious Education Program.[15] This program brings families together for eight two-hour sessions to celebrate and reflect upon themes related to growth and development, faith, sacraments, family life, and social justice. The materials are structured so that families split into peer groups for the first hour to study the same theme and then come together for sharing and prayer during the second hour. The program has been used as both a basic program and a supplemental one.

4. Family Liturgical Models. Frequently this model is structured so that families come together for Sunday liturgy but experience the major part of the liturgy of the Word in peer groups and then come together for dialogue and the liturgy of the Eucharist. Some parishes do this effectively at one of the Sunday Masses each week during Advent and Lent.

5. Family Communications Models. Some programs such as *Parent Effectiveness Training*[16] and *Paths of Life: Christian Parenting Series*[17] are geared mainly for parents although other activities may be planned for children while parents are attending sessions. Communications programs (or, more accurately, good communication skills) are vital to any family program. For this reason many parishes begin family catechetical programs by first providing family communications workshops.

6. Together in Prayer and Together with Jesus.[18] In this program participants come together for prayer and study. A leader introduces the study topic, then everyone moves into peer learning groups. At the end of the session, they share discoveries and offer prayers in a community setting.

7. Family Experience Weekends.[19] This model gives families an opportunity to study, pray, and play together.

8. Family Scripture Studies.[20] Family scripture studies, varying in content, purpose, and interaction enable families to see the relationship between Scripture and daily life.

These are but a few of the ways family catechesis can be implemented in a parish. The key to successful implementation is to match the program with the needs and goals. This means that all published programs will probably have to be adapted to meet local needs. The adaptation will give people a chance to use their own creativity and assume real ownership for their program.

For successful implementation of a program many people will need to be involved. In fact, the more people involved in getting it off the ground, the more successful the program will probably be. This means committees will be needed for publicity, recruitment, the organization of materials, welcoming, future planning, and refreshments.

While it is important to sell the idea of family catechesis to as many people as possible in a parish, people should not become dejected if flocks of people do not become part of the program. No program meets everyone's needs. If a small group is ready to begin, start there. To avoid having family catechesis be labeled as elitist, it is important that all have an opportunity to participate. At the same time, lack of numbers should not stop some things from beginning.

The more facets of family catechesis a parish can develop, the better the program will be. If people are not ready to come together as a whole family to learn and pray, they may be ready for a communications workshop, or a family potluck, or a family film night, or a family Lenten supper. All these are different aspects of family catechesis, because they all can help families grow in faith.

Step VII. Evaluate. Evaluation should not be left until a program is over because adjustments frequently have to be made even in a successful program. For this reason it is good to have some sort of evaluation after every session, especially if the program is new. These can be done informally through discussion as people are having coffee or by asking people to fill out evaluation sheets, or by using a telephone committee to call some participants at random to get reactions and suggestions. Along with evaluation should go an ongoing planning committee who will seriously study the evaluative remarks and make adjustments in future plans where feasible.

There are no foolproof recipes for family catechesis, but there are both abundant challenges and resources which can be juxtaposed to enrich family faith life and ultimately the life of the Christian community.

SUMMARY

1. Family catechesis refers to any number of ways that a family as a unit, or individual family members, grow in faith. The focus is generally on the family as a unit. Family catechesis includes proclaiming the message of the gospel, motivating to service, bonding in community, praying, and worshipping.

2. There is a strong foundation for family catechesis based on historical, sociological, and theological research. The strongest catechetical

tradition in the Church points to family catechesis. Sociologists point to the family as the place where religious values are transmitted.

3. Effective planning is the key to successful catechetical programs involving the family. Accurate needs assessments, effective goal-setting, and creative implementation, along with ongoing evaluation are key steps in the planning process.

CHAPTER NOTES

1. Department of Education, U.S. Catholic Conference. *Sharing the Light of Faith: The National Catechetical Directory for Catholics in the United States* (Washington, D.C.: U.S. Catholic Conference, 1979).
2. William C. McCready, "Parenting: A Sociological Perspective," *New Catholic World* (November/December 1979), p. 244.
3. Ibid., p. 245.
4. Kenneth Keniston and The Carnegie Council on Children, *All Our Children: The American Family Under Pressure* (New York: Harcourt, Brace, Jovanovich, 1977).
5. Teilhard de Chardin, *The Divine Milieu* (New York: Harper and Row, 1965).
6. Leslie A. Hart, *How the Brain Works* (New York: Basic Books, 1976).
7. "Decree on the Laity" (No. 11), "Christian Education" (No. 3), "Constitution on the Church" (No. 11), in *Vatican Council II: The Conciliar and Post Conciliar Documents* (Northport, N.Y.: Costello Publishing, 1975).
8. *Sharing the Light of Faith,* op. cit., para. 177.
9. Ibid., para. 178.
10. National Conference of Catholic Bishops, U.S. Catholic Conference, *A Vision and Strategy: The Plan of Pastoral Action for Family Ministry* (Washington, D.C.: U.S. Catholic Conference, 1978).
11. National Conference of Catholic Bishops, U.S. Catholic Conference, *Sounds of the Family: A Pastoral Listening and Planning Workbook* (Washington, D.C.: U.S. Catholic Conference, 1979).
12. Department of Education, U.S. Catholic Conference. *Family-Centered Catechesis* (Washington, D.C.: U.S. Catholic Conference, 1979).
13. Margaret Sawin, *Family Enrichment with Family Clusters* (Philadelphia: Judson Press, 1979).
14. Center for Family Learning Teams, Inc., P. O. Box 42, Mt. Vernon, VA 22121.
15. Program published by Paulist Press, 545 Island Rd., Ramsey, NJ 07446.
16. Dr. Thomas Gordon, *Parent Effectiveness Training* (New York: David McKay Co., 1970).
17. Jean Marie Hiesberger, ed., *Paths of Life: Christian Parenting Series* (New York: Paulist Press, 1979).
18. Published by Twenty-Third Publications, West Mystic, CT 06355.
19. Materials available from William Sadlier, Inc., 11 Park Place, New

York, NY 10007, as well as Twenty-Third Publications, West Mystic, CT 06355.
20. Materials available on family Scripture from Paulist Press, Ramsey, NJ 07446, and Our Sunday Visitor, Inc., P. O. Box 920, Huntington, IN 46750.

SUGGESTED READINGS

DeGidio, Sandra, OSM. *Sharing Faith in the Family.* West Mystic, Conn.: Twenty-Third Publications, 1980. The author of this book has built its content on sound religious education principles. She also separates principles from specific designs. There is a good annotated bibliography.

Sawin, Margaret. *Family Enrichment with Family Clusters.* Philadelphia: Judson Press, 1979. This book offers a practical guide to religious education through family groupings. It is especially good on ideas for getting people to know one another better, and is excellent in terms of communication skills.

United States Catholic Conference, *Family Centered Catechesis.* Washington, D.C.: U.S. Catholic Conference, 1979. This booklet is especially good on needs assessment.

Parish as the Environment for Sacramental Preparation

Maureen A. Kelly

Program Coordinator for the Center for Pastoral Life and Ministry in Kansas City, Missouri, Ms. Kelly has served as Diocesan Director of Religious Education and a member of the Worship Commission in Grand Island, Nebraska, and as national religion consultant for Silver Burdette publications. She holds an M.A. in theology from the Catholic University of Louvain, Belgium, and has written extensively on sacramental preparation.

Sacraments and Renewal

On December 4, 1963, the Church promulgated the "Dogmatic Constitution on the Sacred Liturgy." That date marked the beginning of the renewal and revitalization of the Church's liturgy. Eleven years after that document, all of the rituals had been revised.

As a part of renewal, pastors and pastoral staffs began educational programs for parents of children who were preparing for first penance and First Eucharist. Yet there was little realization that what Ralph Kiefer later said about the implementation of the *Rite of Christian Initiation of Adults* was true about the renewal of all the rites:

> The attempt to reform the rites of initiation has issued in the promulgation of rites which are, historically and culturally speaking, a massive rejection of the presuppositions both of pastoral practice and of most church-goers regarding the true meaning of Church membership. This is a revolution quite without precedent. . . . Such an approach is either suicide or prophecy of a very high order.[1]

During the 1960s and 1970s many parishes put their *doing* far ahead of their *being*. For the most part, reform took place but not renewal. Programs became the question, the answer, and the cause of burn-out for pastoral staffs and parents alike. The questions were: "How do we schedule all these programs?" "How do we motivate parents?" "Do we mandate attendance?" Parents had other questions, including: "Why do we have to go to these meetings?" Attitudes were in transition on the part of those who were doing sacramental preparation and on the part of those who were receiving it.

The questions began around sacramental preparation programs for children with parental involvement, but they expanded into marriage preparation, pre-baptismal programs for parents of infants, and the initiation of adults into the Church. The pragmatic questions of the last two decades are still being asked; but as parishes experience the implementation of the *Rite of Christian Initiation of Adults* and have experiences of sacramental preparation programs which touch participants' lives, the questions become more profound and can be boiled down to: "How do we introduce a conversion process into sacramental preparation programs?"

Old attitudes and symbols die slowly within the hearts of pastoral staffs and parishioners no matter how up to date theology or pastoral practice may seem. Parishes which reform their liturgies and sacramental programs are to be commended, not criticized. It is out of this experience of doing that people are beginning to see the whole of sacramental life and process and to develop renewed attitudes and new structures for sacramental preparation.

A New Emphasis

The change of rites was a symbol of a more basic shift. It is not primarily a change in how to do the rite or to prepare for it, but rather a shift in the foundation: How are we as a sacramental people? How do we, as Church, make Jesus present? How do we facilitate, in sacramental preparation, the faith that is "expressed and deepened in worship"?[2]

The practice of sacramental preparation in the first half of the twentieth century had specific emphases:

1. The focus was on individuals whether children or adults.
2. The catechesis for sacraments was in objective, legal terms.
3. Sacramental preparation ordinarily followed a school model.

In designing and developing sacramental preparation programs today, parish staffs need to let go of these former emphases and enable parishioners to let go as well.

The post-conciliar years have produced the foundation for a shift in these emphases, at least in theory: First, the renewal of ecclesiology and sacramentology is well noted in the theology that underlies the revision of all the rites, in that they all stress communal celebration of the sacraments. It becomes more apparent in the *Rite of Christian Initiation of Adults* that not only are they celebrated as a community but that the community is the catechizer and the preparer.[3] The notion that sacraments are things done to individuals by individuals who mediate for God is unorthodox. The notion that sacraments are prepared for by individuals is also suspect, an idea that has implications for sacramental preparation programs.

Second, the movement of the notion of sacrament from sign to symbol, object to action, "magic" to mystery, and thing to encounter definitely affects the content of sacramental preparation programs. Formerly people seemed to be satisfied with teaching about how the sacraments worked. As Richard McBrien noted:

> Accordingly it seemed to make little difference if the congregation failed to group the meaning of the words and rituals of the Eucharist and other sacraments, so long as the sacraments were validly administered by an authorized minister, using the prescribed matter and form to a properly disposed recipient.[4]

Today the Church instructs:

> Those who have charge of the religious instruction of children ... should be careful when they are introducing them gradually to the mystery of salvation, to give emphasis to instruction on the Mass. Instruction about the Eucharist ... should aim to convey the meaning of the Mass through the principal rites and prayers. It should also explain the place of the Mass in participation in the life of the Church.[5]

The Church has moved the traditional content of sacramental preparation programs away from concentrating on bread and wine, the form of absolution, or the matter of oil to the action of the sacrament and the community.

In some ways the third shift sums up the first two and becomes the critical issue facing parishes in the process of sacramental preparation. As people begin to sense that there is a connection between the seven sacraments, that they are not seven isolated moments, that they are celebrations of radical and ongoing conversion in the life of the Church and the individual, the task of sacrament preparation programs become conversion and not instruction. As James Dunning[6] puts it:

> Both catechesis and liturgy ... have the following priorities. They
are:

More centered on:	Than on:
Conversion	Knowledge
Personal Change	"Changes in the Church"
Heart	Head
Growth in Community	Growth in Private
Journey	Arrival
Adults	Children
Faith	"the" faith
Imagination	Logic
Right Hemisphere of the brain	Left Hemisphere
Appreciation	Information

Mystery	Fact
Values	Law
Gift	Problem

Taking all of this into consideration, what are some things a parish must do in order to be successful in sacramental preparation?

Sacramental Preparation and Parish Renewal

The effectiveness and success of a given sacramental preparation program cannot be isolated from the way faith is lived in a parish or from the quality of its liturgy. The first step, as difficult and extraneous as it may seem, lies not in choosing the best textbook program but rather in parish renewal.

Parishes can learn something about renewal by looking at some of the programs on the market.[7] The programs combine small group activities of discussion and scripture study with large group activities. The heart of any of these programs is a content and method that has to do with community building.

This type of approach begins to help people talk about faith in their lives and leads to the "aha" experience of connecting liturgy to life. It takes theological jargon (like paschal mystery, conversion, dying and rising, and being reconciled) and brings it into the fiber of the lived experience of the marketplace. The integration of parish liturgies and homilies to the overall formational program is also a significant component of any process.

Parish renewal always calls forth a ministering community. The success of parish renewal, from the beginning planning stages into ongoing development, depends on training lay leaders who will work with parish staffs in planning and implementing renewal processes. Training is important if lay leaders are to experience both competence and confidence. Besides training, structures that foster mutual accountability need to be set up between pastoral staffs and lay leaders. To be effective in sacramental preparation, the pastor and staff have to realize that they cannot do it alone, nor are they supposed to.

There is another aspect to parish renewal which is critical to sacramental preparation. It revolves around the fact that there is remote preparation for sacraments as well as immediate preparation (that is, "the program"). The remote preparation is probably more crucial than immediate preparation. It is the preparation that occurs where most people live their lives — in family; and experience the Church — in liturgy. It is time for parishes to be as concerned about ongoing family ministry and development of liturgical ministry as they are about the immediate programs.

The test of how serious parishes are about this remote preparation will be apparent in their budget. However, many of the pragmatic and attitudinal questions about programming will disappear if parishes seriously consider these areas. Parents will begin to experience support from the local

Church not only for themselves but also for the development of their children's faith long before it is time for First Communion. Perhaps at that point parishes will realize in practice what they have held in theory: that parents are the primary educators of their children.

Parish staff people involved in sacramental preparation need to take on "the mind" and attitude expressed by the renewed rites, that is, attitudes of welcoming, inviting, and journeying. Programs will have to be offered without a legalistic, paternalistic, or messianic attitude. It is the role of the staff to provide opportunities. Genuine renewal cannot be legislated.

The RCIA Model

The most successful programs for adults or children will be those that follow a catechumenate process.[8] They will be evaluated on the following criteria:

1. Are they being done in "the midst of the community"? Does the parish know there are members preparing for baptism or confirmation? Articles in the parish bulletin or newsletter make people more aware. Other means of making sacramental preparation more public to the community are: praying for those preparing for particular sacraments during the Eucharist, and calling forth groups for specific recognition during the Liturgy.

One parish liturgy committee combined this calling forth with the Advent theme of waiting. The invitation was extended to those preparing for marriage, the birth of a child, confirmation, and First Eucharist to be present at a particular Liturgy on a specific Sunday. The homilies integrated the experience of waiting and preparing with the liturgical season and an understanding of sacramental celebration as process and gift. The groups were then called forth, blessed, and promised the support of the community.

2. Does the catechesis for the program involve a sponsoring element? In the case of children, the sponsor is usually a parent. Parishes which have committed themselves to this provide other adult sponsors in cases where the parent cannot or will not minister in this capacity. As parishes become more aware of the community's responsibility to all those it initiates, the question of refusing sacraments (most significantly, baptism) to young people whose parents' practice of the faith is in question becomes clearer. Once the child has been welcomed into the community, that community has a responsibility to follow through.

The sponsoring role is well developed in adult initiation. It is very apparent in children's initiation and preparation for reconciliation. An area which seems to be developing and needs to be supported and attended to is the sponsoring in marriage preparation. Parishes in the Diocese of Kansas City-St. Joseph have developed, with the help of the Office of Marriage and Family Life, lead couples. These couples are chosen by the pastor or parish staff because of the strength and witness of their own sacramental marriage. They are trained in listening and counseling skills, and given background in theology of marriage and Church teaching. They are the ones to whom engaged couples are sent for marriage preparation.

3. Does the program provide for a variety of ministers? In other words, who does the program? Are there ministers of hospitality whose role is to welcome and make comfortable? These people stand at the door and welcome the participants, introduce strangers to each other, provide name tags, refreshments, and in some instances baby-sitters.

Who are the catechists? Is it always the professional staff person, or has the staff person been an enabler for others? Mention has already been made of the ministry of sponsor. Does the program incorporate people who minister in the areas of prayer and liturgy? The question for parish staffs is how to get these people. Many parishes have been successful in recruiting people who have been through the program before by asking at the end of the program for volunteers for these areas.

A pastoral associate who was in charge of pre-baptismal preparation in a large parish invites couples back with their baby after they have been through the program. These couples act as greeters and catechists in the first session of the new program, welcoming the nervous parent- or parents-to-be, sharing formally and informally their experience of the process they have been through, both of birth and baptism. Her comment after she began doing this was: "What a difference! We break down all kinds of barriers and really form a support group."

Some parishes integrate youth service projects in youth ministry and confirmation programs with babysitting or music ministry for liturgy and prayer services. Others identify people who are sick or shut-ins and invite them to be the "pray-ers" for a specific group or individual. This is most successful when there is some communication between the "pray-er" and the preparer. People who are pessimistic about recruiting volunteers must reflect on the fact that a basic adult need is to be needed. A personal invitation is very successful in recruiting volunteers, as is giving the person a specific task with which he or she feels comfortable. Affirmation and support along the way keep the volunteer going.

4. Does the content and method of the program integrate ordinary experience and tradition? Is it suitable to the developmental level of the participant and does it flow out of an understanding of the basic theological themes that underlie the rite? Programs that invite conversion are usually ones that respect the experiences of the participants and probe those experiences through storytelling, faith-sharing, prayer, and celebration.

Recognizing Adults

In cases where adults are participating, program planners should take seriously Malcolm Knowles' principles of adult education and James Fowler's stages of faith development. Malcolm Knowles identifies the adult learner as one who comes to the learning experience with high motivation, a developed self-concept, and experience which needs to be respected. For purposes of clarity, distinctions should be made among the adult who comes for his or her own preparation for Christian initiation, the adults who come for marriage preparation, and the parents who are "required" to participate in sacramental preparation for their children.

In each of these cases there are some general norms that flow out of Knowles' theory. They are:

1. Programming spaces need to be environments that are conducive to adult learning. Elementary-school classrooms do not meet this need. Homes do, as do rooms in a parish plant that are attractive and furnished for adults. Comfortable rooms in the rectory or convent often can provide the atmosphere for adult learning.

2. Basic to the content of any of these programs are the experiences that the participants bring to it. The role of the catechist in these situations is to find ways to facilitate the telling of these experiences and to connect them to Catholic tradition. Malcolm Knowles' insights in this area are valuable:

> Because an adult defines himself largely by his experience, he has a deep investment in its value. And so when he finds himself in a situation in which his experience is not being used, or its worth is minimized, it is not just his experience that is being rejected — he feels rejected as a person.
>
> These differences in experience between children and adults have at least three consequences for learning: (1) Adults have more to contribute to the learning of others, for most kinds of learning; (2) adults have a richer foundation of experience to which to relate new experiences (and new learnings tend to take on meaning as we are able to relate them to our past experiences); and (3) adults have acquired a larger number of fixed habits and patterns of thought, and therefore tend to be less open-minded.[9]

The adult who comes for sacramental initiation through the RCIA usually arrives highly motivated for the process, with his or her experience but not with what one might term "the baggage" of pre-conciliar days. Probably that is why parish staffs who minister in this area find the process so satisfying and rewarding.

The parents who are "required" to be part of a sacramental preparation program for their children are too often heard to say: "How boring," "It was a waste of my time," or "I still don't know what to do to help my child prepare." The first two comments usually point to a program that did not take the adult into consideration in the planning of content and in a method that involved him or her. The third comment points to a program that did not integrate the faith formation element with the practical "how to's."

Parishes also might reflect on the question: Is adult education the only way that parents can be involved? A well-integrated sacramental initiation program for children will always involve ritual. Rituals which are well celebrated often affect the faith formation and development of the adults as much as, if not more than, parent sessions.

In today's society of working couples and single parents, time for family becomes a precious commodity. Successful parishes will provide options. For example, parish staff or lay leaders will go out to homes for visitation of parents or to do some family catechesis.

Some parishes provide family cluster programs where several families join together to reflect and learn about the sacraments together. Other parishes provide a basic preparation program every year which is family-oriented and families choose if "this is the year" for them. This necessitates giving up a set age or grade level for sacramental preparation.

It is obvious from what has been said that successful sacramental programs are those which provide for community building, a comfortable atmosphere, a respect for persons, and time for prayer, reflection, and growth.

The answers are not simple because what the Church is about in sacramental preparation is complex and speaks of the whole of Christian life and the mystery of person.

SUMMARY

1. The revision of the sacramental rites signaled a change not only in how we do sacraments and sacramental preparation but also in our view of what Church and sacraments are.

2. Successful sacramental preparation demands a shift in emphasis from the individual to the community, from sacraments as objects to sacraments as actions, from instruction to conversion.

3. Parish renewal is integral to successful sacramental preparation because remote preparation is even more crucial than immediate preparation.

4. The process and model of sacramental preparation provided by the RCIA is useful for other sacramental preparation processes.

5. All sacramental preparation programs deal with adults. To be effective, programs need to be based on principles of adult learning.

CHAPTER NOTES

1. Ralph A. Keifer, "Christian Initiation: The State of the Question," in *Made Not Born* (Notre Dame, Ind.: Murphy Center for Liturgical Research, 1976), pp. 149-50.
2. *Sharing the Light of Faith: National Catechetical Directory* (Washington, D.C.: U.S. Catholic Conference, 1979), No. 113.
3. Richard Linz, "The Catechumenate: The Community as Catechist," in *Christian Initiation Resources,* Vol. 1, No. 1 (New York: William H. Sadlier), pp. 8, 9-93.

4. Richard P. McBrien, *Catholicism,* Vol. II (Minneapolis: Winston Press, 1980), p. 734.
5. "Instruction on Eucharistic Worship," Sacred Congregation of Rites (Rome: May, 1967), No. 14.
6. James B. Dunning, *New Wine, New Wineskins* (New York: William H. Sadlier, 1981), p. 37.
7. Ibid., p. 105.
8. "Renew" (Paulist Press), "Christ Renews His Parish" (Sadlier), "Genesis II" and "Romans VIII" (Intermedia Foundation).
9. Malcolm S. Knowles, *The Modern Practice of Adult Education* (Chicago: Follett Publishing Co., 1976), p. 44.

SUGGESTED READINGS

Dunning, James. *New Wine, New Wineskins.* New York: William H. Sadlier, 1981. While this book focuses on the *Rite of Christian Initiation of Adults,* the principles Dunning uses are very useful for all sacramental preparation.

Groome, Thomas H. *Christian Religious Education — Sharing Our Story and Vision.* San Francisco: Harper and Row, 1980. Although scholarly, this book offers major insights on the relationship between the Church's story and the personal story of individuals. It may be the most important book in the area of religious education in the 1980s.

Ministry with Handicapped People: A Mutual Effort

Mary Vernon Gentile, RSM
and
The Rev. Patrick P. Cullen

A Sister of Mercy of the Union of the Baltimore province, Sister Mary Vernon has served as the Associate Director of the Apostolate with Mentally Retarded Persons for the Diocese of Birmingham, Alabama. Currently she is the president-elect of the National Apostolate with Mentally Retarded Persons (NAMRP).

Father Cullen is a priest of the Diocese of Birmingham. He has served as the Director of the Diocesan Apostolate with Mentally Retarded Persons since 1970, and is past president of NAMRP. He is also diocesan liaison of the Emmaus spirituality program for priests of the Diocese of Birmingham.

In downtown Anywhere, U.S.A., urban renewal is taking place. Interestingly, several old hotels are being remodeled and rejuvenated to serve as apartments. Notable among the changes to these older structures is the manner in which the hotels are being prepared to house elderly and handicapped people who want to live in the downtown section of the city. Ramps, railings, and automatic sliding doors are being installed; kitchens and bathrooms are being equipped so that people occupying these apartments can be self-sufficient. In short, all is being done to make sure that the tenants, with their own specific needs, feel at home.

Down the street from one of these apartment buildings, a church is also being remodeled. Storm windows are being installed; stained glass is being repaired; the organ is being moved to the front of the church; a day chapel is being designed in one of the sacristies. Curiously enough, there is no *outward* manifestation of changes in this building that would aim at incorporating the handicapped people who live up the street. The parish does not seem to have the same goal in mind, namely, incorporating handicapped people into the parish community.

Such situations make one wonder if handicapped people are recognized as members of that parish community. Is the door of the parish open to them? Throughout this country, are handicapped persons incorporated into the life of local parishes? Are they allowed full participation in the life of the Church?

Church Documents

The answers to these queries stem from an even more important question: Should the Church bother to incorporate persons who are handicapped into the community? The answer is simple: Christians should bother because Jesus bothered with all people. As the bishops wrote: "The same Jesus who heard the cry for recognition from the handicapped of Judea and Samaria two thousand years ago calls us, His followers, to embrace our responsibility to our own handicapped brothers and sisters. . . ."[1]

There are compelling and powerful bases for ministry to "fringe people" — to societal outcasts — in Scripture. *The Pastoral Statement of U.S. Catholic Bishops on Handicapped People* points out that Jesus was concerned for handicapped people and adds: "The Church that Jesus founded would surely have been derelict had it failed to respond to His example in its attention to handicapped people."[2]

Sharing the Light of Faith: National Catechetical Directory speaks to the need of recognition of persons with handicapping conditions, stating that the goal of specialized catechesis "is to present Christ's love and teaching to each handicapped person in as full and rich a manner as he or she can assimilate"[3] in order to help them "overcome the obstacles they face and achieve as much integration as they can into the larger community of faith."[4] Pope John Paul II made the same point in his "Apostolic Exhortation on Catechetics." Referring to the handicapped, he states, "They have a right, like others their age, to know the 'mystery of faith.' "[5]

When the term "handicapped person" is used, it is employed in the same manner as in the *National Catechetical Directory,* where it is said to include "the mentally retarded, those with learning disabilities, the emotionally disturbed, the physically handicapped, the hard of hearing, the deaf, the visually impaired, the blind, and others."[6]

What the Church Is Doing

The statements are clear. The real question is: What does a family actually find when they look to the parish or local Church community? There are some very elementary statistics available concerning the real situation throughout the United States. The United States Catholic Conference has published two documents which contain this information.

The first reported that 43% of the parishes responding provided special help to slow learners, mentally handicapped, or learning disabled people; 25% provided some kind of services to emotionally disturbed or socially maladjusted people; only 14% provided services for the blind or the deaf. While 44% made some effort to eliminate physical barriers from parish buildings, only 11% provided special liturgies. Very few parishes provided any kind of special education program, not of a catechetical nature, for handicapped people. The range was: 8% for preschool; 18% for school age; 13% for adults; and 8% for the elderly.[7]

The second document sought to determine diocesan priorities in regard to religious education. With 78% of the dioceses in the country responding, only 42% had any explicit reference to the needs of the handicapped, while 11% had an implicit reference. Almost half of the dioceses made no mention of the need.[8]

The statistics support the United States bishops' statement that "efforts to bring handicapped people into the parish community are more likely to be effective if the parishes are supported by offices operating at the diocesan level."[9] What happens in the parish is often a reflection of the priorities of the diocese.

The statistics also show that, at best, families have less than a fifty percent chance of finding a catechetical program that takes into account the needs of their handicapped child or family member. The percentage chance drops much lower when it comes to liturgical considerations or other activities for handicapped people. This is the reality families face.

New Directions

In recent times Church leaders have become aware of the situation and are beginning to address the whole question of the full integration of handicapped people into the life of the total parish community. Difficulties arise because programs of religious education and liturgical celebration aimed at reaching a population of people who are handicapped will not, of themselves, create incorporation of them into the mainstream of the local ecclesial community. They may be prepared to enter the parish community by means of religious education and an awareness of liturgy, but the person who is handicapped must be met by a community of welcome — a community with a positive attitude.

Many people value the position of handicapped people in society, expressing themselves as Pope John Paul II does, saying that "on reflection one may say that a disabled person, with the limitations and sufferings that he or she suffers in body and faculties, emphasizes the mystery of the human being with all its dignity and nobility. When we are faced with a disabled person we are shown the frontiers of human existence, and we are impelled to approach this mystery with respect and love."[10]

In reality, though, the person who is handicapped is most often met with fear, disgust, and repulsion. These reactions, while prevalent in society at large, are also found in Christian churches and communities. They may present themselves in the form of openly failing to initiate programs or provide means of incorporation. More often, the reactions are disguised in the form of misguided beliefs, such as: the individual's diminished mental, emotional, or physical power guarantees that he or she is in no real danger when it comes to eternal salvation; or, he or she cannot make a genuine personal choice with regard to faith or love; or, he or she cannot know what it means to live a life of faith; and he or she "will get to Heaven anyway." The truth is that the handicapped person achieves salvation in exactly the same manner as any other Christian — through the life of the Church, her worship, the sacraments, and all that the parish can afford to give each member in an atmosphere of true welcome.

The notion of welcome and its positive effect is the foundation of the *Pastoral Statement of U.S. Catholic Bishops on Handicapped People*. In this text, the bishops say that "the parish is the door to participation for handicapped individuals, and it is the responsibility of the pastor and lay leaders to make sure that this door is always open."[11] Further, "the parish must make sure that it does not exclude any Catholic who wishes to take part in its activities."[12]

In order to achieve adequate incorporation, the bishops feel that certain positive actions may be necessary (for example, a census to find people with disabilities may need to be made). One often hears that there are too few people to warrant a program.

The options of the pastor and lay leaders of a parish concerned about a person who is handicapped are: to develop a parish program to meet his or her needs; to develop an area program in cooperation with neighboring parishes; or to seek someone to work individually with the handicapped person. All efforts should aim at incorporating the person who is handicapped into his or her own worshipping community. In this regard the bishops state that "no parishioner should be excluded on the basis of disability alone."[13]

They further stress that the most obvious obstacle to parish participation is the physical design of the buildings. Can a person who is in a wheelchair get from the parking lot of the parish church to the sanctuary, alone? Is the rest room accessible? Again, the bishops' statement points out that "mere cost must never be the exclusive consideration, since the provision of free access to religious functions for all interested people is a clear pastoral duty."[14]

Public Worship

With regard to the liturgy, certain elements stand out in recent Church documents. The "General Instruction on the Roman Missal" states that any liturgical action must take into account the nature and circumstances of the assembly.[15] This includes taking into account the psychology and abilities of all those involved in the celebration, both handicapped and non-handicapped. Sometimes, in our efforts, we forget that this also suggests giving some consideration to the priest celebrant and his individual psychology and abilities. In order to celebrate authentic liturgy with handicapped people, a priest does not have to do violence to his own personality.

On the other hand, as the above mentioned "General Instruction" points out: "In planning the celebration, the priest should consider the spiritual good of the assembly rather than his own desires."[16] The sensitivity to the implication of this statement is demonstrated by the use of the word "adaptation" in more recent Church documents. The *Directory for Masses with Children* makes the point that "it does not speak directly of children who are physically or mentally retarded because a broader adaptation is sometimes necessary for them."[17] According to the *National Catechetical Directory* "Masses (and all other sacramental celebrations) for handicapped persons require special adaptations. Each handicapping condition calls for a different approach."[18]

These considerations lead to the question of specialized liturgies, or liturgies which take into account groups with special needs. In providing for the fuller participation of handicapped people in the ritual and for their better understanding of the symbols within the liturgical action, their particular abilities and disabilities must be considered in the planning and celebration of the specialized liturgy.

Let it be noted that this is not an either/or situation. Properly used specialized liturgies and regular parish liturgies serve to complement each other. The use of specialized liturgy has often led to eventual participation on the part of the handicapped person in the regular parish liturgy. In some cases it has even led entire families back to the practice of the sacraments. The trauma surrounding the birth of their handicapped child, the embarrassment of the particular handicapping condition, and sometimes the unwelcome attitude of the parish community has driven many families away from the practice of the faith. However, while defending the validity of specialized liturgies, the bishops also caution against allowing them to further the isolation of the handicapped person. As such, specialized liturgies "should never entirely replace the integration of the handicapped person into the larger worshipping community."[19]

It is also necessary to reflect on the didactic or teaching function that liturgy performs. The "Dogmatic Constitution on the Sacred Liturgy" states that "although the sacred liturgy is principally the worship of the divine majesty it likewise contains much instruction for the faithful" (No. 33). The *National Catechetical Directory* also mentions the close relationship between liturgy and catechesis.[20] They prepare and flow from one another.

The liturgy transmits doctrines, beliefs, and values which in turn shape the person's life. The notable thing is that liturgy involves the whole person. It does not depend upon one sense; it does not even depend on intellect alone. Because of this, liturgy takes on an extraordinary importance in the life of many handicapped people. The first duty of Christians is to gather to celebrate. People do not send their heads or brains to the celebrations; the whole package goes to the celebration: the cognitive, the affective, the psychomotor aspects of the personality. If one part is not functioning, communication can occur through the other channels. Thus liturgy for handicapped people is not just a nice addition to the regular catechetical program. In many cases, it is the best, and at times, the only form of catechesis available because many handicapped children and adults will not be involved in a formal catechetical program.

It is vitally important to stress that all forms of liturgy should be completely accessible to handicapped people "since these forms are the essence of the spiritual tie that binds the Christian Community together. To exclude members of the parish from these celebrations of the life of the Church," the bishops state, "even by passive omission, is to deny the reality of that community."[21] In other words, where handicapped people are unable to participate in the parish worship life, even if this exclusion is unintentional, there is, in fact, in that place *no* Christian community.

Handicapped individuals can and should participate in a more active role in liturgical actions, if provisions and training are made available to them. Liturgy interpreted simultaneously in sign language, large-print, or Braille Mass books and hymnals are examples of the necessary provisions. A person who is blind, with the use of a Braille text, could function as a lector. A person confined to a wheelchair could do one of the scripture readings. There is no reason why a deaf person could not be a special minister of Communion at the Eucharistic Liturgy. Surely, a person who is mentally retarded could bring up the gifts or serve at the altar. We have to create the opportunities for handicapped and non-handicapped people to join hands and break down the barriers that separate them.

A Plan of Action

Who is actually responsible for bringing these provisions to the foreground and thus facilitating implementation in the parish community? According to the bishops: the pastors and lay leaders have this responsibility![22] They must first feel the genuine concern for people who are handicapped. Nothing will ever get started or implemented unless they feel this concern.

The following is a suggested plan. Once the need for help is determined, a group of people (handicapped and non-handicapped) needs to be formed to serve as advocates for the parishioners who are handicapped in one way or another. One of these advocates should serve on each parish council committee to bring the needs of this special segment of the parish to light. This type of constant reference to people with handicapping conditions should bring about a degree of integration but should also suffice to sensitize members of the council to the needs and contributions of this population. The expressed concern will "spill over" to the rest of the parish in time.

Obviously a census of the parish should be taken to identify the members who may have handicapping conditions. With this accomplished, programs to meet the specific needs of these individuals should be designed. The authors, for example, most frequently utilize the *Journey With Jesus* program published at Cardinal Stritch College, Milwaukee, Wisconsin.[23] It has been developed with children and adults who are mentally retarded. It is a sacramental program, comprising three cycles (Eucharist, reconciliation, confirmation) and three levels (readiness, preparation, sacramental living) for each cycle.

There is also in this program a Gospel Study Cycle which takes the Sunday readings for liturgy and constructs a lesson for each. The program includes a lesson, paraliturgy, notes for the teacher, and notes for the parent, plus a director's manual for the exclusive use of the person designated to initiate and direct the activities. This director's manual contains a lengthy and explicit section on how to start a program. This would serve as a valuable reference even if a parish did not intend to utilize the *Journey With Jesus* program, or if a program was being designed for people with handicapping conditions other than mental retardation.

In addition to the catechetical program, the handicapped should also be included in the social events of the parish, and not automatically excluded because of their condition. To say that a blind teenager *cannot* go skating with the youth group is presumptuous. The fact may be that the person is not able to skate, but he or she, nonetheless, may enjoy being part of the group and sharing in the activities to the degree possible. The individual should always have the opportunity for participation presented to him or her. It is unfortunate that many times handicapped people, especially in their adult years, are deprived of participation in social events because of a lack of transportation. Parishes serious about incorporating handicapped people into social events must be aware of this need and be willing to provide transportation.

An adequate program for and with handicapped people should absolutely be centered in the worship of the parish. This aspect is the one place where the priest of the parish must take the leadership role in initiating and sustaining incorporation of these members of the parish. Handicapped people need the priesthood. They need the spiritual gifts which the priest was entrusted with by virtue of his ordination. Only the parish priest can bring the handicapped person into the full sacramental life of the Church. Teachers represented by that parish can only go so far.

Nowhere is that need more evident than in the liturgical life of the parish. Thus the incorporation of handicapped people into the liturgical life of the parish community demands not only the good will of the priest but also his physical presence. The physical presence of the priest to his handicapped parishioners is not just a nice thing to do, it is demanded by the Gospel. This is the beginning of full incorporation; it is also its end.

SUMMARY

1. The basis for ministry to and with handicapped people is found in scriptural accounts of Jesus' ministry with marginal people.

2. The term "handicapped people" includes those who are mentally retarded, and those who have learning disabilities or emotional disturbances. It also includes individuals who are physically handicapped, hard of hearing or deaf, visually impaired or blind, and all others whose disability sets them apart from the rest of the parish.

3. Studies show that ministry to handicapped people is a felt need. The available statistics show that families have less than a fifty percent chance of finding a catechetical program that takes into account the needs of their handicapped child or family member. (The percentage drops much lower when it comes to liturgical considerations or other activities for handicapped people.)

4. While the need for ministry to and with the handicapped is being more frequently addressed, the initiation of programs of catechetics or involvement in liturgy will not bring about incorporation unless the fear of handicapped people is eliminated and an atmosphere of welcome is established.

5. The bishops in their *Pastoral Statement* concerning handicapped people stress that this segment of the community looks to the parish as the door to participation in the Church. They further emphasize that it is the role of the pastor and lay leaders to make certain that this door is never closed to anyone wishing to participate in the life of the Church.

6. Specialized liturgies for and with handicapped people serve to complement regular parish liturgies, but should never replace them. The handicapped person needs to be part of the larger worshipping community.

7. Since liturgy involves the whole person — the cognitive, affective, and psychomotor — communication can occur, even if one or more channels is affected by a disabling condition.

8. Liturgy has a teaching function, and as such is a necessary ingredient in a total catechetical program designed to include the handicapped.

9. In order to facilitate incorporation, a census should be taken to discover individuals in need of assistance and to develop suitable programs accordingly. Buildings need to be examined with a view to removing physical barriers; and necessary provisions should be made to create active involvement in liturgy, for example, liturgy interpreted simultaneously in sign language, Braille or large-print hymnals; adaptations in liturgy should be made where deemed necessary and appropriate. A group of advocates should be formed at the parish level who would call to mind the needs of individuals who are handicapped in all areas of the local parish community. Inclusion in the social aspects of the parish is also a requisite for full incorporation.

10. An adequate program for and with handicapped people should be centered in the worship life of the parish. This is the aspect of parish life where the priest takes the leadership role in initiating and sustaining incorporation of those who are handicapped. The handicapped need the priesthood and the physical presence of the priest(s) in the parish.

CHAPTER NOTES

1. United States Catholic Conference, *Pastoral Statement of U.S. Catholic Bishops on Handicapped People* (Washington, D.C.: U.S. Catholic Conference, Publications Office, 1978), p. 1.
2. Ibid., p. 2.
3. National Conference of Catholic Bishops, *Sharing the Light of Faith: National Catechetical Directory for Catholics of the United States* (Washington, D.C.: U.S. Catholic Conference, Department of Education, 1979), No. 195, p. 118.
4. Ibid., No. 196, p. 119.
5. Pope John Paul II, "Apostolic Exhortation on Catechetics," *Origins: N.C. Documentary Service* (November, 1979), No. 41, p. 339.
6. *National Catechetical Directory,* op. cit., No. 195, p. 118.
7. United States Catholic Conference, *A National Inventory of Parish Catechetical Programs* (Washington, D.C.: U.S. Catholic Conference, Publications Office, 1978).
8. Andrew D. Thompson, Ph.D., and Rev. Robert Stamschror, *A Survey of U.S. Diocesan Statements and Objectives for Religious Education and Catechesis* (Washington, D.C.: U.S. Catholic Conference, Department of Education, 1979).
9. *Pastoral Statement,* op. cit., p. 9.
10. Pope John Paul II, "Vatican Statement: The International Year of Disabled Persons," *Origins: N.C. Documentary Service* (May, 1981), p. 747.
11. *Pastoral Statement,* op. cit., p. 6.
12. Ibid., p. 7.
13. Ibid.
14. Ibid.
15. "General Instruction of the Roman Missal," *The Sacramentary* (New York: Catholic Book Publishing, 1974), No. 3, p. 20.
16. Ibid.
17. "Directory for Masses with Children," *The Sacramentary* (New York: Catholic Book Publishing, 1974), No. 6, p. 53.
18. *National Catechetical Directory,* op. cit., No. 138, p. 78.
19. Ibid.
20. *National Catechetical Directory,* op. cit., No. 113, p. 66.
21. *Pastoral Statement,* op. cit., p. 7.
22. Ibid., p. 6.
23. Sr. M. Sheila Haskett, O.S.F., Ph.D., *Journey With Jesus* (Milwaukee: Cardinal Stritch College, 1975).

SUGGESTED READINGS

Haskett, Sr. M. Sheila, O.S.F., Ph.D., *Journey With Jesus*. Milwaukee: Cardinal Stritch College, 1975. This represents a complete program of special religious education prepared for people who are mentally retarded.

John Paul II, Pope. "Apostolic Exhortation on Catechetics." *Origins: N.C. Documentary Service* (November, 1979), pp. 330-47. This document is a reflection on the 1977 international Synod of Bishops which had catechetics as its theme.

————. "Vatican Statement: International Year of Disabled Persons." *Origins: N.C. Documentary Service* (May, 1981), pp. 747-50. This statement was issued by the Vatican in response to the efforts of the United Nations for the International Year of Disabled Persons.

National Conference of Catholic Bishops. *Sharing the Light of Faith: National Catechetical Directory for Catholics of the United States.* Washington, D.C.: U.S. Catholic Conference, Department of Education, 1979. This text provides the principles and guidelines for catechesis in the United States.

Thompson, Andrew, D., Ph.D., and Rev. Robert Stamschror. *A Survey of U.S. Diocesan Statements and Objectives for Religious Education and Cathechesis.* Washington, D.C.: U.S. Catholic Conference, Department of Education, 1979. This survey was designed to identify the priorities presently found in diocesan statements of catechetical goals and objectives.

United States Catholic Conference. *Pastoral Statement of U.S. Catholic Bishops on Handicapped People.* Washington, D.C.: U.S. Catholic Conference, Publications Office, 1978. This is the first official statement of the U.S. Catholic bishops on ministry with handicapped people.

Ecumenism: Staying Together Apart

The Rev. John Mueller

Ordained for the Diocese of Cleveland in 1959, Father Mueller has served in four parishes. He has been active in the Priests' Senate of Cleveland and has worked for fifteen years in the diocesan Tribunal. Presently he is pastor of a parish in Akron, Ohio.

The Priority

Ecumenism did not begin with the Second Vatican Council, but it received its greatest impetus (for Catholics, at least) from the Council. There were great expectations and great fears. The original expectations may not have been met and the fervor may have subsided somewhat, but almost every parish community has an ecumenical aspect today. It may be positive or negative, progressing or retreating, bold or timid, warm or hostile. But the churches *are* much more aware of each other. Will this parish be a leader? a follower? an observer? Is ecumenism a parish goal or a by-product? Will it be the desire and prayer of the people or the "duty" of the pastoral team, or will we resolve the question by establishing the ever-popular committee and forgetting it?

The History

The human race has an affinity for dividing and splitting, and a compulsion to combine and centralize. Judaism in Jesus' time had theological and political factions and emerging Christianity became another break. Jesus could speak of the "other sheep that are not of this fold" and proclaim that "there shall be one flock, one shepherd" (John 10:16). All recognize the "other sheep." Most hope for "one flock, one shepherd." Many, however, disagree on just whose flock he meant and what "one" means.

In 1910 there was a beginning among Protestants who recognized the scandal of a controverted Gospel. These concerned people met in the Congress of Edinburgh which was followed by meetings in Amsterdam (1948), Evanston (1954), New Delhi (1961), Uppsala (1968), and Nairobi (1975). From these efforts came the World Council of Churches (which has never attempted, or claimed, to be a universal "super-church") and many attempts to unite or combine different denominations. Similar desires are today expressed by churches not affiliated with the World Council.

The Roman Catholic Church, at first hesitant to become deeply involved for fear of dogmatic relativism, gradually entered the movement. Pope John XXIII introduced a new mood in the Vatican Council. As he told the representatives from the many churches invited to observe: "We do not intend to conduct a trial of the past, we do not want to prove who was right and who was wrong. All we want to say is: Let us come together. Let us make an end of our division."

The Theology

Archbishop John Quinn commented in 1975: "It is noteworthy that the Vatican Council did not begin its treatment of the Church with the 'people of God,' as is frequently but erroneously asserted. The Council began with the Church as mystery. It was the Church as mystery which was to underlie the whole conciliar teaching. It is a reality hidden in God, made manifest in Christ Jesus and spread abroad in the power of the Holy Spirit."[1]

"Ecumenical" has long been used to mean universal or whatever pertains to the whole Christian church, for example, the ecumenical councils. Today, it increasingly means the activities which promote unity among Christians. Strictly speaking, "ecumenical" refers to relations between the various Christian churches; whereas "interfaith" refers to the relations between the Christian churches and religious traditions that are not Christ-centered.

Cardinal Suenens has stated: "The unity of the Church, then, is compatible with a pluralism on the liturgical, canonical, and spiritual planes. But it uncompromisingly requires a fundamental unity in faith. I do not say in theology, for provided that the faith is safe and intact, the Church welcomes a plurality of theologies."[2] This is not to say that unity should be based solely on experience without reference to doctrine. Such a unity would not be the same as that envisioned by the New Testament.[3]

Cardinal Suenens continues: "There is no such thing as a vague, unspecified Christianity, a kind of residue of the differences. . . . Our divisions, which remain a scandal, do not entitle us to define the essential and the secondary in relation to the hazards of history. The first law of ecumenism is to respect the sincere faith of one's fellow Christian; we are already offending his faith when we classify as secondary everything that divides us."[4] The challenge is to expand our understanding of the Church as mystery, not captured by images. An understanding of Church in this light allows for a humble confidence that is not ashamed of differences in belief. Further, it can acknowledge common faults while working toward unity.

The Parish

There are so many and diverse parishes across the country that it becomes almost impossible to make general observations. There are many different kinds of parishes, from the tired parish of the inner city to the vibrant "monster" parishes of the suburbs; the "weekend only" church in the mountains; the nationality parish and the mixed-nationality parish; the "open" parish; the campus parish; and many more — and your parish. Add the variables of the environment within which your parish exists. Do you coexist with many Protestant denominations? with one particularly? Are you the majority in the community, or a substantial minority, or a small minority? Are you a beloved/respected/feared/despised element of the community? Are you growing/surviving/dwindling? Programs and possibilities will vary widely, but there are opportunities in every situation.

Before a Church can reach out, it has to look within. What is its philosophy? What are its fears, its prejudices, its enthusiasms, its commitment? Where are the people — intellectually, emotionally, spiritually? Sometimes, the biggest and greatest program of ecumenism will never even manifest itself formally outside of the parish. The job, like Paul's, may be merely to plant the seed within people and have the greatness to let another Apollos water it, trusting God to make it grow (1 Corinthians 3:6).

The first question is: What is the end result? The place to begin is at home. Do you know those who work in the ministry in your little world — that realm of influence your parish exists in, whether a suburb, a neighborhood, a whole city, a town, or a "hoot 'n' a holler down the road"? Do you know their names, denominations, beliefs, programs, family? Have you ever invited them over — not that vague non-invitation: "Let's get together sometime," but a specific invitation, whether for dinner, prayer, or to discuss some problem? It is better to do this "one on one" first than to gather a group of people who are all strangers to each other and attempt "instant fellowship."

In many circumstances, Catholics are feared, because they are perceived as being different: better educated, for example, or supported by a large, mysterious structure. The goal, therefore, is not to impress but to "set at ease." A sense of humor is invaluable unless it becomes irritating, embarrassing, or smothering. Genuine interest and gentle appreciation build more bridges than a canon law degree or "hitting them with some Latinisms." Obviously, no one can strike up deep, eternal, meaningful friendships with everybody; but it is important to take the initiative.

Communication

In the community's interaction, there are two main ways to communicate. There are opportunities to do things together, and there are opportunities to understand differences. Most common efforts revolve around community problems which affect everyone. For example, cooperation could center on attempts to provide a food bank for an area or collect money for a fuel fund. It could be for joint prayer at Thanksgiving or efforts to lobby city council for proper lighting in a neighborhood. These types of projects usually begin with and follow the leadership of the clergy and only gradually expand to include interested parishioners; but often the links established become long-lasting. "Share programs" (such as those of prayer for unity or peace or to celebrate some event — as when the Iranian hostages were freed) are "safe" beginnings in an area where people feel awkward if they have not worked together before.

The visible presence and witness of Catholic priests, sisters, and lay professionals on civic boards, task forces, and committees can be a valuable encouragement to the laity to participate as long as (1) they are in a field in which they have competence and something to offer, and (2) they never neglect their primary ministry, which is to enable and inspire people to respond — not to do it for them or keep them from participation. The interesting fact is that most Catholics interrelate with people of other faiths on every level — work, school, neighborhood — except on the religious level.

People communicate in the supermarket, on the bus, at a bar, but suddenly feel uncomfortable if invited to pray together or to discuss religion. Some people might feel insecure or afraid when the subject comes up. One way to begin to overcome this is to create situations that put people at ease. To invite a minister from another denomination to talk to adults about his or her particular Church (history, liturgy, beliefs) and answer questions gives the audience a chance to know a new person. It also gives the minister a chance to meet real-life Catholics. It is especially valuable, after the minister has left, for the group to reflect on what they heard and how it relates to their own faith. To invite specific churches to come for a tour and explanation of church buildings, liturgy, symbolism, offers the same opportunity. Many denominations request this for their confirmation classes.

It is not out of line to try to get articles in the local newspapers, especially if it concerns an ecumenical event. Many radio stations would welcome participation of the Catholic clergy in the "minute meditation" type of public service broadcasting.

Obstacles to Dialogue

One of the most difficult obstacles to widespread dialogue is the insecurity many people feel when it comes to expressing their beliefs verbally. After all the preaching, teaching, explaining, and answering that has gone on for years, many parish leaders just assume that everybody has "got the picture." To dispel that notion, just ask twenty people at Mass on the feast of the Immaculate Conception what the feast means. Or ask a group of adults just what makes Catholicism different from other Christian (or even non-Christian) groups. The responses will not be reasons to give up. The point is that ecumenism begins with self-understanding.

An important advantage of dialogue is the realization of how the Catholic Church "comes across" to others. An image of triumphalism, thoughtlessness, and even stupidity can do as much to return the Church to the days of the Reformation than the events that led up to it.

Cardinal Suenens wrote: "In the past, it was necessary to fight fiercely for the recognition of every man's duty, and hence freedom to follow his duly enlightened conscience, for this freedom is a basic human right that all must respect."[5] So much of the hurt and injustice of human history — the religious wars, the Inquisition, the Westphalia Agreement — have been caused by the open or subtle imposition of "my" will, "my" conscience, "my" belief on "you." Dialogue can only be dialogue if each person is free and respected.

Cardinal Suenens continues: "In our current language, the word 'proselytism' has become increasingly synonymous with pressure, manipulation of consciences and violation of freedom. Clearly, this type of proselytism is the very negation of ecumenism. In any discussion, the first duty must always be to understand what the other is really believing and to avoid any distortion of his belief."[6] Catholics in general do not manifest some of the high-pressure "enthusiasms" of other denominations. This could stem from a sense of the Church's not having to prove itself. It has been around for a long time and it is big (and right). Or, it could stem from an unsureness which makes the Church hesitant to argue, especially if it means trading Bible quotes (with chapter and verse).

The Challenge

With so many pitfalls and so much misunderstanding from the past, is ecumenism worth the effort? It is precisely because the possibilities are so great that ecumenism is such a worthy challenge.

What works? There are many things, from formal covenants between parishes to joint social ministry projects, from elaborate public ecumenical prayer/witness services to sharing a panel presentation; from praying together privately to talking together; from guest speakers to FRIENDSHIP — the day-by-day opportunity of every Christian to care, to understand, to work, to share meaning.[7] Ecumenism is not nearly so much a series of projects as it is a desire and attitude and belief in Jesus' desire for unity.

If the whole ecumenical apostolate is limited to a few petitions in the General Intercessions during Church Unity Octave in January, the parish's relationship with the separated brothers and sisters will be minimal. If people do not believe in the power of the Holy Spirit to effect unity, all projects will be fruitless busywork. The prayer that springs from faith and the action that springs from desire is each person's contribution. The unity will be God's gift.

There is a plaque that says:
"To come together is a beginning.
To stay together is progress.
To work together is success."

SUMMARY

1. Ecumenism is just one of the many priorities of every parish. Whether conscious of it or not, each parish is involved in ecumenism.

2. Factionalism has been a part of Christianity from the beginning. In

this century, the Protestant churches were the first to move toward unity, with Catholics hesitantly following after Vatican Council II.

3. The theological starting point for ecumenism is the Council's presentation of the Church as a mystery. Strictly speaking, ecumenism is the working together of Christian churches to bring about a fundamental unity of faith among them.

4. Because parishes are so diverse around the country, each parish must look within itself before it can become seriously ecumenical. Then it must decide what it wants the end result to look like.

5. Practically, most parish ecumenical efforts revolve around those things that churches can do together and those times when they try to understand each other's traditions.

6. A major obstacle to dialogue is the insecurity many Catholics feel when they try to articulate their faith. Feelings of superiority and attempts at proselytizing also get in the way.

7. Although many things "work" in ecumenism, the fundamental basis is the desire for unity which flows from belief in Jesus' desire for unity.

CHAPTER NOTES

1. Archbishop John Quinn, "Characteristics of the Pastoral Planner," *Origins: N.C. Documentary Service* (January, 1976), p. 439.
2. Cardinal Leo Suenens, *Ecumenism and Charismatic Renewal* (Ann Arbor: Servant Books, 1978), p. 11.
3. *Theological Renewal* (April-May, 1977).
4. Suenens, op. cit., pp. 11-12.
5. Suenens, op. cit., p. 69.
6. Suenens, op. cit., p. 71.
7. The Glenmary Research Center in Washington, D.C., has studied and documented many projects that are particularly useful in rural areas. The Center's contributions in the areas of ecumenism and evangelization are well known and respected.

SUGGESTED READINGS

Suenens, Leo, Cardinal. *Ecumenism and Charismatic Renewal.* Ann Arbor, Mich.: Servant Books, 1978. This small book by a well-known leader in both ecumenism and the charismatic renewal is an excellent summary of the history and the theology of both. He likewise strives to show the relationship between the two. It is written with clarity and depth. It does not stop with merely theoretical aspects but includes many excellent pastoral insights.

Guidelines for Ecumenical and Interfaith Activities for the Diocese of

Cleveland. Diocese of Cleveland, Ohio: 1979. This policy statement and guideline written by Bishop James Hickey, now of Washington, D.C., is both scholarly and pastoral. It is broad in its scope and specific in its applications. It reflects an openness and warmth which is edifying as well as practical.

Idea Book for Small-Town Churches. Washington, D.C.: Glenmary Research Center, 1976. This is a how-to book drawn from experiences and experiments of many parish communities. Written primarily for rural and small-town situations, many of the practical plans can be adapted to just about any parish.

Social Ministry

Suzanne Golas, CSJP

A Sister of St. Joseph of Peace, Sister Suzanne heads the Department of Human Concerns of the Archdiocese of Newark. She has taught in Catholic schools and been involved in parish ministry. Her present position involves helping to develop parish social action efforts. She was a member of the team responsible for implementation of RENEW, an archdiocesan effort at parish renewal which emphasizes spirituality, justice formation, and social action.

After surveying dioceses throughout the country, the National Conference of Catholic Bishops' Committee on the Call to Action Plan issued a statement in the fall of 1980. The committee reported that "bishops feel strongly that social justice is not a priority for white middle-class Catholics and their parishes."[1]

Parish ministers have frequently observed that social action or social concerns committees in parishes are often the weakest committees, least sure of their purpose and goals. Why that is the case may not be as important as how to change the situation. However, since people make the how-to's work, it is important to look briefly at people who make up the Catholic Church in the United States.

An Immigrant Church

For the most part, American Catholics are a people of rather recent immigrant, foreign background. They have worked hard, often in the face of hostility and with a sense of alienation, to participate and share in what they perceived as the "American dream." Today, statistics show that, socioeconomically, professionally, and educationally, many Catholics have achieved their goal.

In the process, however, they have often taken an uncritical position toward American secular values. And as they have become mainstreamed in a highly technological and increasingly complex society they have also seen how the complex social evils and needs of society have become less the concern of close, personal, ethnic parish communities and more the responsibility of government agencies.

It is time for American Catholics to examine more closely their responsibility to the needy, the sick, the alienated, and the oppressed. Hopefully, the Church has "come of age" and is now able to critique more consistently the values, systems, and structures that sometimes support social ills, rather than social progress.

Despite its upward mobility, the Church remains diversified. There are still ethnic parishes. Many Catholics are blue-collar, middle-class workers. The most recent newcomers, though often materially poor, enrich the Church with a culture in which different values are emphasized. All of this can be of great help in any efforts to understand the Church's social mission, and to respond with a fresh vigor that is rooted in the gospel and the teachings of the Church.

The Scriptures

Jesus says: "Seek first his kingdom and his righteousness, and all these things shall be yours as well" (Matthew 6:33).

The Justice of God

The justice of which Jesus speaks is rooted in the Old Testament. For Israel, justice can be described as fidelity to the demands of a relationship. In contrast to modern individualism, the Israelite of the Old Testament was in a world where to "live" was to be united with others in a social context, by bonds of family or covenant relationship. This web of relationships — king with people, family with tribe or kinfolk, community with resident alien and suffering in their midst, and all with the Covenant God — constituted the world in which Old Testament life unfolded.

Justice was related to the Covenant. Yahweh initiated a quality of relationship with his people and demanded a similar quality of relating in the way his people dealt with one another.

This justice of God was personified, made incarnate, took flesh in Jesus.

The Kingdom of God

The kingdom of God is not a place, not an abstraction, not something purely of the future, nor entirely now. The kingdom is both the "already" and the "not yet."

The kingdom is about a new relationship with God made possible now, in and through Jesus. The sign of and testimony to this relationship is the manner in which people deal with one another.

The kingdom is the power of God active in this world confronting the powers of evil and transforming the world into a place of love and justice, a place of right relationships. The kingdom is very much rooted in this world as Jesus is incarnate and rooted in this world. Jesus made present the love

and saving mercy of God to those whom social structures of the time classified as outcasts. He chose to align himself with the poor, sinners, orphans,
and widows.

In the Gospels the proclamation of the kingdom is followed by the calling of the disciples. Discipleship involves commitment to following Jesus in
living the quality and kind of life Jesus led by:

- Working for right relationships among people.
- Confronting the powers of evil, including persecution, exploitation,
poverty, and ignorance.
- Aligning oneself with those in need.

What Does the Church Say?

The Church has always taught the importance of service as described
in the corporal works of mercy. However, it was only at the end of the nine-
teenth century that the Church began to articulate Catholic social doctrine
in Pope Leo XIII's 1891 encyclical, *Rerum Novarum.*

Richard McBrien defines Catholic social doctrine as "a clearly discernible body of the official teachings on the social order, in its economic
and political dimensions. It is concerned with the dignity of the human person as created in the image of God, with human rights and duties which pro-
tect and enhance this dignity, with the radically social nature of human existence, with the nature of society and of the state, with the relationship between society and state . . . and with voluntary associations, e.g., labor unions, which serve as a buffer and a bridge between state and society."[2]

It is unfortunate that many Catholics, including clergy and religious,
are ignorant of the principles of Catholic social doctrine as presented in official Church documents such as *Mater et Magistra, Pacem in Terris,* the
Second Vatican Council's "Pastoral Constitution on the Church in the
Modern World" and the Third International Synod of Bishops' *Justice in
the World.*

Those Catholics who have recognized the importance of these documents often complain that: "You never hear social justice from the pulpit,"
and "Social issues are not part of our parish's adult education program."

The challenge of social concerns committees, of parish ministers and
educators is to understand Catholic social doctrine and to communicate it
by relating it to the political, economic, and social realities of everyday life.
Current events leave no doubt that these teachings have much to say.

What Should a Parish Do?

There is a man named Al. He's been in a parish renewal group. One
night when the group started discussing social issues and justice, Al said,
"That has nothing to do with my relationship with God. That's Jane Fonda
stuff." Today, Al, with his renewal group, is learning about world hunger
and regularly organizes collections for the hungry at the plant where he
works.

There is a woman named Wilma. She lives in a poor neighborhood in one of the poorest cities in the country. Wilma desperately wanted to work for the good of the city. Today Wilma is a member of the executive committee of a coalition of six parishes that have organized and successfully challenged the city government on issues such as housing and unemployment.

There is a man named John. He chairs his parish social concerns committee. This year John left his position as a sales manager for an industrial products firm in order to work in a diocesan effort to develop parish social concerns committees. He did this at a seventy-five percent decrease in salary.

Al, Wilma, and John represent the diversity of parishes within a large northeastern diocese and within the Church of the United States. They come from a blue-collar, ethnic parish, an inner-city minority parish and an affluent, suburban parish. They share a common faith, a faith, which, for each of them, has prompted a commitment to social involvement. There are other common factors that relate to their commitment. An examination of these common factors provides important insights into how social ministry develops in a parish.

Some of these common factors are:

1. The social involvement of each of them has been awakened or deepened through a *parish spiritual renewal* experience.

2. Each of them is an ordinary *"people in the pew"* Catholic.

3. Their commitment has been nurtured by a *small supportive community.*

Parish Spiritual Renewal

At the Third International Synod of Bishops in 1971 the bishops stated:

> Actions on behalf of justice and participation in the transformation of the world fully appear to us as a constitutive dimension of the preaching of the Gospel, or, in other words, of the Church's mission for the redemption of the human race and its liberation from every oppressive situation.[3]

One of the most important challenges of the Church in the closing decades of this century is the internalization of this statement. For the majority of American Catholics, if social involvement is to be integrated with a spirituality, if they are to understand justice actions as a "constitutive dimension of the preaching of the Gospel," this understanding and integration must be prompted, encouraged, and nurtured in the parish.

There is a great need for liturgy, prayer, and parish renewal programs and movements to include social concerns as an integral part of the expression of faith and the formation in faith. It is important that social efforts be rooted firmly in prayer, Scripture, and the teaching of the Church. This rootedness will support an enduring commitment and the ongoing conversion that is necessary if Catholics are to participate in "the transformation of the world."

Al, Wilma, and John experienced a specific parish renewal program, RENEW. One of the major goals of this program is formation for justice action.[4] For the first time, they saw the relationship not only between direct service to the needy and Scripture, but also the relationship between action for just systems and the gospel. Through a program of prayer, reflection, and discussion, they deepened and broadened their understanding of the social implications of following Jesus Christ. This aspect of Christian living has become such an integral part of their understanding of discipleship that it will be difficult, if not impossible, for them to abandon social concern as they continue to live out their Christian commitment.

Reflection on such experience leads to some practical conclusions for parishes:

1. It is especially important that efforts at parish spiritual renewal include social concern as an itegral part of that renewal — which, indeed, it is.

2. Groups working directly in social efforts should be involved in a process of ongoing formation which includes reflection on the social implications of the gospel and the teachings of the Church. This formation should also encourage personal sharing on the relationship between those social implications and the life of individuals in the group, as well as the life of the group as a whole.

3. Parish staffs, liturgy committees, and spiritual life committees should examine how social concern can be better integrated into the liturgical/prayer life of the parish.

'People in the Pew' Catholics

Al, Wilma, and John are "people in the pew" Catholics. Over the years, they have been involved in the usual parish activities. They have always been "regulars" at Sunday Mass, have served on the parish council, have dug deeper into their pockets on Mission Sunday, and have bundled up the kids' outgrown clothes for the Thanksgiving clothing collection. The pastor and other parishioners view them as good, solid, concerned Catholics.

They are precisely the people who, today, are being challenged to reexamine the social mission of the Church.

Back in the 1960s and early 1970s, socially sensitive and searching parishioners in many parishes initiated that reexamination. Often they were nurtured by movements such as Cursillo and the Christian Family Movment. Unfortunately, all too often, they became suspect in the minds of other parishioners. "Does the Church really belong in 'political' issues?" That underlying question stemmed from an ignorance of Catholic social teaching as well as an underdeveloped understanding of the mission of the Church.

Parishioners involved in social action rapidly found themselves on the periphery of parish life. Sometimes they were labeled as "radicals." Or, viewed as the "social justice people," they assuaged the conscience of the parish and, in the minds of many parishioners, fulfilled its social responsibility.

Often the "social justice people" became frustrated, and they despaired of raising consciousness within the parish. For them, the issues were too crucial to waste time trying to "build bridges." Many of these dedicated people eventually channeled their efforts into groups outside the parish structure.

What can parishes learn from these past experiences? How will ordinary "people in the pew" Catholics be reached? There are some relatively simple answers.

1. Start "where people are."

Often parishioners respond to direct service projects, such as food and clothing collections, phone networks, and visitation of the homebound and concern for the handicapped. These are valuable activities that meet immediate needs. However, there are other types of social involvement that are very challenging even though their success is more difficult to measure. These other areas of involvement usually deal with the systems and structures underlying the immediate needs.

Start "where the parish is at," but be alert to nudge it into other areas of involvement. Also educate the parish to the various ways in which the Church extends its concern.

The following is an outline of ways of being involved in social efforts:

Direct Service: The concentration here is on the immediate needs of people. Examples include food collections, visitation of the hospitalized and the homebound, programs for the elderly.

Advocacy: The emphasis here is on educating people about issues related to injustice, oppression, and poverty and the action needed to change the systems or structures that create or tolerate the injustice. Examples include working for local issues like the implementation of drug-education programs in schools, or low and moderate income housing; working to influence national policy, (for example, food policy, disarmament, programs for the poor). Advocacy relates to what is called "political ministry" and includes writing and visiting legislators to urge them to take certain positions, writing letters to editors — and educating others to do likewise.

Organizing/Empowerment: The emphasis here is on developing people to confront their own issues and to help change systems and structures. Examples include neighborhood associations, co-ops, tenant organizations, organizing around certain issues like housing, security, and health care.

Start "where people are" but encourage them to examine the broader picture and to confront issues as well as immediate needs. For example, a social concerns committee that has successfully established a food pantry could be encouraged to ask the deeper questions about the issues of food and food policy. What are the food problems within their state? What are some key issues on the national level. Organizations like "Bread for the World" issue monthly updates on food legislation and suggestions for letter-writing to congressional representatives.[5] Parish activities concerned with the elderly and the handicapped can lead to a probing of related issues.[6]

2. Issues will come and go. We've noted that the "kingdom" is the "not yet" as well as the "already." Social concerns committees would be wise to concentrate as much on skills as on issues. These skills will enable people to deal with a variety of issues that continually confront socially alert people in a complex society.

Some of these skills are:

• Integrate social action with the life of faith. Some familiarity with Scripture and with the Church's social justice writings will enable people to reflect on their social justice efforts in a faith context. At times it will be helpful to have people share their thoughts on a simple question like: "How do you see the presence of God in our social justice efforts?"

• Surface issues. In the beginning, especially, it is important to attempt projects and to confront issues that will have a reasonably broad base of support in the parish. Raising consciousness and developing concern among parishioners is a priority if the "people in the pew" are to be reached. Choose some projects and issues that have good promise of success and accomplishment. This will increase credibility and encourage added involvement. Surveys, questionnaires, and interviews with a broad spectrum of parishioners can help in the choice of issues and projects.

• Research issues and projects. Develop a familiarity with local, state, national, and diocesan agencies and resources. These sources can lead to the discovery and/or development of more specialized groups. In some parishes, social concerns groups can render a great service by being thoroughly familiar with the service agencies within the municipality and making that information available to those in need.

• Educate, raise consciousness, build constituencies. More will be said about this below.

• Dialogue with those who disagree or are unsure. As social concerns groups move into controversial topics, it is important that they discuss issues with those who disagree without condemning, oppressing, or becoming too emotional. Remember the emphasis is on building bridges and helping people understand.

Some hints here:

a. Know your facts.

b. Listen for points of agreement as well as disagreement. Build as much as possible on areas of agreement.

c. When possible, appeal to self-interest. Make Christian values as concrete as you can.

d. Know when to be satisfied with "planting seeds."

• Learn how government works. Be familiar with local, state, and federal government structures. Know your government representatives. Know how to write letters to your representatives as well as letters to editors. A local social studies or history teacher could give hints on effective letter writing.

3. If "people in the pew" are to respond to social efforts, education must

be a high priority for parish social concerns committees. They must have the patience to spend at least as much time on raising consciousness and letting parishioners know what the committee is doing, as they do in acting on their projects and issues.

Some parishes have successfully tried an "after Sunday Mass" approach. After each of the weekend liturgies parishioners are invited to a hall for a forty-five-minute program plus coffee and discussion. (If time permitted, this could also be done effectively in the church for parishioners who responded to the invitation to remain after liturgy.) The program could include a film or filmstrip presentation, a brief talk and discussion. One parish ran an "Issues of the 80's" program. Over four weekends the parish had the opportunity to discuss hunger, human rights, corporate responsibility, peace and disarmament. Perhaps one of the greatest lessons learned was that these discussions rightfully belong within the parish setting. There was the added symbolic value of having the program immediately following the liturgy.

An added hint — always get a list of those attending. Be alert to a high-interest level. Some "Bread for the World" and "Amnesty International" groups have dated their beginning back to gatherings such as these. These "after Mass" programs have been most successful when publicity has been thorough. Pass out flyers several weeks before the program begins. Include announcements in the bulletin and from the pulpit.

Of course, most scarred social concerns veterans remember the night they sponsored the program on hunger and nobody came. Do not despair. Use existing groups. Take it to the people. Choose your issue, learn your facts, and then "blitz" the parish. Do not just report your project to the parish council. Ask for a half hour to explain the issue. Meet with the staff and do the same. Ask for a slot on the agenda of the school and religious education faculty meetings, the meetings of the Home and School Association and, yes, the Rosary Society, Women's Group, Holy Name Society, and Senior Citizens. Reaching "people in the pew" means building coalitions with all groups. A well-planned half hour can stimulate interest and even involvement. A word of warning — be sure that the organizations know that "What St. Philomena's Is Doing About Hunger" is on their agenda. Avoid suspicions that they ahve been "tricked or trapped."

Current events can sometimes cry out for a public prayer response. Churches in many dioceses were filled when liturgies were celebrated for the four American women murdered in El Salvador.

Finally, whether the parish emphasis is on the Thanksgiving clothing collection or on lobbying for the poor, continually look for opportunities to educate. Use the bulletin, the bulletin board, and the newspaper. Use scripture passages and quotations from the Church's social teaching in connection with your announcements. That will help parishioners hear the good news of your social efforts within a context.

Speak to your clergy about proclaiming the Church's social mission in homilies. The sensitivities on this issue are real — so keep the dialogue gentle and open — but be persistent.

Small Supportive Communities

Al, Wilma, and John are "people in the pew" Catholics who experienced a parish renewal that included the social responsibility of Christians. For each of them this sense of a social responsibility has been nurtured within a small supportive community.

These small communities are not separate from the parish. They are an integral part of the life of the parish. They provide an experience of communal love, challenge, and support which is difficult to realize in large parishes.

Within their small communities, Al, Wilma, and John share prayer and reflection on Scripture and their life experience. They also learn together. Their communities are not settling into a sterile, complacent passivity, because they are committed to an outreach that will improve life for those who are in need.

Commitment to the social responsibility of the Church is difficult. Gains seem insignificant. Eventually, such commitment leads one into controversy, challenges values, and threatens the status quo.

The understanding support, the sense of a common mission, and the shared faith that can be experienced in a small Christian community encourages perseverance.

Social concerns groups in parishes have an important and challenging task. Having a community of faith and support will strengthen them to embrace that task.

An Added Word

"Network" is a popular word today. It's an "in" word that merits attention. Social concerns groups should develop a solid experiential understanding of that word. Begin by asking questions like: "What's already going on in the parish?" "What's going on in other parishes in town, the deanery, the dioceses?" "What are other churches and synagogues doing?" "What's the town doing to address social problems?" "Who are other involved groups?" "What can we learn from all these?" "Where can we join forces?" "How can we collaborate?" "How can we form a network?"

The problems are many and complex. Solutions will be the result of many good people working together.

* * *

Early in the Gospel of Luke we read of Jesus proclaiming his mission: "The Spirit of the Lord is upon me, because he has anointed me to preach good news to the poor. He has sent me to proclaim release to the captives and recovery of sight to the blind, to set at liberty those who are oppressed, to proclaim the acceptable year of the Lord" (Luke 4:18-19).

Bringing glad tidings to the poor, liberty to captives, sight to the blind, and release to prisoners can be an overwhelming task in the face of the suffering and oppression that afflicts so many. The temptation is to stand paralyzed before the task. Yet our faith tells us that we have not been called to do the impossible.

Ultimately we believe, in the words of Isaiah, that when these things are being done: "Then shall your light break forth like the dawn, and your healing shall spring up speedily; your righteousness shall go before you, and the glory of the Lord shall be your rear guard" (Isaiah 58:8).

SUMMARY

1. Parish social concerns efforts are often an underdeveloped part of parish life.

2. United States Catholics are relatively new arrivals in this country. They have worked and struggled to share in the "American dream." They have tended to be uncritical about the secular values of the society of which we're becoming a part. Today, Catholics are being challenged to a serious acceptance of social responsibility.

3. Both the Old and New Testaments teach the concept of justice. Justice in the Old Testament was related to covenant and to a relationship between God and his people. Jesus is the personification of justice. The "kingdom" of which he preaches is the power of God active in the world, confronting the powers of evil and transforming the world into a place of right relationships.

4. Discipleship means following Jesus in living and working for right relationships.

5. Catholic social doctrine is "a clearly discernible body of the official teachings on the social order, in its economic and political dimensions." Many Catholics are unfamiliar with this doctrine.

6. Parish social efforts should flow from a spiritual renewal that integrates faith, prayer, and social efforts.

7. Groups working in social efforts should be involved in a formation process that roots their efforts in Scripture and the teaching of the Church and that helps them integrate their efforts with their spirituality.

8. The liturgical/prayer life of the parish should reflect a sensitivity to the Church's social mission.

9. Emphasis should be placed on raising the awareness of ordinary Catholics to social responsibility.

10. It is important to "start where people are." This often means direct service projects. However, it is also important to encourage parishioners to move into the more difficult area of advocacy.

11. The Church is involved in social efforts in several ways. Some of these include: (a) Direct Service: The emphasis is on immediate needs.

(b) Advocacy: The emphasis is on educating people about issues and acting to change systems and structures. (c) Organizing/Empowerment: The emphasis is on developing people to deal with their own issues.

12. Skills are as important as issues, since good skills will enable people to deal with many different issues.

13. Important skills for parish social concerns people include:

- Integrating social action with the life of faith.
- Surfacing workable issues for study and action.
- Researching issues and projects.
- Educating, raising consciousness, building constituencies.
- Dialoguing with those who disagree or are unsure.
- Knowing how systems work.

14. Educating must be a high priority if ordinary Catholics are to realize their social responsibility. Educational approaches include:

- Programs after weekend Masses.
- Reaching existing groups — getting a place on the agenda of staff and parish council meetings, faculty meetings, Home-School Association, Holy Name, Rosary Society meetings.
- Prayer/liturgical events.
- Use of the bulletin, bulletin board, and the newspaper — and homilies.

15. Small communities which share faith, Scripture, learning, and life provide the support and challenge that enable parishioners to work on social issues and projects.

16. It is important to join forces with groups already working on issues and projects.

CHAPTER NOTES

1. National Conference of Catholic Bishops Ad Hoc Committee on the Call to Action Plan, "A Survey and Report on Diocesan Implementation of: To Do the Work of Justice: A Plan of Action for the Catholic Community In the United States" (September, 1980), p. 16.
2. Richard P. McBrien, *Catholicism,* 2 Vols. (Minneapolis: Winston Press, 1980) pp. 937-938.
3. Synod of Bishops, *Justice in the World* (Washington, D.C.: U.S. Catholic Conference, Publications Office, 1972), p. 34.
4. RENEW is a parish spiritual renewal program which was developed by the Archdiocese of Newark, New Jersey, and which is presently being implemented in dioceses throughout the country. (See Suggested Resources and Readings, below.)
5. Bread for the World is a Christian citizens' movement that seeks to influence government policies related to the issue of hunger. Bread for the World, 207 E. 16th Street, New York, NY 10003.

6. Elderly and Handicapped. For a helpful packet of materials on the handicapped, contact the United States Catholic Conference, Department of Social Development and World Peace, 1312 Massachusetts Avenue, N.W., Washington, D.C. 20005.

SUGGESTED RESOURCES AND READINGS

Catholic Committee on Urban Ministry (CCUM), Box 551, Notre Dame, IN 46556. CCUM is a national network of clergy, laity, and religious who, in urban, rural, and suburban areas, are engaged in ministry for social justice. CCUM sponsors conferences, summer institutes, and issue workshops. Especially helpful is the CCUM Education for Justice Team which is available for weekend workshops, presenting the biblical and moral basis for justice action; a social analysis framework and practical organization/empowerment techniques.

Network, 806 Rhode Island Avenue, N.E., Washington, D.C. 20018. For those interested in political ministry, Network is a Catholic social justice lobby that addresses issues before Congress that affect the poor — and the powerless. Network services include publications (a bimonthly journal and periodic Action Alerts), workshops, an annual legislative seminar, and training seminars for people in social justice work.

RENEW. This is a parish renewal program that integrates information for social action with spiritual renewal. Through Scripture, prayer, liturgy, and the development of community, parishioners develop a deeper understanding of discipleship. RENEW originated in the Archdiocese of Newark, New Jersey, and is presently being implemented in dioceses throughout the country. The magazine *Renew* is published by Paulist Press, 545 Island Road, Ramsey, NJ 07446.

A RENEW Service Team assists dioceses, vicariates, or large clusters of parishes wishing to implement RENEW. Contact:
Office of Pastoral Renewal
One Summer Avenue
Newark, NJ 07104

BOOKS

Fagan, Harry. *Empowerment Skills for Parish Action*. Ramsey, N.J.: Paulist Press, 1979. This is a guide for helping parishes and neighborhood groups to organize themselves into effective social action agents.

Haughey, John C., ed. *The Faith That Does Justice*. Ramsey, N.J.: Paulist Press, 1977. This book examines the Christian sources for social change and provides excellent background for the parish minister.

O'Brien, David J. and Thomas A. Shannon, ed. *Renewing the Earth*. Garden City, N.Y.: Image Books, 1977. This is a collection of major Catholic social documents on justice and peace. An overall introduction probes the background of the Church's social teachings. There are also introductions to the individual documents placing them in a historical context and reviewing their impact on Christian life.

Sider, Ronald J., ed. *Cry Justice — The Bible on Hunger and Poverty*. Ramsey, N.J.: Paulist Press, 1980. This book brings together a collection of biblical texts related to hunger, justice, and the poor. A good reference for scripture reflection and sharing.

PERIODICALS

Salt, Claretian Publications, 221 West Madison, Chicago, IL 60606. This magazine advertises that it is "for grassroots Christians seeking social justice." The ad is accurate. *Salt* is very readable information on ordinary people who are involved in social efforts.

Sojourners, 1309 L. Street NW, Washington, D.C. 20005. This magazine concentrates on the role of the Christian and specific justice issues. It stresses a biblical foundation for justice action.

Parish Administration as Ministry

The Rev. John R. Gilbert

Ordained for the Archdiocese of St. Paul-Minneapolis in 1956, Father Gilbert is pastor of The Nativity of the Blessed Virgin Mary Church in Bloomington. His professional degrees include a doctorate in education from the Catholic University of America, and a licentiate from the University of Louvain. He has spoken and published extensively on parish ministry and Catholic education.

If an observer were to spend a week in a parish, ministry is what that person would see. The observer would see a parish staff working with youth, ministering to the elderly, counseling, preparing couples for marriage, bringing communion to the sick, preparing liturgies, leading worship and prayer, teaching the young and the elderly, assisting families in need, meeting with a variety of parish commissions and committees, and being with those who are sick, suffering, and dying. This kind of behavior is the visible side of parish ministry, the outer skin.

Administration is the inner skin of parish ministry. It is not so much seen as its effects are felt, sometimes dramatically. If parish administration is done well, the parish is able to minister well. If it is done poorly, ministry will suffer. The effects of bad administration surface rapidly in troubled staff members, poor programming, and disheartened parishioners.

Some people who are very interested in ministry find administrative work unappealing. They consider working with youth as ministering, but question the value of administration. Such an attitude is very shortsighted. Good administration makes good ministry possible. Poor administration limits the possibilities for ministry.

While there are different ways to organize a discussion of parish administration, the notions of vision, structure, and management provide a cohesive framework. Vision is important because the parish must know where it hopes to go. As one of the sages once said, "If you don't know where you're going, you're liable to wind up someplace else." Structure is equally important because the vision must be shared and directed toward specific results. Management of time, personnel, and finances gives reality to the vision.

Vision or Money: Which Comes First?

Before getting into any discussion of vision, it is necessary to point out a common fallacy in parish administration. Some people argue that money is the keystone to successful administration. They say that vision without financing is an illusion. There is no doubt that it often takes money to make the vision functional. In the Church, however, money without vision often leads to greed.

Vision precedes financial support. A parish, a school, a diocese, or any institution needs a vision if it is to generate financial support. The professional fund raisers know this very well. When an institution approaches a company or a diocesan finance director for help with raising money, the first question is always: "What is your vision?" The professional fund raiser might not use the word "vision." He may talk about "the case." Regardless of the words used, the concept revolves around a vision for the future.

From the point of view of the parish, the thesis is simple. Parish administration that works on vision will find the finances to support that vision. The contrary is also true. The administration that puts finances first and spends little or no time developing a vision will find its finances less and less able to support its work.

Vision

If someone unexpectedly gave a parish with a clear vision a million dollars, that parish would know exactly what it would do with the money. Such a parish is also more likely to get a million dollars.

Recently a school completed its five-year plan, its vision for the future. Its plan was simply but attractively printed and then made available to all the parents and friends of the school. At one home and school meeting the principal talked about the five-year vision and the work that had gone into creating it. After her talk, a couple whose children had long since graduated came up to speak with her. They told her that during the years when their children were students they had hoped that the school would have the resources to go on from one year to the next. As far as they were concerned, the school's goal was to survive. They told the principal that they were very happy to hear that their school now had a future, and wanted to express their gratitude for her leadership in forming a vision for the school. The next week they mailed her a check for $50,000.

A high school in downtown Cleveland regularly informed its alumni of its plan and its vision for the future. Recently an alumnus who was completely unknown to anyone currently at the school proposed that they name the new library after his father, one of the school's first graduates. He offered $500,000 toward the building of this library.

Having a vision is the first key to success. In order to get somewhere, people have to know where they are going. If they know where they are going, they can tell other people about it. If other people hear about it, they can respond and support it. Unfortunately, the work of creating and presenting a vision is given a low priority in many parishes. People speak of it as secular or managerial, materialistic or beneath the pastoral ministry. In reality, forming a vision should be seen as an opening to the work of the Spirit, as an expression of the living heart of the Christian community.

Currently two parishes are having to reduce their staff while at the same time seeing their school in immediate danger. The finance committees of these parishes are saying things like: "You can't get any money these days, not with the financial crunch." Statements like that become self-fulfilling prophecies, which cause the mission of the parish to suffer and good ministers to be released from their jobs. Ministry suffers because people do not take the time to dream dreams, to create visions, and to give direction to the parish.

If this discussion were not about the Church, but about a profit-making business, the attitude would be completely different. A manager in a business who is visionless will not be manager for long. The same thing should be true in regard to stewardship in the Church.

In one parish that takes the work of planning seriously, the parish council decided in 1976 that among other things it wanted to have a new church by 1980, plus one additional staff person for youth ministry by 1979. At that time the parish had a large school, a $50,000 religious education program, and a $420,000 debt. The council was talking about spending a million dollars for a badly needed worship center and additional staff.

Some people in the parish thought that the council had lost its collective mind. Others said it was a move to close the schools. Many said: "It's not a bad idea." Five years later the parish had its new church. Enrollment in the school was higher than it was (in a community where the general school population was declining by approximately eight percent per year), the religious education program is funded at more than $60,000 a year, and the new youth minister is a popular and successful asset to the community. Finally, the average Sunday income doubled during the five-year period.

Vision sets the goal, charts the course. Without vision and planning there is nothing to present to the local Church, nothing to call them to. Parishes without vision soon discover that people are reluctant to support a rudderless parish with their hard-earned money.

Structure

Structure and vision go together, since structure is really a part of the vision. Vatican Council II called for structures in the Church that would allow for shared decision-making. These kinds of structures develop and announce the parish vision. For example, if the structures are such that the pastor makes all the decisions, that pastor is stating to his community his vision of Church. Those pastors who are uneasy with decision-making councils and boards because they fear that mistakes will be made or that their own authority will be undermined are, in effect, announcing their vision of Church.

If the structures of the parish are such that the parishioners really make decisions about the direction of the parish, the pastor is saying to them that he believes that the whole Church is led by the Spirit, that they are adult members of the community of faith, and that they are competent to use their talents in such a way that will help the parish grow.

This kind of parish would, of course, have a large number of people in decision-making roles. One parish has over one hundred people who are involved in making decisions on an ordinary basis: fifteen people are members of the council, twelve are on the finance commission, nine on the school board, nine on the religious education board, twelve on the adult education board, twenty are on the liturgy commission, seven are members of the social action commission, five are members of the social activities commission, seven are on the maintenance commission, nine are on the special committee to study the space needs of the parish, and another seven work on the committee for youth ministry.

In this particular structure, the main work of the council is to develop a vision of the parish, while each board, commission, or committee works on one-year objectives which translate that vision into a year-by-year plan. This kind of parish structure has a number of advantages. First, it draws a large number of people into the decision-making process of the parish, since each board or commission sets policy for its own area of ministry.

Second, it helps develop a sense of community in the parish, since parishioners develop ownership for the work of the parish. It would be difficult to overemphasize the value of this sense of belonging, leading, and participating under this structure. In a parish of fifteen hundred families, three hundred to four hundred of them would have been involved in some leadership role over a period of a very few years.

Third, each person on the parish staff has a group of consultants with them to discuss, plan, and carry out his or her particular area of ministry. A staff person also becomes accountable in a personal way to the members of this board. At regular meetings they monitor objectives and prepare annual reports for the council on the progress they are making.

Fourth, consensus-type decision-making fits in very naturally with this structure. The parish staff is not free simply to move ahead with ideas that they come up with, since each board or commission is involved in setting policy. At first glance such an approach may seem to be a disadvantage in that it slows down the staff. This, however, is only an apparent disadvantage. This type of structure forces people to include dialogue and education in the decision-making process.

While some people would see this type of parish organization as being very new, it flows from a very traditional reality. It was available in the 1950s through the writings of Gerard Philips of Louvain and the French Dominican Yves Congar. This theology emphasizes the notion of the community of faith. In the Church, lay people who are gifted by the Spirit and reborn in the Lord share in the life of Christ. While these authors acknowledged the role of the ordained priest, they pointed out the great dignity and irreplaceable ministry of the people of God.

Both of these great thinkers were very prominent in the writing of the Vatican Council's "Dogmatic Constitution on the Church." They reminded the Church of its own tradition of lay people as "a holy people," a people called to service who share in the priesthood of Jesus. It is this traditional and rediscovered theology of Church which is at the root of today's parish council, pastoral council, liturgy commission, school board. The parish priest who enters into serious shared decision-making is not changing the Church, he is rediscovering it in the local community of faith. The pastor who enters into shared decision-making is creating structures to open the power of the Spirit to his parish community.

Unfortunately, it does not always work that way. One pastor said recently: "We don't have any immediate problems now, so we don't need any council meetings. We've suspended them until the next problem comes along." This approach is crisis management in a negative sense. It reflects the tendency some people have to seek advice only in crisis. Crisis management may indeed be needed from time to time, but the best form of crisis management is good planning.

Some people do not plan because they think the process is too difficult. One very simple method of planning is to have each member of the council write out the three best things they can think of about the parish community and the three areas in which they see the need for the greatest improvement. Once this information has been gathered, the council can reflect on these particular areas and turn them into a mission statement or a statement of purpose.

Vision and structure go hand in hand. One is there for the other. Just having them, however, is not enough. Nothing happens unless the vision is communicated.

Communicating the Vision

Depending on the gifts of the people who staff the parish, and the makeup of the parish community, the various ministries present in that parish will be loving and powerful. Strangely enough, most of the parish would probably be completely unaware of just how effective most of that ministry is. The reasons are clear. People do ministry, but they do not communicate it. They do not tell other people what they are doing.

The Catholic Church in the United States is poorer for this fact. The reality is that thousands of extraordinary ministries are going on in the parishes around the country with little or no knowledge of what is going on in other parishes.

A vision is worthless until it becomes a communicated vision. Only then will it become a source of power and inspiration, a vehicle for the work of the Spirit. If the vision of individual parishes and the mission of the Church in general is going to be communicated, new forms are necessary.

Diocesan newspapers in some places may be an adequate vehicle for communicating the good news lived out in parishes, but that does not seem to be the norm. The same thing is true within the parish. The parish vision should be communicated to all the parishioners.

The parish should write about its dreams and mail them to the parishioners. It should write about its life as a parish community and distribute it door to door. It should prepare a newsletter on the parish that tells the parish story month by month.

The parish should not wait for other people to come in to find out about it. It should write about itself, and submit the article to the local newspapers. It should take some pictures of its meetings: divorced persons supporting one another, a widows' group, liturgical planning committees, school boards in action, and meetings with guest speakers — and see that they get passed around.

Many people still think that the Church only operates on Saturday and Sunday, with the rest of the week being given over to rest and relaxation. The parish should publish its schedule of events with an explanation about the adult enrichment program, the catechumenate, the retreats, the youth meetings, the Lenten programs, the family programs.

The first premise of communication is that no one else is going to tell the parish story except the parish. Granted that many parishes are inexperienced in this thing, inexperienced communication is better than no communication. Perhaps the parish could think about establishing a communications commission to spread the good news around.

Management

Along with developing the vision and structure of the parish, management of personnel, time, finances, and conflict is an ongoing responsibility of parish administration. Personnel, time, and finances are all limited resources, and the sense of stewardship demands that they be used well. Conflict is a part of the human condition, and a good administrator will work to bring about healing and reconciliation in challenging an unhappy situation.

• *Personnel Management.* The greatest resource in any parish is personnel. Therefore it must be treated carefully. Good personnel management requires time, study, and effort, especially as the number of staff people in parishes increases. The following are some simple suggestions for practical parish personnel management.

1. Take the time to develop a good hiring process for the parish. The better the hiring process, the less likely the necessity to fire people. Every hiring process should include a search committee that is developed from the parish council and the board or commission that is going to have to work directly with the staff person being hired.

2. Make an absolute rule that no one is hired to a staff position without the consent of both the board or commission with whom the person is going to have to work and the existing staff. The only way to ensure this consent is

for each new staff person to meet with the assembled staff, share a vision of ministry, and ask and answer questions. It also means that everyone must listen to everyone else, and not go forward with the hiring process unless there is a favorable consensus. This process takes time, but in the long run it saves time by avoiding problems that would crop up later.

3. Each candidate for any position in the parish should be given a detailed job description in advance, along with the contract he or she would be expected to sign and all pertinent diocesan policies. In the enthusiasm of hiring new people, the process sometimes becomes abbreviated and important information is not communicated ("We thought you had your own car"). Nothing should be hidden, no matter how innocently.

4. The pastor should spend time with each individual staff member. Most parishes are not team parishes in the strict sense of the word. Therefore it is important that the pastor take time to discuss each staff person's specific ministry on an ongoing basis. One hour a month is not exorbitant. This meeting allows potential conflicts to be defused and the pastor and the staff person to support and encourage one another.

5. Staff meetings should be scheduled a year in advance and very carefully planned. Staff meetings take up a lot of time and should be planned so as to gain maximum benefit. Items for the agenda should be requested well in advance and the completed agenda handed out in advance.

6. The parish staff should pray together regularly. All staff gatherings should be conducted in as prayerful an atmosphere as possible. Occasionally the staff should go away from the parish for days of reflection to strengthen the inner life of everyone.

7. Parish staff should also play together occasionally. Parties and meals together (including spouses) are a great help to a staff coming to know one another.

8. The staff should have a midyear day for review. Each staff member should be given a chance to tell everyone else how things are going, and to receive feedback.

9. Two or three days should be set aside sometime in the early spring for planning for next year's ministry. This meeting is crucial, and requires the best preparation possible. Prayer, play, reflection on ministry, setting of specific objectives for the year, and in certain settings sharing of household chores, are all part of this gathering.

Personnel management is a key to successful parish ministry. Parish ministers are the most priceless resources available. They should be treated as such.

• *Time Management.* To the professional staff of a parish, time management refers to the techniques of making the most efficient use of time available. Both the job description and the ordinary way people interact with one another on the parish staff are critical parts of the management of time. A job description limits the scope and direction of each person's ministry so that he or she knows where time has to be spent. Working together doubles the effectiveness of individuals, and helps make the maximum use of time.

There are a number of principles that help in time management.

1. A staff person should delegate as much as possible to the volunteers who work with him or her. Volunteers should be trained and then encouraged to do as much as possible. This kind of freedom can only be given if the parish staff members do not see themselves as the only competent people in ministry in the parish.

2. Staff members should not overcommit themselves. One way to help limit involvement is for each staff member to take on no more than three objectives per year. If a staff member reaches a limit, he or she is asked to drop one program of lower priority before beginning another. Focus is very important in time management. Many people debilitate their ministry by doing too much because they are unfocused.

3. Staff members should not overschedule. For many parish ministers the weakest point in terms of their ministry is their inability to take time off. No one is absolutely indispensable. No one has to work all the time. People committed to the gospel also need the discipline of being able to say no. Overwork eventually leads to burn-out, which will show just how indispensable any individual is.

4. Staff members should consider the secretary as a professional associate, not simply as a typist. Everyone on the parish staff will get more from their time if they will allow their associate-secretary to make decisions, to answer questions, to handle large numbers of matters that can be handled competently by the secretary.

While there are techniques that can be learned to help people make better use of their time, most good parish administrators today need to encourage people to work less rather than more. The value of any event is not necessarily determined by the amount of time that goes into it. In every parish, the amount of ministering that needs to be done far exceeds the capacity of the staff in that parish. Realism, then, is a necessary component of good time management.

• *Financial Management.* Finance is very important in the parish. Money represents people's time and energy, and, therefore, must be treated carefully. Not to take stewardship seriously indicates a lack of concern for the people who contributed the money.

The following might be a financial agenda for the Catholic parish today.

1. The parish has to develop the notion of tithing among parishioners. People must come to know that the parish belongs to them and that they have responsibility to support it. Just as they pay their house payments, car payments, fuel and electricity, so they support their Church. It is important to remember that an essential ingredient in tithing is financial disclosure. The parish that tells people they must support it because they own it must also give them accurate financial data.

2. Parishes have to develop efficient finance committees to oversee the development of budgets, to monitor expenses, and to effect solid financial planning for years to come.

3. Parishes need to develop programs that help parishioners with their wills. In the average parish, more than half of the families do not even have a will, much less a will that leaves something to the Church or one of its institutions.

4. Parishes have to be encouraged to look beyond themselves to the work of the universal Church and the diocese. Just as individual people and families are asked to contribute a percentage of their income for the work of the Church, so must each parish set aside a certain percentage for the work of the broader Church.

5. Parishes have to communicate with graduates of their parish schools and invite them to share the future vision and life of the school.

6. Parishes have to develop better and more regular means of communication with their larger contributors so as to share the future vision of the parish community with them. (Such communication in no way presumes a watering-down of the gospel message.)

7. Parishes have to start considering the need for "directors of development." A number of parishes, especially those with schools, have operating budgets that border on $1,000,000 per year. Such large expenditures point to a need for financial management assistance.

8. Parishes need to think about endowment programs, especially for schools.

9. Parishes should not be afraid to ask diocesan personnel to help in those areas where the parish does not feel adequate.

10. Parishes must make sure that financial planning is in line with the vision and structure of the parish.

• *Conflict Management.* Managing conflict is the most difficult area of administration. Conflict avoidance is one of the main reasons why so many pastors prefer to work alone, without parish councils and without parish staff. Many pastors go to unusual lengths to make sure that the "ship sails smoothly." Unfortunately, that sometimes means that the ship does not move.

Conflicts occur in every parish, in every life situation. The real question is how individuals handle the conflict so that it enhances the work being done. The following ideas offer some help in this area.

1. The best form of conflict management is adequate planning. Many people get into "crisis management" because they move from one crisis to another. Crises can best be avoided by forming a vision and planning for the future. Financial planning is especially useful in this area. Good budgeting procedures, accurate income projections, and contingency funds for unforeseen expenses help keep conflict at a minimum.

2. Good hiring procedures help avert personnel crises; yet no matter how good the planning in this area is, personnel difficulties are bound to

arise. Every parish should have some kind of internal arbitration system. For example, conflicts could be referred first to the pastor, and then if they remain unsolved, to the parish council. If they cannot be resolved at this level, they could move to diocesan arbitration and mediation procedures. If there are good personal relationships in the parish, the need for arbitration is dramatically reduced.

3. Many crises and conflicts revolve around complaints of parishioners in regard to liturgy, education programs, speakers, and other activities. The staff person most concerned with this activity should be the one to handle the situation. Other people would be wise to stay away. If the crisis cannot be resolved by the staff person and the one making the complaint, then perhaps parish arbitration procedures could be used.

4. Crisis management in the parish should be governed by the overriding principles of reconciliation and healing. People who have been hurt often lash out in anger. The appropriate response in the parish is not anger or defensiveness, but acceptance of the individual person. By working to understand different experiences and points of view, many problems can be solved quickly. Where people are involved, crisis management is usually more a question of reconciliation than it is one of right and wrong.

SUMMARY

1. Vision is the foundation and starting point for all good parish administration.

2. Good structures which allow the vision to be communicated and shared is the second step in administration. It does no good to keep "the good news" a secret.

3. Good parish administration requires good management skills. Parish personnel are the greatest resources a parish has. Good personnel management is a matter of justice, since it allows people to carry out their ministry effectively.

4. Time is also an important resource that must be managed. Good time management helps eliminate burn-out, and allows individuals to make the most creative use of their gifts for others.

5. Money represents people's time and energy, and must be treated respectfully by the parish. Finance committees are essential to the smooth running of any contemporary parish.

6. Conflict management is usually difficult for people in ministry. It is, however, in this area that much healing and reconciliation takes place.

SUGGESTED READINGS

Kilian, Sabbas J., OFM. *Theological Models for the Parish.* New York: Alba House, 1977. A historical and theological examination of the parish, this book offers reflections on five models of parish.

O'Neill, John J. *The Essentials of Planning.* Washington, D.C.: U.S. Catholic Conference, 1975.

―――― and Edie Frost Johnson. *The Essentials of Organization.* Washington, D.C.: U.S. Catholic Conference, 1977.

――――. *The Essentials of Management.* Washington, D.C.: U.S.Catholic Conference, 1978.

These three companion publications offer clear and comprehensive materials in the areas of planning, organization, and management. They are recommended for the group that wants to have concise information available for further study.

Scheets, Francis Kelly, OSC. *Parish Management Information: PMI Planning Manual for Total Parish Planning: An Integrated Approach Employing a Decentralized Method.* Published by the Office of Fiscal Planning, Diocese of Fort Wayne-South Bend, Indiana, 1974. This manual provides a step-by-step process for total parish planning and is based on the principles of collegiality and subsidiarity. The book provides a concrete planning process, planning tools, timeliness, and worksheets for various committees.

An Overview of the Steps in Program Planning. This concise, six-step overview of program planning provides groups with a means of discussing planning in a logical manner. The booklet is designed to ensure that planners arrive at programs which arise out of the real lives of people and that the programs actually resemble the ones planned. Copies may be ordered from:

Church Leadership Resources
United Church of Christ
Box 179
St. Louis, MO 63166.

Communication in the Parish

Margaret McBrien, RSM

A Sister of Mercy of Philadelphia, Sister Margaret has taught in Catholic schools on the elementary and secondary levels, and was publicity director for two Catholic hospitals. She is currently Minister of Religious Education at the Cathedral of the Sacred Heart, Richmond, Virginia. She holds a master's degree in communications from the University of Notre Dame.

Communications are at the very core of what the Catholic Church is and does. By its nature the Church is a large communications system spanning centuries and continents. It has one message to communicate: the good news of Jesus Christ. The Church has an obligation to present the gospel message as clearly, completely, and effectively as possible.

That obligation rests with the entire Church, not just with its "official" members. Regardless of how effective Pope John Paul II is with the use of media, each person in the Church has the obligation to proclaim the gospel in his or her own circumstances.

The Word of God

As with other Semitic cultures of its time, Israel believed that the spoken word had a reality distinct from the person who spoke it. While drawing its power from the person, the Word once spoken takes on a new reality that helps to bring about what the words themselves signify.[1] God's Word has creative power, as in the creation account of Genesis when God said, "Let there be light. And there was light" (Genesis 1:3).

It is, however, in the prophetic writings from the Hebrew Scriptures that the Word of God receives the greatest emphasis. The Word of God is given to the prophet in some dramatic fashion. For the prophet Jeremiah it is through the Lord's extending his hand and touching his mouth, saying: "Behold, I have put my words in your mouth. See, I have set you this day over nations and over kingdoms, to pluck up and to break down, to destroy and to overthrow, to build and to plant" (Jeremiah 1:9-10). The Word of God as given to the prophets had absolute power. As spoken by the prophet, it does not merely communicate truths, but actually *creates events and molds history*. History becomes a process which is governed by the Word of God. At the same time, the Word of God renders history intelligible.[2]

In the New Testament, the Word takes on new meaning. The Letter to

225

the Hebrews begins: "In many and various ways God spoke of old to our fathers by the prophets; but in these last days he has spoken to us by a Son" (Hebrews 1:1-2). The Gospel according to John begins with an exalted hymn to the preexistent Word of God, a Word that "became flesh and dwelt among us" (John 1:14). According to the New Testament, in Jesus God the Father has spoken his final word. Thus Jesus accomplished in his person all that the Father wishes to be accomplished.

The Church

The Church continues to proclaim the salvation that Jesus brought, to make known the mystery of God revealed in him. As it is preached and lived by the Church, the Word of God builds up the Christian community.

Following the specific instructions in the "Decree on the Means of Social Communication" from Vatican Council II, in 1971 the Church issued a pastoral instruction on the means of social communication. One of the most significant statements in that document says: "Communication is more than the expression of ideas and the indication of emotion. At its most profound level, it is the giving of self in love. Christ's communication was, in fact, spirit and life. In the institution of the Holy Eucharist, Christ gave us the most perfect, the most intimate form of commitment between God and man possible in this life, and out of this, the deepest possible unity between men. Further, Christ communicated to us his life-giving Spirit, who brings all men together in unity" (No. 11).

The document further stresses the relationship between the freedom to express one's own opinion and the right to be informed. Only if an individual has consistently accurate information can that person live in the real world. There is no possibility of true economic, political, cultural, or religious freedom without the possibility of accurate information. In today's world, knowledge is power. All people have the right to the information necessary for them to lead authentic lives (No. 28).

Communication looks simple, especially when it is done between people who speak the same language and are from the same culture. Yet in a very complex world where people are being bombarded with immense amounts of sensory data, effective communication is very difficult to achieve.

In its simplest form, communication is a process whereby a "sender" tries to transfer intentional meanings to a "receiver" by means of verbal and nonverbal symbols. The problems arise because both the sender and the receiver have various "filters" through which the intended meaning must pass by way of verbal or nonverbal symbols. These filter systems are the experience, attitudes, prejudices, and genetic heritages of individuals. Words change meaning based on context, connotation, pitch, tone, and facial expression.

A good communicator, therefore, whether a sender or receiver, has to work hard at communicating accurately. The effective communicator knows the formal system of communication (for example, the organizational chart). That person also knows the informal communications system, which is often more effective than the formal one.

Effective communication also demands some kind of feedback system. In the case where two people are speaking to each other, there is, if the communication is honest and open, relatively effective and immediate feedback. In dealing with large groups, however, a built-in opportunity for feedback is not always present and must be built in.[3]

Parish Communications

Communications are at the very core of what every parish is and does. The parish has an advantage over the worldwide Church for obvious reasons. Its size limits the number of symbols used in communication, simplifies the formal and informal communications systems, and increases the opportunity for feedback.

Since the celebration of the Sunday Eucharistic Liturgy is the central event of parish life, what goes on during that time will reveal much about the total life and spirit of a parish community.

Messages Picked Up on Sunday Morning

Buildings have a language all their own. Bright, cheery, uncluttered church doorways are inviting. Plants in the vestibule of the church can express llife, tranquillity, and familiarity (provided they are alive and well; dead plants say something else). Wheelchair ramps and sturdy railings tell the handicapped and elderly that they are cared about and welcome. Clear signs and/or available maps indicating the location of other parish buildings such as rectory, school, convent, parish office, or senior citizens' center, provide easy access for the unfamiliar.

Environment is one of the most significant symbols in any communications process, yet it is often paid the least attention by communicators. Both the physical and psychological environments contribute significantly to the success or failure of communication.

A person who is too hot, too cold, unable to see, or unable to hear, will be distracted from the total worship experience. Adequate heat, ventilation, and lighting are expensive but necessary. A good sound system in a church will not make a homily effective; but a bad sound system will negate the good effect of the very best homily.

Lack of attention to these basic factors can result in large numbers of people being cut off from the total experience of liturgy. The way church buildings are maintained and decorated tell the parish at large something about its own self-image. Cleanliness and simple beauty do not cost much money. Dark, dingy, paper-strewn foyers with month-old flyers and backdated magazines usually depress the spirit. A makeshift lost and found that includes one lost glove, a pair of prescription sunglasses, and a pink comb, usually has a negative effect as well.

Since the first parishioners that most people meet coming into the church are the ushers, their function is particularly important. Many parishes now talk about "greeters" rather than ushers. The name is unimportant. What is important is the friendliness, openness, and helpfulness that the ushers exhibit to parishioner and non-parishioner alike.

A quick glance around the church before the liturgy begins will reveal some very significant information. A congregation that knows one another, one that has a sense of genuine community, cannot hide the fact. Friendliness and warmth are rooted in shared experience. Parish suppers, home Masses, community nights, and coffees connect people that normally would not socialize together. Most parish projects have the same bonding effect on participants.

One such project, a parish auction, was designed primarily as community building activity, and only secondarily as a fund raiser. Several weeks before the auction, twenty to thirty parishioners were contacted and asked to donate some personal talent or service. One family donated their house on the river for a week's vacation. A mechanic donated an oil change; a secretary thirty pages of typing; a dentist offered a diagnostic checkup and cleaning treatment; several of the women in the parish offered to make dinners. Teenagers offered to baby-sit or rake leaves. Even the pastor offered to wash and wax a car. All of these items were listed on a large poster placed in the back of church. An announcement was made after Mass encouraging people to sign up and to be very original and daring. They responded.

Compiling the list generated a lot of fun, enthusiasm, and personal interaction. It provided great conversation starters, and affirmed many personal talents. Young and old turned out for the bidding. Connections were made between parishioners and nonparishioners, between the rich and the poor, between parishioners of different interests, different ages, different races. This one activity provided an entry into the parish system for many who had previously been on the periphery. Gradually some of those who met and worked at the auction became adult education committee members, RCIA sponsors, or special ministers of the Eucharist.

Eucharistic Ministers

The eucharistic experience builds on and is built on experiences just like this one. Eucharistic ministers, lectors, cantors, and altar assistants send out very definite signals about a parish. If the majority of these are women, subtle sexual bias results. "This is a women's church — it is not for men," or "Women are active here, men are passive." In terms of age, sex, race, the composite of ministers should reflect the makeup of the total worshipping community. When a lector says, "Let us pray to the Lord," the congregation will more readily identify with "us" when that lector is a sixty-year-old woman one week, a young black man the next, a middle-aged business executive the next. All levels of the group should be represented in these roles of worship.

Broad-based participation requires extra work on the part of parish leadership. People need to be encouraged to participate. They must be actively recruited to be lectors, eucharistic ministers, cantors, and altar assistants, and they must be trained. To get them to the point where they communicate "we know what we're doing, we're comfortable doing it, and it is very important to us" takes time and effort. Workshops for lectors and cantors usually provide self-confidence and encouragement. These training sessions also help participants to be less self-conscious in the roles assigned at Sunday Liturgy.

That notion seems to be the key to all good ministry — not getting in the way of the message — or, stated more positively, delivering the message is what it is all about. When people know what to do and when to do it, they are able to facilitate prayer because they become transparent. They act almost like a camera lens, which serves to focus all attention in one direction. Cantors who sing off-key or eucharistic ministers who run up to the altar at the wrong time draw attention to themselves.

The Priest-Celebrant

The most difficult communication job in the parish belongs to the priest-celebrant. He is the one who has to find that delicate balance between personalism and transparency. To the best of his ability he has to be loving, warm, sensitive, and challenging, because he represents Christ. Yet his personality must not get in the way of the message he preaches.

The fact remains that the personalism with which the priest celebrates the Eucharist and the words and style of his homily are the most effective means of communication in the parish. It is understandable that many parish priests do not want to hear how important they and their sermons are. A recent article states, "There is an extremely powerful relationship between the quality of Sunday preaching and return to the center of the church." Referring to young people, the same article states, "They are no longer attracted to or driven away from the church by the sexual, or authority, or feminist issues. They are rather attracted to or driven away from the church by the quality of Sunday preaching."[4]

For many Catholics, the sermon is the only form of religious education any of them receive. This means that what is communicated in the Sunday homily constitutes the most current religious curriculum for entire families.

What practical suggestions can be offered about this powerful communication vehicle? Only one seems appropriate. Whatever brings about the awareness on the part of the celebrant of the importance of the homily should be encouraged. Once a priest confronts the fact that this ten- to fifteen-minute time period is critical in his ministry, he will find the time, the materials, the guidance and prayer, that he needs to do the best job he is capable of doing.

The Parish Bulletin

The parish bulletin is an obvious communications medium with a very limited function. At the same time it says a lot about a parish. If it is used well it can be very effective. What can a visitor tell about a parish from reading the bulletin? Many names and a variety of activities usually say, "There is a lot of life here." If a parish is socially involved, the announcements will indicate it. Outreach to the sick, the elderly, widowed and divorced, say, "You are a part of us and we care about you." A summary of parish council meetings and weekly finances promotes a sense of ownership and belonging for all parishioners.

These guidelines for a parish bulletin may be helpful.

1. Clarify its purpose. Bulletins are primarily vehicles of information. They differ from newsletters, magazines, devotional guides, and who's who tabloids. Effective bulletins provide basic, accurate "who, what, when, and where" information.

2. Every parish bulletin should contain the name, complete address, and phone number of the parish church and office, a liturgy schedule, and the names of parish staff members.

3. Names of parishioners should be spelled correctly. Extra effort to double-check spelling pays off. Misspelling names is insensitive, and may be interpreted as, "You're just one in a million around here."

4. Avoid editorializing, that is, injecting personal opinion into announcements. Also avoid judgmental, pedantic, or alienating statements. People have different interests, talents, and abilities. How they use them in the parish must always be a matter of personal freedom, yet some parish bulletins read as though every good parishioner will run a booth at the carnival, attend the CYO meeting, and bake three cakes for the annual card party.

5. Use the principles of good design in layout and choice of type. Uncluttered space and clear, legible letters invite reading. If the typing is sloppy, the print crowded together, and the ads for local funeral homes more prominent than anything else, the chances of the notices being read diminishes. Good graphics improve a would-be bulletin one hundred percent. Clear black-and-white line art is available from several commercial art companies.[5] Transfer letters, which can be obtained at a local art store, are easy to use and add a professional touch to a publication. An artistic parishioner could use these to create a wonderful masthead for a parish bulletin.

6. Make sure all groups within the parish know how to get their messages into the bulletin. Publish the print deadline in the bulletin occasionally.

7. As people's schedules become more complex, parishes might consider publishing a monthly calendar with the bulletin on the first Sunday of the month.

Visitors

One group that parishes communicate with on a regular basis, but which they do not generally acknowledge, is visitors. Depending on the location of the parish, at any given Sunday Eucharist there are a number of visitors or people who have just moved into the parish. Acknowledgment of their presence is important. Perhaps the cantor, in welcoming people before Eucharist begins, could give a special welcome at each Liturgy to those people who are visitors. The written word in the form of a card in the hymnbook rack can also be effective. Below is a sample of such a card used in the Cathedral in Richmond (originally brought back to the parish by a parishioner who was on vacation in Maine).

WELCOME TO THE CATHEDRAL
OF THE SACRED HEART

Are you a tourist visitor?
 Can we help you find accommodations, restaurants, places of interest, or help with route directions?

Are you a guest relative?
 Thank you for joining us at worship and be assured you're always welcome when you return.

Are you new to Richmond?
 Would you like someone to call to help you meet folks in the neighborhood?

Are you new at Cathedral?
 Would you like to join us permanently? Can we be of service? Please call us at 555-1212.

Are you a registered parishioner?
 Do you have any suggestions? Or questions? Or remarks? Or anything we could do for you?

_____

Name _____
Address _____
Zip _____ Phone _____
 Please place this card in the collection or give it to an usher.

Christmas and Easter are special times to be aware of visitors. The parish has an unusual opportunity to proclaim the gospel to many Catholics (as many as fifty) who only come to church several times a year. As frustrating as it may be to see so many people come on these few occasions, the parish has to make a special effort to communicate to people who still have a spark of faith that they are welcome at church.

 These are times for the parish to remember that Jesus welcomed everyone; they are also times to think of new and creative ways to encourage the Christmas and Easter people to return to the church on a regular basis. One pastor, every Christmas and Easter, tells the people who are there what has been going on since the last big feast. He does it in a very positive way and concludes by saying, "This is what you missed. We think we have a good thing going here, and we would like you to join us."

Messages Picked Up on Monday Morning

Parish communication, like religion, is not limited to Sunday morning. The business of maintaining a parish goes on twenty-four hours a day, seven days a week. How the parish communicates within and without should be consistent with the gospel and its mission to preach.

While it would be difficult to prove, the main communicators in any parish are probably the members of the parish staff. The priest and the other people who serve the parish set the tone for everything that happens in the parish. Where truly excellent communication is going on, parish staff members work diligently to communicate effectively. They reflect together, and with the parish council, on how and what must be communicated.

Very often the tone is set by simple things. It can be proclaimed over and over from the pulpit on Sunday that Christians must love one another, care for one another, be sensitive to one another's needs. Those statements have to be backed up by sensitivity on the part of the entire parish staff. It is extremely important that phone calls be returned within a reasonable time. It is important that people keep their promises, no matter how unimportant they may seem. For someone on the parish staff to tell a parishioner who is sick that he or she will be by to visit on Wednesday morning is a sacred trust. Not to follow through communicates exactly the opposite of what is proclaimed from the pulpit.

Speaking of the sick, it is important to enlist the help of parishioners in communications. Some parishes have formal networks, others telephone committees. At the very least, parishioners should feel free to call the parish when they think someone needs help. For example, the following bulletin notice serves a practical need. It also serves as a notice that the parish staff needs help.

IS THERE ANYONE SICK AMONG YOU?

If you are going to the hospital, or if someone in your family is in the hospital, or if you know of a parishioner in the hospital, please call the parish office and let us know. None of the hospitals in our area notify churches that their parishioners are there and only five out of sixteen list patients by denomination (but not parish). Also, if you know of a parishioner sick at home for an extended period, please call us. We need your help.

Parish Secretary

The parish secretary is a key communicator in any parish. The secretary is the first person people meet when they come to the office or call on the phone. How the door and telephone are answered is an indication to the caller of how welcoming and concerned the parish really is. At that time, the secretary personifies the entire parish. Some parishes have reputations for being unusually friendly simply because the parish secretary is so friendly on the phone.

Big business and parish work are different. While both value efficiency and good public relations, the latter requires a pastoral dimension. That should be made clear to a secretary. Fortunately there are many wonderful people in these positions who need very little guidance or training, since they are already sensitive, discreet, and prayerful people.

Arrangements for weddings and funerals, and all the circumstances surrounding these occasions, are dependent on communications. The pastoral quality of these communications often has far-reaching effects on the faith development of those involved. More than a few people are brought into the Church because of good experience at these times, and more than a few leave because of bad ones.

It is helpful to remember that family and close friends involved in these events are usually operating out of a heightened emotional intensity, so whatever directions or instruction must be given should be clear, sensitive, and direct.

These occasions contain great potential for evangelization. Non-Catholics who are active in their own churches, people who have some slight affiliation with another church, and the completely unchurched attend these events. Some are hearing the gospel proclaimed for the first time in many years. It is an opportunity and an obligation for parishes to welcome all people into their churches.

Conclusion

None of what has been said is brand new, but all of it is important. Some parishes are doing a very fine job in many of these areas, some are doing well in one or two areas, but few parishes are doing a perfect job in all areas. It might be helpful for a parish staff and a parish council to do a communication study of their group. Identifying areas of strength and weakness is invaluable to good planning for the future.

For many people, "the medium is the message," that is, *how* the Church proclaims what Jesus said *is* the message they hear.

SUMMARY

1. Communications are at the very core of what the Catholic Church is and does. Each person in the Church has the obligation to proclaim the gospel in his or her own circumstances.

2. The Word of God has great power. It does not merely communicate truths, but actually creates events and molds history. History becomes intelligible through the Word of God. The Word of God builds up the Christian community.

3. Accurate information is absolutely indispensable to life in this world. Knowledge is power.

4. Good communication requires accuracy, feedback, and takes place best in a relatively small community.

5. Environment is one of the most significant symbols in any communications process, and all aspects of the environment must be evaluated in terms of their enhancement of, or detraction from, the process.

6. In order to foster the closeness that is integral to good communications, parishes should devote attention to events at which people can socialize and get to know each other.

7. The various ministers at Sunday Eucharist play a very important role in communicating the gospel message. They must be chosen and trained carefully for their role.

8. The priest-celebrant is a central figure in the communication process, and his weekly homily a key reason why people flock to, or stay away from, his parish.

9. The parish bulletin is important and can be effective if done with taste, clarity, and consistency.

10. Christmas and Easter are special times to proclaim the gospel message to people who generally do not attend church at any other time.

11. The parish staff's role of communicating cannot be overemphasized.

12. As with Christmas and Easter liturgies, weddings and funerals are other excellent opportunities for communicating the gospel message to alienated or unchurched Catholics.

CHAPTER NOTES

1. John L. McKenzie, *Dictionary of the Bible* (Milwaukee: Bruce Publishing, 1965), p. 938.
2. Ibid., p. 939.
3. For a fuller explanation, see James Owen, *The Effective Manager* (Washington, D.C.: Management Education Ltd., 1978), pp. 41-54.
4. Andrew M. Greeley, "Parish, Priest, and the Young Catholic," *Parish Ministry II* (January/February, 1981), pp. 1-2.
5. These graphics are available from: Logos Art Productions, Inc., 33 E. Wentworth Avenue, Suite 217, West St. Paul, MN 55118, and from Artmaster, 1420 N. Claremont Blvd., No. 111, Claremont, CA 91711.

SUGGESTED READINGS

Communicate! A Workbook for Interpersonal Communication, 2nd ed. Dubuque, Iowa: Kendall Hunt Publishing, 1978. No one book can possibly contain all there is to know about any subject. This book, however, comes closer than most. As important as its broad scope is its practicality. It covers the whole area of communications and gives concrete ways to communicate better. If it is a one-book situation, this is the book.

Organizing Parish Councils, Boards, and Committees

The Rev. Robert W. Wilson

Father Wilson was ordained for the Diocese of Dallas-Fort Worth in 1957. He has served as an associate pastor in that diocese, as the Director of Vocations, and as Dean of Students for the University of Dallas. He has also served as superintendent of schools for the Diocese of Fort Worth, and is currently vicar for education and pastor of St. John the Apostle Parish. Father Wilson holds a Ph.D. in counseling psychology.

In one parish the pastor said, "We have only two organizations here, the men's club and the ladies' guild." He saw that as a virtue, uniting the parish, even though only a small minority of people attended. Most parishes find that organizing people into many groups does two things: it forms community and it achieves the mission of the parish as Church. This section will deal with the need for organization (how to involve, motivate, and keep people active), and will propose a possible model for linking organizations together.

Committees vs. Communities

Vatican Council II in its "Decree on the Apostolate of the Laity" calls for lay people to be "nourished by their active participation in the liturgical life of their community, (to) engage zealously in its apostolic works, (and to) spread the Word of God. . . . The parish offers an outstanding example of community apostolate, for it gathers into a unity all the human diversities that are found there. . ." (No. 10).

Since the Council, forming community has been the primary concern of many Church men and women. Lay community formation was achieved by the Cursillo, the Marriage Encounter movement, and in some places the Better World movement. The Latin American success with *"Comunidades de base"* ("Basic Communities"), although not satisfactorily replicated here, continues experimentally in many places.

This concern for formation of community seems appropriate, at least if that is the model of Church that the parish follows. Father Avery Dulles suggests five models with many submodels.[1] He sees community not only as an end in itself (although he demonstrates that it appropriately could be), but also as a means to achieve the apostolic mandate of the "Decree on the Apostolate of the Laity."

That this decree declares the parish to be an outstanding example of the community apostolate comes as a surprise to no one who has ever worked in a parish. Although people may live out their Christianity for a time in educational settings, practically everyone that gathers to break bread eventually gathers in a parish, whether traditional or experimental, large or small, well organized or poorly organized.

In all but small parishes it is a misnomer to call the gathering of people at Sunday Mass a community. The term implies some "I-thou" sharing, as Martin Buber defines such relationships. Buber also wrote about another kind of relationship, the "I-it."[2] In the "I-it" relationship the other person or persons perform a function. Sadly, Sunday liturgies all too often provide an "I-it" relationship for people. They come to do a variety of things — worship, fulfill their Sunday obligation, be inspired, hear a good homily, or all of these and more. However praiseworthy, all of these make up the "it" of the "I-it" relationship.

It is the fortunate Catholic parish in which everyone at a Sunday Mass knows everyone else. Only when the worshippers enter into a relationship with each other is the "I-thou" achieved. We attempt to achieve the sense of a worshipping community in the renewed liturgy through singing together, communal responses, and the gesture of peace. In fact the "itness" of the people at worship is diminished by these humanizing elements. Nevertheless, in the final analysis, to become community, people must come to know each other.

The solution is to see the larger parish as a "community of communities." Perhaps the ideal would be to have a parish broken into many "basic Christian communities." Although the South American success with *"Comunidades de base"* has not been experienced in the United States, various types of parish divisions into faith-sharing groups have taken hold.[3] In larger parishes where people feel anonymous, and in developing areas where people are separated from their extended family, the need for a primary community enhances the development of these neighborhood faith-sharing groups. (See the next chapter for a more thorough treatment of "base communities.")

However, the fact is that many, even most, American Catholics, have not yet become involved in primary faith communities. They are searching for something but have not found it. Parish organizations could provide the answer. They may be social groups like a bowling league or bridge club. These are "being" communities, secondary rather than primary. Others are service oriented, such as the altar society, the liturgy committee, or the St. Vincent de Paul Society. Although these are "doing" communities, their task is accomplished partially by the working community formed by the participants.

At Sunday Mass if every parishioner recognizes some of the people from his or her neighborhood community, from his or her bridge club, or from his or her involvement in one of the apostolic liturgical or formation committees of the parish, an "I-thou" community of worshippers has been gathered. The community of committees has gathered to break bread. Therefore the principles of recruitment and motivation espoused below have the dual purpose of community formation for its own sake, and accomplishment of the mission of the parish.

The communities within the larger parish community will be as varied as the needs of the body. It was of this that St. Paul wrote: "If all were a single organ, where would the body be? As it is, there are many parts, yet one body" (1 Corinthians 12:19-20). The well-organized parish will have the parts interconnected, a good parallel to St. Paul's analogy.

What Organizations?

The similarity between St. Paul's body and the parish is in the diversity of the parts. However, it should not be inferred that each body is going to have the same parts. What is appropriate in one parish will be inappropriate in another. To have a Guadalupana organization in a predominantly black parish, and no Knights of St. Peter Claver would be ludicrous.

Communities within the community arise from needs. For example, hardly anyone would quarrel that there is an ongoing need for strengthening the family in religiosity, in communications, in parenting. The Christian Family Movement (CFM), begun by the Crowleys, flourished in the 1950s and 1960s.

While still a factor in some areas, CFM is all but dead as a national force for family renewal. The CFM introduced a movement from Spain at its 1967 national convention. Since then Father Calvo's Marriage Encounter has become the most vibrant force for couples' renewal, if not family renewal, in the United States. The times were right.

Yet, Marriage Encounter may not be the right renewal agent for a particular parish. Who decides what organizations? Most appropriately, the people themselves decide. They will always do so by their attendance or lack thereof. They vote with their feet. The pastor and/or the parish council, after whatever decision-making process they use, may decide that an adult mixed softball league will form community in the parish. If the people like it, the project will fly . If not. . . . All parish leaders have experienced the disappointment of bad guesses.

'Being' and 'Doing' Communities

A "being" community is one in which people gather just to be together. "Being" communities usually utilize social activities, personal formation, or special interests of people to bring them together.

Whatever form they take, such communities are needed for their own sake. To form an "I-thou" relationship is a good in itself. Parish decision-makers will usually find it easier to begin any organization or group after polling people about their wants and needs. Although formation of social or athletic groups is a beginning, it is more important to form "being" groups around faith, whether in neighborhood groups, in Bible study groups, in prayer groups, or in whatever spiritual or formation format.

The parish leaders also have to determine what "doing" communities are relevant to their parish. These are the groups that fulfill Vatican II's mandate to do apostolic works and spread the Word of God. Some, like a hospital visitation committee, would seem helpful, wherever the parish. Others, like a committee to assist senior citizens in activities or programming, will depend on the demography of the parish.

It is usually helpful to break the parish up into several areas of concern. One system is to consider worship, formation, service, and administration separately. Some make social life a fifth area. By assessing parish needs, committees for each area could determine what service or "doing" communities are needed, for example, a St. Vincent de Paul Society, a shut-in visitation group, a blood bank.

The same would be true of the "being" communities, both those gathering people for social activities and those gathering them for prayer or study. An organization chart showing a multiplicity of possible communities is included at the end of the chapter.

Research and Planning

Decisions on what "being" communities a parish needs are best made after a poll of the people. Polls can usually be devised inexpensively with professional advice from sociology departments of local colleges. One system is to pass out a brief questionnaire to be filled out at all Masses. Return on mailed questionnaires is always low. Another method is to target several "typical" neighborhoods, and hold house meetings to find out what people think.

The surefire method is to encourage groups of people to set up whatever "being" communities they want, so long as they are open to everyone in the parish. The best people to start a bowling league, a softball team, a bridge group, a study group, or a square-dance club are the people who are excited about the activity. If research turns up needs for several "being" communities, including the most basic ones, the faith communities, people enthusiastic to start them must still be found.

Such polls can also discover what the parishioners want done about religious education, social service, worship, and administration. The members of these committees would be well advised to assess the needs of the parish on an ongoing basis through brief annual polls.

Another planning technique used by business[4] is the following nine-grid chart:

**Needs of the Apostolate Fulfilled
by This Group or Activity**

	Low	Average	High
Parish's Ability to Continue or Start This Group or Activity — Low			
Average			
High			

The members of a committee such as worship could do two exercises with this grid. First, they could list all the *current* groups or activities at the appropriate cross-reference point on the grid. For example, "Our need for lectors is high, and our ability to recruit and train them is high." Or, "Our need for an altar society is average, and ability to recruit membership is low."

After all the existing activity and organized committees are charted, the commission members would make a new grid and list the *nonexisting* groups or activities that might fulfill the apostolate of their area. This is best done in a three-year projection, that is, "What groups or activities will we need within the next three years to fulfill the mission of our committee, and what is our capability for getting them started?"

After the two exercises are completed, the committee leader or the facilitator passes out the chart of suggestions based on management principles (see below).

The suggestions in each of the nine grids are geared to existing activities. However, they can be rephrased to apply to projected new groups or activities. Obviously, the right-hand column, high needs of the apostolate, deserves the greatest attention on the part of planners and decision-makers.

What Do the Organizations Do?

For the "being" communities this question is unnecessary. Families relate to each other. Faith communities share faith values. People in bridge groups enjoy each other at recreation. However, it would be good for each group to have a clear statement of purpose written out to help new or prospective members know what they are all about. Some call this a "mission statement." An example would be: "The bridge group is made up of members of St. Pius X Parish and their guests, and meets every first Monday to play duplicate bridge. There is a $1.00 charge to cover expenses. There are

**Needs of the Apostolate Fulfilled
by This Group or Activity**

		Weak	Moderate	High
Parish's Ability to Continue or Start This Group or Activity	**Weak**	*DISINVEST* Drop this activity now and redeploy resources.	*PHASED WITHDRAWAL* Drop this activity over a period of time.	*DOUBLE OR QUIT* Tomorrow's opportunity: Need large resource infusion or get out.
	Moderate	*PHASED WITHDRAWAL* Drop this activity over a period of time.	*CUSTODIAL* No major commitment of resources.	*"AVIS"* Try harder to improve capability.
	High	*OLD STANDBYS* Maintain this activity but add no further investment.	*GROWTH* Maintain this activity and grow with the need.	*LEADER* Give absolute priority to these activities; spend all resources necessary to meet the needs; expand capability.

no officers, but one person is selected each year to take care of arrangements."

"Doing" communities have a greater need for a clear statement of purpose, and they also need to set clear goals. These are the steps to take: First, write a mission statement (as suggested above). Second, set a long-range goal, that is, a desired condition the committee wants to bring about within three years. Third, set objectives, action plans for the current year, designed to bring the group closer to the goal. Fourth, design any action steps or programs needed to achieve the objectives. Fifth, decide "who will do what by when," a definition of accountability.

If there are not enough members of the committee to achieve the action steps, recruitment of people interested in the work is easier because of the clarity. If additional cash resources or parish space is needed, the committee has to negotiate with the pastor, the finance committee, the secretary who reserves space, or whatever appropriate person or group in the parish.

Usually, each step will take a two-hour meeting, although it is possible to accomplish the necessary tasks at one all-day meeting. An example of this process, using the evangelization committee of a parish, follows:

Mission Statement: Evangelization is the ministry of spreading the good news to those alienated from God and Church as well as to those searching for meaning in their lives.

This ministry will be accomplished by the witness of a community of Christ-like, praying people who will reach out to others to help them realize their value as people and enable them to express their faith in the contemporary world.

Note that the mission statement is broad in scope. It is a description of the way the group would like things to be.

Goal: By three years from (*date*), there will be an ongoing process of homecoming for the alienated Catholic. (Note that the goal is action-oriented, describing a desired condition whose function is to fulfill the mission statement, but is still general.)

Objectives: (1) Within six months from (*date*) our committee will have had the opportunity for inner renewal and witness by becoming a prayer community. (2) Within six months from (*date*) we will have formulated a process of homecoming. (3) Within six months from (*date*) we will have decided upon and implemented a process of identifying non-churchgoing Catholics within the parish boundaries. (4) Within one year from (*date*) we will have implemented the first of the ongoing process(es) of homecoming for non-churchgoing Catholics within the parish boundaries. (Note that the objectives are more specific than the goal.)

Action decisions: (1) To achieve objective number one we will meet for prayer every first Thursday in the parish hall for one and one-half hours of prayer, with leadership alternating. (2) To fulfill objective number two, six members, namely _____ , _____ , etc., will study homecoming processes utilized elsewhere, such as "Come Home for Christmas," and will make a recommendation to the whole committee by (*date*) for a final decision. (3) To achieve objective number three, three committee members, _____ , _____ , and _____ , will meet with the pastor and parish secretaries to study existing records and parish census, and recommend to the whole committee whether a door-to-door census is needed. (4) To achieve objective four, we will do some type of outreach program within the year, depending on the recommendations made by the groups appointed above. (Note that the action decisions are flexible. Depending on the recommendations made by the research groups, action will be taken or further research done as is appropriate to achieve what the committee set out to do.)

Most organizations do something like the above, whether formally or informally. Often the most neglected element is evaluation. It would be wise to put an evaluation date on the calendar for each objective, and the goal itself. On a date six months later, the group would ask: "Have we had the opportunity for inner renewal and witness by becoming a praying community? What did we do well? Poorly? What can we change? Add? Leave out?" The same can be done for each objective adopted.

Leadership of Committees

The leader of a community can be elected or appointed. It is usually best to do so for a term of office. Leaders are the servants of the community whether it is "being" or "doing." They see that meetings are called, rooms are reserved, that members are consulted, that the needs of the group are met, and that the purpose of the organization is accomplished.

Usually, ongoing groups elect their leadership annually or biannually. This is a good system, although it sometimes causes the election of the most popular member and not the most competent. It helps if the duties of the leader are clearly spelled out in a constitution, in bylaws, or some working document.

Often "doing" communities are task forces appointed by the pastor, the parish council, or the commission in charge of an area of parish life. For instance, the purpose of the finance committee may be to run a stewardship drive each year. The appropriate person (pastor or parish council lay leader) will have as his or her major contribution the appointment of the leader of that "doing" community. It is a task force to raise sufficient finances for the parish budget for the coming year. The head of the task force will have as part of his or her duties the recruitment of other leaders, such as team captains, who in turn will recruit workers.

One of the most creative tasks of top leadership is the appointment of the right person or persons to task-force leadership. Two criteria will help. First, look for those who have been successful at lower level activities, either in the same task force in the past, or in similar acivities. Second, look for someone who is enthusiastic about the project, whose energies are generated by the challenge, and who will accept the challenge as a personal goal or commitment. The person who does not use his or her Sunday offering envelopes will make a poor stewardship leader. However, this same person may be an enthusiastic gatherer of people to start an outreach program to elderly shut-ins. What turns him or her on? Talk to people and look at their daily activities. Also, sometimes one just has to take a chance. If you judge someone competent and are able to challenge him or her with a task, you have discovered a new leader.

Leadership training for organization heads is extremely important.[5] Leadership training includes such things as the use of the goal-setting exercises outlined above. Training in clear communication could be provided by behavioral scientists from local colleges. Training in working with different types of people could be offered by psychologists. Techniques of decision-making and efficiency could be provided by management experts. Formation in prayer and spiritual life could be provided by clerical and lay leaders in spiritual renewal. This latter skill in particular might be shared with the membership of all the parish communities. Small parishes which cannot afford the cost of outside experts for leadership training usually do so by banding together as a cluster of four or five parishes, or perhaps as a deanery. It is advisable to group leadership together as much as possible for training purposes.

Recruitment and Motivation of Membership

If "being" communities are fulfilling their purpose, little recruitment will be needed. Those who want to play bridge will gather to play bridge, if leadership is appointed or elected to see that this happens. The leaders of prayer groups or faith-sharing communities will have to explain carefully what they are doing. If people are attracted by charismatic prayer, they will gather to experience this form of community. If they are attracted by Bible study they will gather to do it. However, "basic" communities will have to explore ways to gather people since their purpose is difficult to explain. If people feel that their basic needs of faith-sharing have been met, they will return. Usually these will work best with a beginning and an end, perhaps in major penitential seasons.

The key for leaders of "doing" communities is to find people who like doing what the group task is all about. Sometimes membership can be gathered by guilt-producing statements like "every good parishioner will work on the carnival," but not for long and not with much enthusiasm. Find the people for whom a particular project has meaning. Some people like to visit hospitals or rest homes, and want to do it for themselves as much as for the people they are visiting. Others who feel awkward in a hospital room would spend countless hours in the parish buildings with hammer in hand.

The major task for the parish council and/or pastor is to identify parish needs. Once needs are identified, the pastor or council chairperson recruits people who are energized by that need. Instead of begging for CCD teachers in September, it is far easier when the chairperson of teachers shares his or her own experience of joy in teaching children about God, and engenders enough excitement (and frequently courage) in others to experience this joy.

Get in touch with people's idealism. What are their dreams? What enables them to see themselves as effective, as personally valuable and important, as serving others? Whether it is counting the Sunday collection or carrying groceries to the poor these people will stay with the task, especially if it is for a definite term, like one year. The art of the parish leader is putting together needs and people who are fulfilled by meeting these needs.

After Recruitment, What?

After the community or task-force leader has recruited group membership, two vital tasks remain. The first is training for the task. Before undertaking recruitment, the leaders need to have determined what kind of training is necessary: Who will do it? How much it will cost? When should it be done? The volunteers have a right to know what to expect. "What do I say and do when I visit someone in the hospital?" is a natural question.

Recruitment is easier when the committee members not only know what the expectations are, but also that they will be trained to meet them. Some even suggest signing contracts, such as: "In exchange for your service of teaching grade-school CCD weekly, the parish will provide you with a teacher's guide and two hours a week of group lesson planning with the guidance of the DRE."

The second job for leadership is support (some systems call it maintenance). It can be as informal as the pastor's saying, "You're doing a great job, stewardship workers," or as formal as an award or certificate given for a year's service on the committee. Hospital volunteer groups (including candy stripers) award five-year pins, ten-year pins, and so on. Whether the support given is formal or informal, it must be systematic and planned, so that all the bases are covered.

Burn-Out

Burn-out is the result of putting out more energy than one takes in. The power plant that puts out more electricity than the energy source that supplies it soon runs dry. So does the person.

Most people burn out after a while, unless they have a change of pace, a diversification, or a change of activity. Some people may be energized by the same activity forever. They will need occasional vacations, but no new directions. Others will need an entire change of activity.

If all committees are appointed or elected for terms of one or two years, burn-out is usually avoided. Those that are not motivated or energized by the particular activity move on to something else..

The Community of Communities

Each community, whether "being" or "doing," has been seen as a separate entity with needs for goal-setting, leadership, membership recruitment, and support. Back to St. Paul's statement "There are many parts, yet one body" (1 Corinthians 12:20), there is also a concern about how the different parts are interconnected.

Medium- to large-size businesses have organization charts showing how various departments are interconnected, perhaps through divisions under vice-presidents. Likert and Likert have devised an organizational system that is not the traditional pyramid, with workers reporting to straw bosses, who report to managers, who report to vice-presidents.[6] Their description is more akin to a group in which community is more important than lines of authority, and interconnection is not based only on a superior-subordinate relationship.

The system is simple. One person has to be willing to belong to two groups. He or she is the linkage person. For example, a lector would belong both to the group of lectors and to the liturgy committee. The two groups are linked by this person, who keeps both informed of what is happening with the other.

This linkage is one way that a parish can be a community of communities interconnected among its various parts.

Many parish councils divide the four areas of ministry in the parish into worship, formation, service, and administration. The four areas (sometimes called commissions) could be linked to the parish council by commissioners who serve both on the commissions and on the parish council. The commission, or division (for example, worship), would be made up of people from each of the various areas of worship, such as ushers, lectors, musicians, and special ministers of the Eucharist. The chairperson of each subgroup or committee, or preferably another subgroup committee member, would belong to both groups. He or she would belong to the larger and more general group, in this case the worship commission, and the smaller, more specialized group, for example, the lectors. This is the key concept. The person involved belongs to *both* groups. He or she does not necessarily chair either. Both groups can independently elect their own chairpersons.

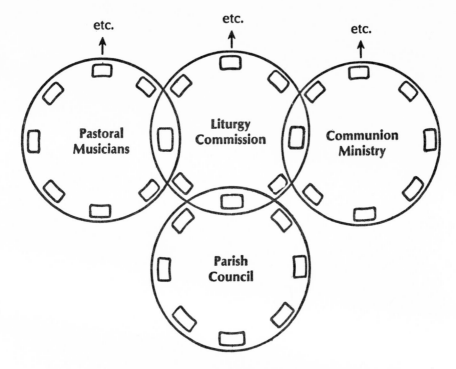

The chart above is graphically descriptive of the concept. The major purpose is that all more particular ministerial groups be represented on more general policy-making groups such as the worship commission and the parish council. The more general group does not "run" the more particular group.

The breakdown could extend as far as necessary. For instance, the "musicians" described above may be one member each from seven different singing groups including adult choirs, children's choirs, or folk groups. They would meet to coordinate pastoral music planning in an overall way, but each particular group would have to gather to plan and practice.

The Parish Council

Many parishes place the ministerial organizations within the parish council framework. The above four divisions are typical, with some adding a fifth commission of "social" or "fellowship." Frequently, certain council members are "in charge" of one of the four areas. They may have been elected specifically for that area of parish life, or they may have been appointed by the parish council chairman after having been elected at large. Nevertheless, they see themselves as responsible for effective ministry in one of the areas of worship, formation, service, administration, or fellowship. Their task will be to set up as many permanent committees (or subcommittees) in their area as necessary for the effective carrying out of the particular area of parish life.

In this model, it is important for the council member to be aware that he or she is wearing two hats. When in council session the members are policymakers, concerned with the overall direction and vision of the parish. When doing committee work the parish council hat is left at the council meeting place. The person then becomes a committee member, focusing on getting a particular job done, fulfilling a specific need of the parish, and, in this one area, living up to parish vision and goals.

Another way to approach ministry is for the parish council to be entirely policymaking, that is, to concern itself with long-range planning, major parish directions, major decisions, and leave up to the pastors, pastoral staff, and the committees themselves, the recruitment of people for the ministerial work of the "doing" communities.

The parish council as part of its policymaking and long-range planning may wish to set up an organization chart of desired committees (and subcommittees). This work is done best in conjunction with those already working on a commission, or if one is not yet set up, with those working in the area of ministry that will be covered by the ministry.

In the first approach above, the parish council members are both policymakers as a council, and administrators as commission heads. In the second approach all are "at large" representing the interests of the whole parish. One alternative would be to have a majority elected at large, but with one commissioner from each commission also sitting on the council. Another would be to link an at-large elected council member with each commission, but not put him or her in charge of it.

Whatever system of parish council election is followed, the interconnectedness of linking the council with the commissions is the key concept. The commission is then linked with each committee, and each committee with each subcommittee, as far down the line as interlinking "doing" communities is needed. A chart depicting this structure is found in the Appendix (see p. 252).

The Role of the Commission

The commission is primarily a communications vehicle. If a quarterly or monthly meeting does nothing more than acquaint the parish council member or members with the activities, the successes and failures, and the problems of all committees gathered, the commission is a success. On the surface, this may seem a waste of time in a small parish where everyone communicates all the time; in reality, it is not. Only by formalizing input to the parish council can committees be sure that they are being heard. The beauty of the linkage system is that the parish council member belongs to both groups, and hears reports from committees not as an outsider, but as a member of the commission.

The commission would also take on any project that is too broad for a particular committee. For instance, the renovation of the church needs the input of musicians, service ministers, parishioners involved with arts and environment, and all involved with the liturgy. The commission apparatus would be the appropriate place to gather such information. The worship division might be delegated by the parish council to gather opinions from all parishioners.

The Parish Staff and Parish Organization

The staff may be the pastor and a part-time secretary, or it may be a large group of priests, religious, and laity working together. Many parishes with a large staff that would include job titles like "Director of Religious Education" and "Youth Minister" are incorporating volunteer parishioners into ministries at staff level, for example, a ministry of evangelization or of adult enrichment. The concept is that such a person has the same responsibilities as paid staff members.

What is the role of a pastor and/or a staff in a linkage system described above? The answer usually depends on the local parish. One system is to see the pastoral staff in charge of absolutely nothing, but acting as resource persons to the various commissions and committees. The old CCD structure had the priest as "moderator" or "chaplain," but not running the CCD board or the teachers. He was the resource person. Where leadership has been developed sufficiently in a parish, such a system would seem the best. In a small parish it is probably the only system. The pastor simply cannot spread himself so thin as to run everything from grounds care to First Communion preparation. Country pastors have long been adept at delegating people to run the various ministries and giving them support and backup. A clear chart of organizations showing their linkage would be helpful.

In larger parishes the pastor and staff sometimes become program administrators. The parish council makes policy, and the staff administers it, making all day-to-day decisions. The pastor is seen as chief administrator and the staff as associate administrators. This works well, especially when volunteer parishioners are willing to enter ministries as "staff" members. As lay people become more trained and willing to assume leadership of the various commissions and committees, staff members can take on more of a helping, resource role. DRE's can do teacher training, perhaps for several parishes, rather than administrative duties such as teacher recruiting and doorlocking.

As laity take over more of the work of the Church, as has been happening gradually, paid professional staff members may decrease in number rather than increase. In our sacramental Church, priests will always be needed for liturgy and for other sacramental ministries. Larger parishes usually prefer to have some professionals to work full time at particular ministries. However, nationwide, more Catholics are taking responsibility for the ministries within their parishes. When this happens, the pastor becomes more pastoral, less administrative. The lectors, for instance, report to the head lector, perhaps elected by them, who reports to (is linked to) the liturgy commission, which reports to (is linked to) the parish council.

The pastor and the staff are needed to keep this system going by helping with recruitment and support, but they are not seen as administratively "in charge." Nevertheless, as the day-to-day pastoral ministers most in contact with all the people, they are leaders, providing vision, inspiration for the people to live up to the vision, and support in difficulty. In almost every parish, the amount of leadership and responsibility assumed by the people is the amount they are encouraged (or enabled) to do so by the pastor and pastoral staff.

The Appendix (at the end of this section) shows how a parish might chart its organizations according to four or five commissions. Only a newly founded parish will have the luxury of starting from scratch. In that case the parish council, the pastor, and staff can meet together in order to set priorities through a planning process such as the one suggested above. The establishment of committees is the final implementation of goals and objectives on an action basis.

Boards of Education: A Special Concern

The preceding model for parish organization is based on a desire for broad participation among the members of the parish community. It has been devised from experience. Different dioceses, however, have a variety of organizational models.

Because so much time, energy, and money goes into the parish's educational effort, the kind of decision-making process used in this area is especially critical. While the model proposed earlier works, other models are also available. The National Catholic Educational Association has proposed a board model that has been used successfully in different areas of the country.

This model presumes that the parish council has a standing education committee that deals with all education within the parish. Its major functions would be: "(a) to identify the faith community's educational needs, (b) to formulate these needs into goals, (c) to recommend programs to meet these needs/goals, and (d) to present these goals and program recommendations to the council for acceptance and authorization."[7]

Existing alongside the parish council's education committee is a board of education which has the following specific responsibilities:

- to articulate the educational mission of the local faith community
- to establish goals and objectives for the educational programs
- to determine specific policies which will guide the administrative staff in working toward these goals and objectives
- to review the decisions made by the administration in order to carry out the board's policies
- to evaluate the effects of the board's policy decisions in achieving the board's goals and objectives
- to approve the financial expression of the educational plan, the budget
- to participate in the selection of the administrator, who is the board's executive officer, evaluating regularly his/her ongoing performance, and, if necessary, dismissing and providing for replacement.[8]

The existence of an education committee of the parish council and a specialized board of education might seem to present an environment for educational schizophrenia. In reality, by having specific functions based on the principles of subsidiarity and complementarity, this organizational model offers real efficiency.

Several cautions should, however, be noted. First, both the education committee and the board of education should scrupulously avoid involvement in administration. Second, the education board and the parish council committee must communicate effectively with each other on an ongoing basis lest one group tends to take over the functions of the other.[9]

SUMMARY

1. Every parish is organized, whether extensively or simply. The challenge is for these organizations to become a "community of communities."

2. "Being" communities in the parish may someday follow the experience basic communities in South America have had. Presently they are usually tied into the social life of the parish.

3. "Doing" communities are organized according to some structural vision of the apostolate. One frequent system is to divide parish ministries into worship formation, service, and administration.

4. Research and planning are needed for both types of communities. Research through polling the parishioners is needed for the "being" com-

munities. Planning is needed to decide what "doing" communities are most relevant for a particular parish to fulfill its ministry.

5. Leadership is necessary for the development of "being" and "doing" communities. It is best to elect or appoint leaders for specific terms.

6. Membership of the "doing" communities comes from those interested in and excited about the particular apostolate. Leadership involves putting the right people with the right ministry. The membership deserves training and continuing support from the leaders.

7. The community of communities, that is, the parish, is made up of interconnecting parts. The traditional pyramid organization chart of management is less appropriate to describe this phenomenon than a chart of interlocking circles.

8. The parish council may be entirely policymaking or have members "in charge" of commissions concerned with areas of ministry. If the former system is utilized, the linkage system described above still works if a parish council member (or members) still sits on each commission, but does not run it. If he or she runs the commission (worship, formation, service, or administration) it should be remembered that two hats are involved, policymaking and administration.

9. The pastor and parish staff fit into the linkage system in one of two ways. The pastor, if by himself, or the pastor and staff in larger parishes, may be the day-to-day administrators of long-range policy set by the parish council. Another system is for the pastor and pastoral staff to take on a support role, providing vision, encouragement to fulfill the vision, and a challenge to leadership on the part of the people. Their enablement of people makes this happen.

10. NCEA has proposed a board of education model that allows for participatory decision-making in the educational mission of the parish.

CHAPTER NOTES

1. Avery Dulles, *Models of the Church* (Garden City, N.Y.: Doubleday, 1974), pp. 1-30.
2. Martin Buber, *I and Thou* (New York: Charles Scribner's Sons, 1970), pp. 51-85.
3. Richard Westley, "To Build a Household Church," *Today's Parish* (May-June, 1981), p. 5.
4. Joseph Reilly, "Texas Catholic Conference, Workshop on Parish Management," unpublished paper, 1981.
5. Cyndi Thero, *Parish Councils* (Kansas City: NCR Cassettes D-22, 1981).
6. Rensis Likert and Jane Gibson Likert, *New Ways of Managing Conflict* (New York: McGraw-Hill, 1976), pp. 183-201.

7. Mary-Angela Harper, *Putting It All Together* (Washington, D.C.: NCEA, 1979), p. 8.
8. Mary-Angela Harper, *Ascent to Excellence in Catholic Education* (Waterford, Conn.: Croft-NEI, 1980), p. 14.
9. Harper, *Putting . . .* , op. cit., p. 9.

SUGGESTED READINGS

Buber, Martin. *I and Thou.* New York: Charles Scribner's Sons, 1970. This book forms the theoretical basis for the discussion on "being" and "doing" communities.
Likert, Rensis and Jane Gibson Likert. *New Ways of Managing Conflict.* New York: McGraw-Hill, 1976. This work presents conflict management in a positive way. The heart of the process is "linkage," which is easily adaptable to parish life.
Whitehead, Evelyn and James Whitehead. *The Emerging Parish: An Adult Community of Faith.* Kansas City: NCR Cassettes, 1981. The Whiteheads explore the different needs people have and the different kinds of community it takes to satisfy those needs, in terms of the parish.

Appendix

Parish Organization Chart

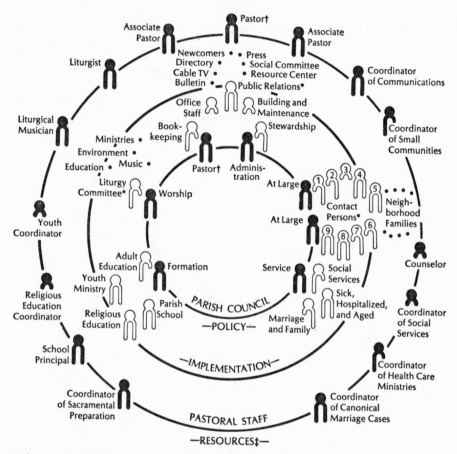

‡ The number of resource people can be increased or decreased according to the size of the parish and/or funds available. In this model they are not "in charge" of ministries but are of assistance to committees which have the responsibility. Some exceptions are obvious, e.g., a pastoral counselor or school principal. Also, many are involved in direct one-to-one ministry with parishioners because of their role in the parish.

† The pastor plays a dual role in this representation: as Parish Council policymaker and as resource person to various ministerial communities.

* These three areas — Public Relations, Contact Persons for Neighborhood Families, and Liturgy Committee — have been expanded to show their functions. Actually, each area of implementation could be extended to show additional groups and subgroups with functions as needed.

Basic Christian Communities: The Local Church Alive

The Rev. J. Stephen O'Brien

Ordained for the Diocese of Richmond, Virginia, in 1965, Father O'Brien has served in various parishes and in different educational ministries in the diocese. A former superintendent of schools and director of education, he holds graduate degrees in theology, education, and the teaching of English. He is currently rector of the Cathedral of the Sacred Heart, Richmond.

In the last three decades, the major theological issue in Roman Catholicism has been the concept of Church. The American Church has had an especially difficult time identifying itself with the different models of Church that have been described since Vatican Council II. Like other Americans, Catholics tend to deal best with concrete, practical, result-oriented models. Most models of Church do not emphasize practical results. The best models emphasize relationships.

On reflection, the relational model is the common experience of Christians — God to people, people to each other. People come to know Church through daily living, through experience. Church is identified by the people who belong to it, by its practices (what the people do). It is in fact best expressed through its people (the pope, bishops, and the lady in the next pew), rather than through theoretical definitions. It is this experience of Church as people related to people in Christ that is at the heart of Basic Christian Communities.

Definitions

It is difficult enough to arrive at a common name for Basic Christian Communities, much less an agreed-upon definition. The original name in Spanish, *comunidades de base,* is translated into English as base communities or basic communities. Later the word *eclesialis* was added to the definition so that there would be no possibility of confusing basic communities with communist organizations. From that addition came basic ecclesial communities or Basic Christian Communities.

There is no authoritative definition for Basic Christian Communities. No one who has written on the subject seems willing to restrict the reality by defining it. There is, however, a description from the National Secretariat for Hispanic Affairs of the United States Catholic Conference:

The CEB is the basic portion of the Church of Christ . . . [It] is a portion of the People of God which constitutes the first and fundamental nucleus of the Church, in which the Church of Christ is truly present and operative at its most basic level, through personal fraternal relationship with the Father, in the brotherhood of Christ and other human beings, through the action of the Holy Spirit, and in the salvation and total liberation of the whole person and of all persons.[1]

Another description of Basic Christian Communities flows from the Church as witness to the resurrection of Jesus. Every person in the Church is a witness to and a sharer in the resurrection, and thereby acknowledges that there is a truly new and different reality after that event. From this understanding flows a longer description of Basic Christian Community (BCC).

1. A BCC is first of all a gathering of people who have a sense of being called to work for God's reign and justice.

2. The people in the community are committed to celebrating the kingdom of God in their own lives. They recognize that dialogue and struggle are necessary to transform human society into an expression of the kingdom. They are still willing, however, to celebrate the kingdom now.

3. The BCC's sense of authority, mission, and ministry has its roots in the history of salvation; yet its focus is on the future.

4. The starting point for the BCC is dialogue about what is important in life — what is repressive as well as what is creative and freeing.

The Need for Small Communities

The need for people to form small groupings within larger communities is directly related to BCC's. These are communities where everyone knows everyone else in the group. The phenomenon is not confined to the Church. *Pro Mundi Vita Bulletin* lists three factors that have influenced the formation of small groups within various societies.

1. The very size of social institutions in countries throughout the world has limited the freedom of individuals as well as the possibility of their forming close interpersonal relationships. Cities today are marked by isolation and anonymity, rather than close relationships.

2. The whole process of alienation is increased because of the breakdown of many of the smaller groups to which people used to belong. For example, many of the socialization functions once performed by the family have been taken over by other institutions. These institutions are large and impersonal, such as the mass media. In the past, educational institutions, unions, the Church, political parties — all of these fostered a sense of community among people. These institutions have grown in size to the point where they often offer little sense of community to their members.

3. People have begun to realize the need for social structures that allow some kind of harmony in lifestyle. Many groups are formed that allow for a certain security on the level of values and authentic relationships. Some

groups are formed to protest the impersonal and inhuman nature of social structures. More often they are formed to set up "an ideal type of small-scale society really capable of replacing a society which has fallen prey to gigantism."[2]

The Church Community

Basic Christian Communities operate off the notion reaffirmed in Vatican Council II that the local Church is a true expression of the Church of Jesus Christ. A 1978 gathering of Hispanic communities used the analogy of a loaf of bread. They stated that "the local Church is not a part of the whole Catholic Church, like a room in a house. The local Church is more like a piece of bread. The piece is truly bread although it is not the entire loaf. The same is true of a particular Church; it is a true Church, although it is not the entire Church."[3]

They cite the "Dogmatic Constitution on the Church" as a confirmation for this position. The Council Fathers wrote: "This Church of Christ is truly present in all legitimate local congregations of the faithful . . . united to their pastors. In them the faithful are gathered together by the preaching of the Gospel of Christ and the mystery of the Lord's Supper" (No. 26).

When the Latin American Church met in Medellin in 1968, it called the Basic Christian Community the "first and fundamental ecclesiastical nucleus, which on its own level must make itself responsible for the richness and expansion of the faith, as well as the cult which is its expression. This community becomes, then, the basic cell of the building of ecclesiastical structures . . . and essential to this building . . . are leaders or directors. They can be priests, deacons, men or women religious, or lay people."[4]

In 1970, Pope Paul VI in his *On Evangelization in the Modern World* recognized Basic Christian Communities as a tool for evangelization and as "a hope for the universal Church."[5] In 1974, the World Synod of Bishops in Rome reaffirmed the importance of Basic Christian Communities to the Church.

When the Latin American bishops gathered at Puebla in 1979, they stated: "As a community, the BCC brings together families, adults, and young people, in an intimate, interpersonal relationship grounded in the faith. It celebrates the Word of God and takes its nourishment from the Eucharist, the culmination of all the sacraments. It fleshes out the Word of God in life through solidarity and commitment to the new commandment of the Lord; and through the service of approved coordinators, makes present and operative the mission of the Church and its visible communion with the legitimate pastors."[6]

Basic Christian Communities Within the Catholic Church

Basic Christian Communities are a growing phenomenon in all parts of Central and South America, Africa, the Philippines, southeast Asia, and northern Europe. People who make up these communities are the poor, the young, the old, intellectuals, workers, housewives — anyone who feels the sense of alienation so prevalent in industrial technical societies.

Pro Mundi Vita Bulletin lists six characteristics of these Basic Christian Communities:

1. Unlike "fraternal faith" groups of the past, Basic Christian Communities begin as strictly grassroots communities. They are made up of groups of people who come together, sometimes spontaneously, to share their faith. Although they may be supported by the institutional Church, they are not formed from above. Even where they are not supported by the Church, they generally have some position in regard to the Church. They may challenge it. They may be a structure parallel to it. Or they may even be on the edge of it.

2. A major reason why people join any group is to form human relationships. Thus BCC's are always small enough so that all the people in the group can get to know one another intimately. In this setting, leadership tends to spring forth from the group.

3. The goal of each Basic Christian Community is to form a community of faith. Even when the Eucharist is not celebrated on a regular basis by the group, it maintains a central place in their prayer life.

4. The community attempts to live a life that flows from the Gospel in such a way that it relates directly to contemporary needs. The group spends a significant amount of time trying to relate the good news to the real world.

5. While groups tend to form around some strong personality, these leaders now take on a role related to group process. The stress may be on conversion or social commitment.

6. It would be almost impossible to list the variety that is found among the different Basic Christian Communities. The composition of the group varies widely in terms of the number of members in the group, their socioeconomic background, their religious state (lay or clerical). There is no unanimity on the number of times they meet or on the depth of their community life. For example, some groups share goods in common. Others do not. Goals are different among the groups, especially in terms of faith and political commitment. Their relationship to the official Church goes all the way from a very close connection to indifference.[7]

How Basic Christian Communities Are Formed

The gathering of the Hispanic communities reported that there are no universal ways to start a Basic Christian Community. There is, however, one common element. The community is always formed by one person relating to another person. As they put it: "This relationship can be initiated through families, work, friendships, common social interests or concerns, for example, concerns of justice or religion. This person-to-person contact helps to reveal the value of brotherly relationships. Regardless of how the CEB (basic ecclesial community) is started, all members eventually have to reach the person-to-person relationship."[8]

They also list four different models that seem to cover the various kinds of BCC's:

1. Some communities gather to begin some form of social action. These people usually have a common goal. What is important for them is to examine that goal in light of the Gospel.

2. Other groups form out of existing Church movements, such as Cursillo, or from the charismatic movement. A group that is formed around Christian marriage might take a special interest in marriage and family issues, such as the rights of the divorced, laws protecting children, and the rights of women.

3. Some groups form because they live in the same neighborhood and attend the same parish. According to the Hispanic communities, "Neighborhood groups have two natural advantages: (a) Community action is easier because of the closeness of the members, and (b) members of the group can relate to their neighbors in a personal and natural way. One of the possibilities for a neighborhood group is promoting an environment of friendship, openness, and mutual support among group members."[9]

4. Some groups form around function, especially official Church ministries. Basic Christian Communities can be made up of catechists or religious.[10]

Focus

The focus of BCC's can revolve around different areas of life (for example, catechesis, liturgy, commitment to today's world, and liberation). Father Jack Ryan, a missionary to the Philippines, has drawn up a schema that gives insights into the different organizational structures of BCC's based on their orientations. While it reflects the Philippine experience, his admittedly oversimplified models are helpful in understanding an experience that is foreign to mainstream American culture.

He divides BCC's into three groups: liturgy oriented, development oriented, and liberation oriented. The aim of the liturgy-oriented BCC is to bring people without a priest together for Sunday worship, and for other prayer activities at other times. The people in this community would come from natural, geographical groupings. The development community's aim is toward the implementation of programs that will help the people in these natural groupings. Their population also comes from small, often rural, communities. The liberation-oriented group aims at raising consciousness and helping to free people from oppressive social and economic structures. The people in this BCC come from similar task groups, such as workers, fishermen, and farmers. The focus may be on organizations of workers in a geographical area.

In terms of the notion of community, both the liturgy-oriented and development-oriented BCC's understand community as flowing from the biblical People of God concept. The development group, however, would also work toward fulfilling some socioeconomic needs of the community, for example, forming cooperatives. Since the liberation group is composed of diverse groups from different geographical and sociological areas, it would work toward the liberation of the larger society.

In terms of concrete activity, the liturgy group would hold liturgical gatherings in which all share. In the development group, the members of the BCC are given ways in which to begin development programs through mutual sharing. They might attend workshops on family, self-awareness, nutrition, or sacraments. In the liberation group, the people discuss their real situation and analyze it in terms of the gospel. The leadership meets to try to arrive at ways to change themselves and whatever structures of the society that are oppressive.[11]

It is obvious from Ryan's brief description that each Basic Christian Community will be different from all others. No two are alike, because the people who make up the groups are different and because their day-to-day realities are different. What makes them the same is that they are built on the understanding that all people are brothers and sisters in Christ Jesus.

Basic Christian Communities and the Parish

An English priest, James Pitt, spent some time observing the Church in Brazil in 1979. One of his descriptions of that Church centered on the archdiocese of Vitoria. Only ten percent of the Catholic population in this archdiocese practiced their faith. In order to make the Church more active in the lives of people, the archbishop asked the BCC's in his diocese to draw up a pastoral plan. The basic principle in that plan is: "As Christians we are called to love our neighbors, which demands that we create the political, social, and economic situation in which our neighbor can develop."[12]

That simple statement expresses the theoretical foundation of the whole thrust of a diocese that is made up more of Basic Christian Communities than of traditional parishes. The parish became too formal and institutional to touch the lives of people. While the structure of parish remains for canonical reasons, the reality of the Church is found in the Basic Christian Communities.

A Basic Christian Community in Action

Actually seeing a BCC in operation is beyond the experience of most North Americans. For those who have not experienced it, James Pitt has described one facet of the activity of a BCC in Brazil, entitled "A First Communion Class in São Mateus." The description is worth quoting in its entirety.

> I went to a First Communion class on the periphery of São Paulo where I experienced a practical lesson in liberation theology.
>
> It was a small group of mothers, eight in all, meeting in one of their houses. The catechist, an American Sister, was taking them through a catechetics program that had been developed by basic church communities in the sector to help prepare children for First Communion. The

program covered 30 themes, and every two weeks the mothers would study one theme as a group, teach their own children individually and then evaluate it as a group.

I went to the meeting, hoping it would be interesting, but little prepared for an experience that would teach me more about liberation theology than anything I had heard or read to date.

The theme of that fortnight was "that Jesus was born poor and humble and shares our life," and the question was "Why?" The women present were all poor. None had had much formal education. Most were migrants from rural areas. All knew real hardship. They could easily identify with a poor family on the move whose baby had been born in a stable. Indeed a one-minute reading of Luke's account of the nativity provoked a one-hour discussion of the injustices, humiliations and hardships that the mothers themselves experienced.

They discussed the terrible health services available in the area and how a local woman's baby had been born while she was waiting in a queue to see the doctor. (The baby died.) They swapped accounts of having to wait in shops while better dressed people were served first and how as domestic servants they were treated without respect by their mistresses. They talked of the high price of food in the local shops.

After an hour the catechist put the question, "Why did Jesus *choose* to be born poor and humble?" "Maybe," said one woman, a mother of ten of whom three had died and only two were working, "maybe it was to show these rich people that we are important too."

A ripple of excitement went through the room. Was God really making such a clear statement about *their* humanity? About *their* rights as people? The discussion progressed, but with an electric charge in the air. Half an hour later, a young woman said, "I think we still haven't got the right answer to the first question!" A complete hush. "I think," she went on, "that God chose his Son to be born like us so that *we* can realize that we are important."

And suddenly I saw what it means to say that the Gospel has the power to set people free, that the Good News to the poor is a message of liberation. For these women, fired by a sudden consciousness of their own worth, of their identification with Jesus Christ, by an awareness of God's love for them ... these women went on to discuss what they should be doing about the high food prices, about how a particular chain of shops had cornered the market and was overcharging, and how they themselves would link up with other catechetics groups and basic church communities across the sector to organize a boycott.

Liberation theology is knowledge of God the Liberator.[13]

Conclusion

The fear that Basic Christian Communities will undermine parish structures in the United States is a common negative reaction. People who have worked with both are not overly concerned. Thomas Peyton does not see parishes and BCC's as antithetical. Parishes are institutions which allow the larger Church to function. Usually a parish is the coming together of many smaller groupings of people, either in neighborhoods or interest groups.

Basic Christian Communities are a way of approaching becoming Church. The focus is relational, on how people relate to one another and to reality. As Peyton writes: "BCC's are gatherings of pilgrim peoples taking a lifetime learning how to become Christian."[14] It is very possible that the Church is once again dealing with the question of charisms versus institution.

The key question is: Will Basic Christian Communities work in the middle-class American Church? The model works in the Third World; it works among Hispanics in this country. There is no guarantee that the model will work in the typical American urban or suburban parish.

There is a danger that some people will set up structures in parishes that they call Basic Chrisian Communities which are, in fact, other forms of organization. BCC's are not mini-parishes. They are not neighborhood groupings or area gatherings of suburban households. Dividing the parish into clusters may be very worthwhile, but the mere fact of division does not create a Basic Christian Community.

Neither do Basic Christian Communities flow out of the community organization model. Very popular over the last fifteen years, community organization has helped many parishes and groups accomplish their purposes. This model, however, is based on conflict. It organizes people around a common issue or a common enemy; people band together to overcome some obstacle that stands in the way of their goals. Basic Christian Communities, on the other hand, are for people. They are for the understanding that all are brothers and sisters. They are a process organized for people to explore their experiences, to examine the reality that surrounds a particular group in the light of the gospel so that all might become free to serve others.

There is no answer to the question concerning the viability of Basic Christian Communities in the American middle-class Catholic Church. The institutional structure of the Church in this country seems to be at odds with such a process. American Catholics have historically not been especially interested in viewing reality in the light of the Gospel, nor have they been patient with processes that are not particularly efficient and do not have immediate concrete results.

At the same time, the principles involved in Basic Christian Communities are certainly needed in the American Church. To introduce those principles into any parish would be to change radically the priorities of the parish and the way ministry is exercised. Whether BCC's will succeed or not is still an open question. Even if they do not succeed, the effort and investigation will help renew the Church.[15]

SUMMARY

1. Basic Christian Communities are difficult to define. Most people describe these communities rather than restrict them by definition. The descriptions include that these communities are: a gathering of people in the Church; a group conscious of the kingdom of God and the necessity of transforming society according to that kingdom; a group whose roots are in history and whose focus is on the future; a group aware of what is important in life.

2. Small groupings of people are a phenomenon in the world today, not only in the Church. These small groups arise from the largeness of institutions, the increase in alienation, and the felt need for harmony in life.

3. Church documents emphasize local Church as a true expression of the Church, which tends to validate the existence of Basic Christian Communities (BCC).

4. BCC's have started all over the world within the Catholic Church as a way people can share their faith, form close human relationships, celebrate a community of faith, apply the Gospel to contemporary issues, experience conversion, and share common goals.

5. There are many different models of BCC's, including those based on social action, those growing out of existing Church movements, and those based on geographical groupings or common work.

6. In one example from Brazil, BCC's have become the basic unit of Church, replacing the traditional parish. In other places, BCC's exist within traditional parishes.

7. BCC's and parishes are not enemies of one another. A more fundamental question for the American Church is whether typically middle-class Catholics can form true Basic Christian Communities. What have been called BCC's in the United States are usually other kinds of small group structures. While there is no answer yet, the American Church would do well to adopt the underlying principles of BCC's.

CHAPTER NOTES

1. National Secretariat and Hispanic Communities, *Guidelines for Establishing Basic Church Communities in the United States* (Liguori, Mo.: Liguori Publications, 1981), p. 104.
2. *Pro Mundi Vita Bulletin* (September, 1976), p. 4.
3. *Guidelines*, p. 105.
4. Medellin, "Joint Pastoral Planning" (10-11), as quoted in *Guidelines*, p. 106.
5. Pope Paul VI, *On Evangelization in the Modern World* (Washington, D.C.: U.S. Catholic Conference, 1976), No. 58.
6. Puebla Document, No. 641, as quoted in "Basic Christian Communities," *Columbian Mission* (November, 1980), p. 3.

7. *Pro Mundi Vita,* p. 5.
8. *Guidelines,* p. 118.
9. Ibid., p. 120.
10. Ibid., pp. 118-20.
11. Jack Ryan, "Models for Community," *Columbian Mission* (November, 1980), pp. 20-21.
12. James Pitt, "Basic Communities of Brazilian Church in Action," LADOC (May/June, 1980), p. 23.
13. Ibid., pp. 11-13.
14. Thomas Peyton, M.M., "Basic Christian Communities and the Parish," National Federation of Priests' Councils (1979), pp. 36-37.
15. For a suggested way to introduce BCC's into a parish, see Peyton, op. cit., p. 37.

SUGGESTED READINGS

Developing Basic Christian Communities — A Handbook. Chicago: National Federation of Priests' Councils, 1979. This book contains a series of eight articles that describe various aspects of Basic Christian Communities in the United States experience.

Friere, Paulo, *Pedagogy of the Oppressed.* New York: Seabury Press, 1970. Many consider this book to be the theological basis for basic communities.

National Secretariat and Hispanic Communities. *Guidelines for Establishing Basic Church Communities in the United States.* Liguori, Mo.: Liguori Publications, 1981. This book grew out of a 1978 meeting of Hispanic communities in the United States involved in basic ecclesial communities. It provides a comprehensive picture of base communities in this country, including the relationship of base communities to parish life.

Pro Mundi Vita Bulletin (September, 1976), pp. 1-32. This short bulletin provides a complete analysis of the phenomenon of base communities throughout the world. It is an excellent description.

Resource Addresses

Abingdon Press, 201 Eighth Ave., S., Nashville, TN 37202.

Alba House, Div. of the Society of St. Paul, 2187 Victory Blvd., Staten Island, NY 10314.

Alban Institute, Mt. St. Alban, Washington, DC 20016.

Argus Communications, 7440 Natchez Ave., Niles, IL 60648.

Association Press, 291 Broadway, New York, NY 10007.

Augsburg Publishing House, 426 S. Fifth St., Minneapolis, MN 55415.

Ave Maria Press, Notre Dame, IN 46556.

William C. Brown Co., 2460 Kerper Blvd., Dubuque, IA 52001.

Capitol Publications, Inc., 2430 Pennsylvania Ave., N.W., Suite G-12, Washington, DC 20037.

Cardinal Stritch College, 6801 N. Yates Rd., Milwaukee, WI 53217.

Celebration Books, Box 281, 115 E. Armour Blvd., Kansas City, MO 64141.

The Center for Contemporary Celebration, 119 N. 6th St., West Lafayette, IN 47902.

The Center for Single and Young Adults in Ministry, Merrimack College, N. Andover, MA 01845.

Charles Scribner's Sons (*see* under "S").

Church Leadership Resources, United Church of Christ, Box 179, St. Louis, MO 63116.

Detroit Institute for Continuing Education (*see* under "I").

Dimension Books, 1 Summit St., Rockaway, NJ 07866.

Diocese of Cleveland, 1027 Superior Ave., Cleveland, OH 44114.

Fides/Claretian, P.O. Box F, Notre Dame, IN 46556.

Fiesta Publishing Corp., 6360 N.E. 4th Court, Miami, FL 33138.

Fortress Press, 2900 Queen Lane, Philadelphia, PA 19129.

Fort Wayne-South Bend Fiscal Planning Office (*see* "Office of Fiscal Planning").

Foundation for Christian Creativity, 1346 Connecticut Ave., N.W., No. 817, Washington, DC 20036.

Glenmary Research Center, 4606 East-West Hwy., Washington, DC 20014.

Griggs Educational Service, P.O. Box 362, Livermore, CA 94550.

Harper and Row Publications, Inc., 10 E. 53rd St., New York, NY 10022.

Image Books, c/o Doubleday and Co., Inc., 245 Park Ave., New York, NY 10017.

Institute for Continuing Education, Archdiocese of Detroit, 305 Michigan Ave., Detroit, MI 48226.

John Knox Press, 341 Ponce de Leon Ave., N.E., Atlanta, GA 30308.

Judson Press, Valley Forge, PA 19481.

Kendall/Hunt Publishing Co., 2460 Kerper Blvd., Dubuque, IA 52001.

Liguori Publications, 1 Liguori Rd., Liguori, MO 63057.

The Liturgical Conference, 1221 Massachusetts Ave., N.W., Washington, DC 20005.

Liturgy, 810 Rhode Island Ave., N.E., Washington, DC 20018.

Liturgy Training Program, 155 E. Superior, Chicago, IL 60611.

Liturgy Training Publications (*same address as preceding*).

The Living Light, 11 Park Place, New York, NY 10007.

Management and Fund Raising Center, 287 MacPherson Ave., Toronto, Ont., Canada.

Management Review, 135 West 50th St., New York, NY 10020.

McGraw-Hill Book Co., 1221 Avenue of the Americas, New York, NY 10036.

National Biblical, Catechetical and Liturgical Centre, Bangalore, 560005, India.

National Catholic Educational Assn., 1 Dupont Circle, Suite 350, Washington, DC 20036.

The National Center for Voluntary Action, 1214 16th St., N.W., Washington, DC 20036.

National Conference of Catholic Bishops, 1312 Massachusetts Ave., N.W., Washington, DC 20005.

National Conference of Catholic Charities, 1346 Connecticut Ave., N.W., Washington, DC 20036.

The National Federation of Priests' Councils, 1307 S. Wabash Ave., Chicago, IL 60605.

NCR Cassettes, P.O. Box 281, Kansas City, MO 64141.

New Catholic World, 1865 Broadway, New York, NY 10023.

North American Liturgy Resources, 2110 West Peoria Ave., Phoenix, AZ 85029.

Office of Fiscal Planning, Diocese of Fort Wayne-South Bend, P.O. Box 390, Ft. Wayne, IN 46801.

Our Sunday Visitor, Inc., 200 Noll Plaza, Huntington, IN 46750.

Pamphlet Publications, P.O. Box 41372A, Cincinnati, OH 45241.

Pastoral Arts Associates, 4331 Sandersville Rd., Old Hickory, TN 37138.

Paulist Press, 1865 Broadway, New York, NY 10023.

Pro Mundi Vita Bulletin, Rue De La Limite, 6, B-1030, Brussels, Belgium.

Pueblo Publishing Co., Inc., 1860 Broadway, New York, NY 10023.

Religious Education, 409 Prospect St., New Haven, CT 06510.

William H. Sadlier, Inc., 11 Park Place, New York NY 10007.

St. Mary's College Press, Winona, MN 55987.

Charles Scribner's Sons, 597 Fifth Ave., New York, NY 10017.

Seabury Press, Inc., 815 Second Ave., New York, NY 10017.

Servant Publications, P.O. Box 617, Ann Arbor, MI 48107.

Society of St. Paul (*see* "Alba House").

Thomas More Press, 225 W. Huron St., Chicago, IL 60610.

Twenty-Third Publications, P.O. Box 180, West Mystic, CT 06388.

U.S. Catholic Conference, Publications Office, 1312 Massachusetts Ave., N.W., Washington, DC 20008.

U.S. Government Printing Office, Div. of Public Documents, Washington, DC 20402.

University of Notre Dame Press, Notre Dame, IN 46556.

The Voluntary Action Resource Center, 1625 W. 8th Ave., Vancouver, BC, Canada.

Volunteer Management Associates, 279 South Cedar Brook Rd., Boulder, CO 80302.

William C. Brown Co. (*see* under "B").

William H. Sadlier, Inc. (*see* under "S").

Winston Press, Inc., 430 Oak Grove, Minneapolis, MN 55403.

World Library Publications, Inc., 2145 Central Pkwy., Cincinnati, OH 45214.